Richard E. Mertzer

D0587805

STRANGER AT THE PARTY

The author in 1935

STRANGER AT THE PARTY

A
Memoir

Helen Lawrenson

Random House
New York

Copyright © 1972, 1973, 1974, 1975 by Helen Lawrenson

All rights reserved under International and Pan-American Copyright
Conventions. Published in the United States by Random House, Inc.,
New York, and simultaneously in Canada by Random House of Canada
Limited, Toronto.

The author wishes to thank the editors of Esquire, *who published parts
of this book and without whose help and encouragement none of it
would have been written, especially Jill Goldstein, who first thought it
was a good idea.*

Library of Congress Cataloging in Publication Data
Lawrenson, Helen.
Stranger at the party.
A memoir.
1. Lawrenson, Helen. 2. Journalists—United
States—Correspondence, reminiscences, etc. I. Title.
PN4874.L28A37   070.4'092'4 [B]   74-23421
ISBN 0-394-48900-4

Manufactured in the United States of America
2 4 6 8 9 7 5 3
First Edition

For Johanna and Kevin

CONTENTS

STRANGER AT THE PARTY

FARRAGO FUNERAL

NO ONE WOULD HAVE REL-
ished the funeral more than my husband, even though it was
his own.

The High Mass in St. Joseph's Roman Catholic Church in
Greenwich Village that November day in 1957 was attended
by an olla podrida of mourners: merchant seamen of varied
origin—Arab, Goanese, Egyptian, Turkish, Scandinavian,
Puerto Rican, American whites and American blacks;
ex-Communist Party members and ex-Condé Nast editors
(in some cases not such mutually exclusive backgrounds as
one might suppose); truck drivers and moving-men; drinking companions from Village bars like the White Horse,
Louis' Tavern, the San Remo, the Kettle of Fish; a sprinkling
of painters, musicians, actors and writers; members of the
Ladies' Auxiliary of the National Maritime Union; a fashion
model who looked like Garbo; longshoremen; Arnold Ging-

rich, publisher of *Esquire*, and his wife; my husband's Irish relatives from the Bronx; a waterfront whore with hair like Shredded Wheat; a fashion writer with a cut-glass accent and indomitable chic; a minor DuPont who had once been infatuated with the dead man. (She met him when she went on a Sarah Lawrence "field trip" to the National Maritime Union headquarters—for a Current Affairs course? perhaps a quick, hopefully instructive look at real live trade union-ists?—during the time Jack was still a vice-president there.)

It was indeed a motley throng that would have tickled Jack's ironic humor, especially when it became even more motley with the sudden and unexpected arrival during the service of a good-looking Jesuit priest who a few years previously had been sent by Clare Boothe Luce, following her own spectacular conversion, to redeem us. Although an unsuccessful proselytizer where I was concerned ("Sorry I barged in where even angels can't get a toehold," Mrs. Luce wrote me, in her sometimes distastefully demotic style), the priest had become a good friend. I asked him to officiate at the funeral, but he was conducting a retreat in an upstate monastery and said he couldn't make it. My children and I were therefore surprised to see him rush onto the sanctuary from the wings (or whatever they're called), look-ing as if he'd thrown on his robes in a hurry, sit down, and open a book. "Look, Mom!" whispered my eleven-year-old son Kevin, nudging me. "There's Father McCarthy! What's he doing sitting there reading a book?" (He was reading prayers for the dead, he told me later.) I was also unpre-pared for the burst of beautiful music, with a superb and thrilling tenor voice transforming and exalting what until then had been a gloomy ritual. I could tell by the murmur-ing and rustling and turning of heads that others were as astonished as I was at the pure tones swelling gloriously in this small, shabby, unfashionable, neighborhood church. I learned afterward that it was the New York Pro Musica, the ensemble founded by Noah Greenberg to perform medieval music, and that the male soloist was reputedly one of the best tenors around. Greenberg was a musician who had been a merchant seaman member of the NMU and a friend of Jack's. He had been in our house a few times but I didn't know him well myself, and I knew nothing of his plan for the funeral. It was a graceful tribute to my husband.

I was in Red Rock Canyon in the Mojave Desert when Jack became ill. I had gone there to do a piece for *Esquire* about the filming of *The Big Country*, a boringly pretentious Western with Gregory Peck, Charlton Heston, Chuck Connors, Jean Simmons, Carroll Baker and Burl Ives, all of whom I avoided, save for perfunctory interviews, and spent my time drinking and gossiping with Charles Bickford, also starring in the movie, and the unit press agent. We three had a fine time agreeing that William Wyler, who was directing the picture, was vastly overrated and, far from being the genius he was usually acclaimed, merely demonstrated the irresistible appeal of invincible banality. Bickford really loathed him, especially the way Wyler would make some poor old bit player do a half-minute scene over and over —thirty-two times, we once counted—so that everyone would say, "My! What a perfectionist Wyler is!" "Perfectionist my ass," Bickford said. "He only does it to show off. It's not only unnecessary; it's stupid and cruel. But he's not worth talking about. Did I ever tell you about the time Julia Faye, wearing black silk stockings and nothing else, came out of a pie at a surprise birthday party for De Mille?"

It was stinking hot in the desert, so when the company knocked off for the weekend I went back to Los Angeles and the Beverly Hills Hotel. I telephoned home, and my daughter Johanna told me that both my husband and Kevin had bad colds. It was during an Asian flu epidemic, so I flew back to New York. It was the first time in our eighteen years of marriage that I had come back from a trip without Jack meeting me at the airport. Instead, Johanna was there. "Papa won't see a doctor," she said. "I'm glad you came home." When we arrived at our apartment, Jack opened the door. "Welcome to our pest-house," he said. I made him go to bed and called our doctor, who gave him a shot of penicillin. The next day he was delirious, and that evening he became unconscious. I rode in the ambulance with him to the hospital, where they put him in an oxygen tent. Even then, it never entered my head that he wouldn't live. (Two weeks before, on his fifty-first birthday, he had said, "I guess I'm good for another twenty years." He looked about ten years younger than his age and aside from the fact that he drank too much and smoked too much, he was in perfect health.) I had come home on Monday. Wednesday morning, shortly before eight o'clock, the telephone rang. It was the doctor. "Jack expired at 7:02 this morning," he said. My reaction, along with shocked disbelief, was one of anger. "Why can't people come out and say the word?" I thought. The ridiculous euphemisms went through my mind: "My mother passed away" . . . "She lost her husband" (as if he were an umbrella) . . . Does it make it any less painful to say something idiotic like that? Are people so embarrassed by death that they cannot bring themselves to say the word? . . . And now the doctor, with his "expired." Why couldn't he say, "Jack died"? I hung up the telephone and walked into the other room, shuddering.

He was laid out in style. Mindful of the slogan "Nothing's too good for the workers!" I chose the Frank E. Campbell Funeral Parlor, undertakers to the elite, from Rudolph Valentino to the more status-conscious members of the Social Register and the Mafia. Still in a state of shock, I suppose, I made the arrangements in a cynical, almost flippant mood, remembering the undertakers' convention I once covered as a teen-age newspaper reporter in Syracuse. It was held in the State Armory, the huge floor covered with coffins and salesmen handing out brochures extolling the beauties of mauve satin linings and solid mahogany. Stands trimmed with ruffled crêpe paper featured embalming fluids, and one of them had a printed sign: ESPECIALLY RECOMMENDED FOR CHILDREN. The high point of the convention was an embalming demonstration performed on the gray corpse of a young man—a vagrant? someone nameless, destined for paupers' field?—by a man wearing a white smock and a high white hat like a chef's. The convention ended with the delegates singing a song about undertakers, to the tune of "Just Let a Smile Be Your Umbrella."

The day before the funeral, the body was on view in the open coffin in a fair-sized room in Campbell's, and people came and went all day. The coffin was at one side of the room, banked with flowers, from elaborate floral pieces (with cards reading "Mr. and Mrs. Henry R. Luce," "Mr. Bernard M. Baruch," "Joan Crawford"), to bouquets from wives and children of fellow workers in the labor movement. Everyone spoke in low, respectful tones, as if in church or a public library reading-room, except my mother, who was her usual loquacious self, a relentless monologuist, eager to impart details of previous family funerals and her own personal history, enjoying what for her was the social event of the season. ("I had such a nice chat with that Mrs. Rutherford," she said later. "I gave her my recipe for baked mackerel.") I was self-consciously playing the gracious hostess, welcoming each visitor (including strangers like the woman with the worried look of a tired dachshund, who kept mumbling unintelligibly), oozing phony charm as I accepted even the most smarmy condolences, thanking people as they left, and all the time incredulous at the stagy unreality of the scene. No one paid much attention to the corpse, aside from a quick, obligatory pause at the coffin where he lay, the honey-colored hair unaccustomedly smooth and slick, the blue eyes closed, the handsome nose, the neat mustache, the lean, distinguished face so familiar yet now irrevocably remote, a rosary twined in the folded, long-fingered, elegantly molded hands. In place of his usual outfit of dungarees, blue work shirt and cloth cap, he wore the navy blue pin-stripe custom-made suit I never could get him to wear when alive ("I'm saving it to be buried in," he would say, laughing), a Sulka shirt, the Bronzini tie we had often giggled over, because when I asked the snobbish salesman, "What do you call that color—ochre?" he replied haughtily, "It's ormolu, madam." It had come in a silk-lined box, together with a scroll describing in ludicrously flowery terms the origin of the design—something to do with

Napoleon, his return from exile, or maybe it was his final burial, with his weeping mother or someone exclaiming "The Emperor is home again!" So of course whenever Jack wore the tie, he would say, as he knotted it, "Well, the Emperor is home again." And here he was wearing the tie in his coffin, my Irish rebel husband, getting the kind of final send-off he would have laughed at, but enjoyed. The previous winter, an old friend, Foghorn Russell, had died of a heroin overdose, alone in a dingy Lower East Side room. Although it was rumored he came from a well-to-do Georgia family, no one could trace any relatives, and he was buried in Staten Island by his union, MFOW (Marine Firemen, Oilers, Wipers) with no fuss, no flowers, no funeral, just a brisk graveside service in the chill gray rain and only three people present. Jack was one of the three, and when he came home, he shook his head and said, "That is no way to go. When I die, I want candles at my head and candles at my feet, surrounded by my weeping family!" Well, he had the candles, but the tears were private.

The funeral was the next day. When we left the church, the children and I rode in one of the black Cadillacs, directly behind the hearse, as we slowly made our way, leading the procession all the way through heavy traffic from Greenwich Village to the Catholic cemetery in the Bronx. When we finally arrived at the cemetery, Father McCarthy, the Jesuit priest, was standing by the open grave. I was so glad to see him there, so grateful for his presence, that, without thinking, I went up to him, lifted the black mourning veil that covered my face, and kissed him. I imagine the other people were pretty surprised. (Afterward, as he and I walked away, toward the waiting limousines, I said to him, "I guess I made a terrible gaffe. I don't think the widow is supposed to kiss the priest at the grave." He patted my shoulder reassuringly and said, "I'm sure God will understand.") With the coffin in the grave and the children and me, our relatives and friends standing around, McCarthy recited the burial service and then added, impulsively, his

8

own unorthodox comment, "You're with the angels now, Jack!"

The *New York Times* ran a top-of-the-page photograph and obituary headed: "Jack Lawrenson, Maritime Leader," with a subhead, "Former Vice President and a Founder of the N.M.U. Dies—Had Opposed Curran." Other papers had short paragraphs, and *The Village Voice* had a feature story, the gist of which was that in many a Greenwich Village and waterfront bar, glasses would be lifted in memorial toasts. But there was not a word in *The Pilot*, the weekly publication of the union Jack had helped found and of which he had been an elected official from the beginning. Nor did I receive any personal word from the union officers or their wives, although they had known and worked with us throughout the years. (I guess this was to be expected. Joe Curran, who turned against the Communists, as soon as he saw on what side his bread would best be buttered, had ordered the union history to be rewritten, leaving out Jack's role, and Jack's face was blacked out in early photographs that showed him standing at Curran's side in the 1936 and 1937 strikes from which the NMU was born.) A labor columnist sent a wire to Curran—"The conscience of the NMU died yesterday"—and for weeks I continued to receive messages from rank-and-file seamen and members of other CIO unions.

It was as if this death had pulled together the mixed threads of our backgrounds into one multicolored pattern. In a way, the funeral was a microcosm of my own life, with the antipodal elements of Park Avenue and the waterfront, from the granitic conservatism of upstate New York village and farmland to the radical Left and what the Scottish poet Hugh MacDiarmid has called "the eternal lightning of Lenin's bones." Yet did I ever really belong in any of these disparate worlds, even though I was a part of them all? Fossicking about in different milieus, never seeking any Grail, have I not always been like Axel Heyst in *Victory*, inwardly the detached observer, no matter how involved I might be outwardly? "It was the very essence of his life to be a solitary achievement, accomplished not by hermit-like withdrawal with its silence and immobility, but by a system of restless wandering, by the detachment of an impermanent dweller amongst changing scenes. In this scheme he had perceived the means of passing through life without suffering and almost without a single care in the world—invulnerable because elusive." I first read these words of Conrad when I was seventeen and, even then, I realized that this was what I, too, was doing, and that for me it was the secret of how to live.

Two

BACKWARD, TURN BACKWARD, O TIME, IN YOUR FLIGHT

NOT FOR ME, THANK YOU. I wouldn't want to be a child again, even for one night. I wasn't miserable exactly but I don't look back on laughing, carefree days, either. I was no merry grig. I was a gloomy grig. Never at ease with other children, wary of grown-ups, I wasn't popular and didn't really yearn to be. I enjoyed being alone, except for my grandmother. My parents were often in Europe, Florida or New York, and my grandmother brought me up. I sometimes say, "I had a very happy childhood going to auctions and funerals." (My grandmother was over sixty when I was born, so the funerals were fairly frequent and she always took me with her, as well as to the auctions she loved—she'd buy anything, whether she wanted it or not, just for the fun of bidding.) The truth is that I was an oddball child.

I was born in 1907. Teddy Roosevelt was President, Edward VII sat on the British throne, and in New York the

Ziegfeld Follies opened at the New Amsterdam Theatre with Nora Bayes singing "Has Anyone Here Seen Kelly?" There was also a financial panic, but none of these events cut much ice in LaFargeville, New York, a village of four hundred inhabitants, seven miles south of the Canadian border, where the only doctor delivered me on a horsehair davenport in the front parlor of my grandmother's yellow frame house.

LaFargeville was named after its founder, John LaFarge, (ancestor of Oliver, the writer, and John, the celebrated stained-glass window artist), who came from France in the early nineteenth century and built a fine stone mansion, set in large grounds with a deer park. (My grandmother nearly bought the place before I was born but decided it was too far from the village and her friends, especially when severe winter snowstorms made the road impassable—those were horse and buggy days. In 1838, the mansion became a Jesuit seminary which later moved to New York as Fordham University.) For some years John LaFarge lived there with his housekeeper and mistress, Miss Betsy Cotter, a tall, robust, agreeably plump young neighborhood woman, but there came a day when he returned from a trip to France, bringing with him a bride. The betrayed Betsy charged like a Valkyrie out of the mansion and down the path to confront the couple as they descended from their carriage. Raising both clenched fists toward heaven, she greeted them with the passionate cry "John LaFarge, is there a God in Israel?!" Village legend did not record his answer, if any, to this presumably rhetorical question. However, not long afterward he did convey to Betsy, for the sum of one dollar, the deed to 129 acres of land, on the dog-in-the-manger condition that she never marry. She didn't, but she gave the land to her sister Ruth, who thereupon married John Rottiers, LaFarge's clerk and agent. I remember their daughter Wilhelmina, widow of a man named Harman, as a jolly old lady with whom I used to play cribbage.

My childhood friends were usually my grandmother's friends, especially summers, which I spent with her at her summer place in the Thousand Islands, on the St. Lawrence River. My social life until I was about thirteen was highlighted by church suppers, strawberry festivals, quilting bees, square dances (Virginia Reels, etc.), Independence Day parades (with a few still-ambulatory Civil War veterans tottering along to the tune of "We're Coming, Father Abraham" tootled on a fife), afternoon card parties at which I played Five Hundred with ladies aged from sixty to eighty, and the previously noted auctions and funerals. I mention Mrs. Harman because her son, John Harman, grandson of John Rottiers, inherited Betsy Cotter's consolation prize land and also became editor and general manager of the Brooklyn *Times* and sheriff of Kings County.

LaFargeville and other communities in Jefferson County bred a fair share of millionaires, among others, Frank Woolworth, the salesclerk in Empsall's Drygoods Store in Watertown who suggested setting up one counter with goods priced at five and ten cents, an idea so successful that he later opened his own store; his early partner, Fred Wickesser (his house was across the road from ours in LaFargeville); and prosperous grain and dairy farmers—all penny-pinching Silas Marner types, closet millionaires, no lah-di-dah life style for them or their womenfolk, inflexibly conservative, anti-Semitic, anti-Catholic (they would have been anti-Negro except there weren't any), God-fearing, Democrat-hating, proud, tough, intolerant ergomaniacs.

Like most places, upstate New York has its fancier historical myths, one of which is that the lost dauphin, the eight-year-old son of Louis XVI and Marie Antoinette, did not die in his Paris prison, as reported, but was spirited away by the Baroness de Feriet, a former lady-in-waiting to the French queen, with the aid of James LeRay, an American whose father had been influential in enlisting French support for the American colonists in our own revolution. The child, who had become demented in prison, according to testimony from those who visited him there, was said to have been brought to upstate New York by the baroness and LeRay, who left him with the Oneida Indians to be reared by them, concealed in the wilderness, his identity secret, to keep him safe from agents of the Bourbons who acceded to the throne. True or false, it is a matter of record that the baroness, reputedly a woman of sophistication and charm, spent the rest of her life in a house she built on land she bought from LeRay near Watertown, on Black River, allegedly remaining there so that she could occasionally visit her royal charge. (More easily confirmed is the story of how Prince Lucien Murat tried to found a city near LaFargeville, about six miles up the Indian River from Theresa. He bought land in 1834, induced a few friends to build there, called the community Joachim, after his father—Napoleon's marshal and one-time King of Naples—and entertained on a scale that required the importation of supplies from New York, all on credit. His vision of a new Paris ended when his creditors lowered the boom and the prince fled to escape court proceedings. Without his impetus, the others drifted away, the buildings crumbled, and the wild grass took over.)

I lived in LaFargeville until I was seven and even after I moved away I often spent holidays there, and every summer for eighteen years I stayed with my grandmother at the Thousand Islands, such a short distance from LaFargeville that we went back and forth a lot. I suppose it's where my roots are, but I don't feel that way. The last time I was there was in the summer of 1970. I stayed in the house on the St. Lawrence River and I spent a day in LaFargeville—the village cemetery where my mother and grandmother and dozens of other relatives are buried, the house where I was born, the other house my grandmother built, into which we moved when I was three, architecturally graceful with its white-columned verandah, the small Episcopal church where my parents were married and where I was baptized and later confirmed—all familiar and unchanged, and yet none of it meant a thing to me. I felt nothing. Not a single twitch of "This is my own, my native land." Breathes there a man with soul so dead? Yes. Me. I listened to the voices among which I grew up—the flat twang of dropping *g*'s—and I felt an alien. Not even the beautiful St. Lawrence River could arouse in me the doubtless satisfyingly sentimental response "I have come home." (I felt more at home the first time I ever set foot in Havana.) I have no wish ever to go back again. I have litttle reluctance in admitting this, because I believe that what most people think is patriotism is often merely jingoism. Besides, I feel I have the right to deny any such obligation without being accused of ingratitude.

Many Americans who are 150 percent patriots are twentieth-century immigrants or the children of immigrants. But one of my ancestors went to Massachusetts from England in 1635 and the first of the others arrived here before our Revolution—those who weren't already here, that is. The Indian blood comes from my mother's side, an ancestor from the Senecas, one of the Six Nations that make up the Iroquois (the Senecas, Oneidas, Mohawks, Onondagas, Cayugas and Tuscaroras.) My family didn't talk about it, even though a glance at the daguerrotypes in the gold-clasped leather-bound family albums reveals unmistakably Indian features. My own sole contact was when I was twelve and played my harp at a church Christmas party on the Onondaga Indian Reservation. I played the "Marseillaise" and "Silent Night," a whimsical combination, but the Indians seemed to like it.

My mother's great-great-grandfather was Baltus Strauch (the name was later changed to Strough), a farmer in Germany who was impressed by the Duke of Hesse into the army and sent to America to fight with the British against the rebel colonists. That particular group were called Hessians. Baltus deserted and made his way on foot, in winter, from New Jersey to the Mohawk Valley in Pennsylvania, where he became a blacksmith. Because he was a known sympathizer with the rebels, a group of his Tory neighbors dressed up as Indians and scalped him, but he survived and lived on into his nineties. Although my sympathy and admiration were totally for his views, I used to infuriate my mother by saying, "I come from a long line of cowards and deserters," because Baltus' grandson hired a substitute to fight in his name in the Civil War and the substitute deserted. Baltus' son Daniel married Anna Wiswell, whose father was one of Ethan Allan's Green Mountain Boys, a descendant of the Thomas Wiswell who emigrated from England to America in 1635. The rest of my mother's line were also of English descent, among them Increase Mather, president of Harvard, and his son, Cotton Mather, clergyman, author, witch hunter.

My father's ancestry was similar to that of my mother. He belonged to the Sons of the American Revolution, just as she belonged to the D.A.R., and they were both considerably more patriotic and less critical than I am. His people on his mother's side were all of English origin, while his father, David Brown, was descended from a German baron (the name was then Braun) who came to America in the early eighteenth century, a dramatic arrival because his ship was wrecked and he swam ashore carrying a bag of gold in his teeth. (All my family have great teeth, and I probably could have made a living hanging by mine, like the lady in Barnum & Bailey's Circus.) The only reason I bother to go into this genealogical bit is to show my credentials, perhaps defensively, for the role of critic and non-patriot and to stave off any reaction along the lines of if-you-don't-like-it-here-why-don't-you-go-back-where-you-came-from? Tracing ancestors is a silly bore, and I certainly didn't dig up the information myself. It's all in the family Bibles. I've never pretended to be a family person and the less I have to do with relatives, the better I like it, for the most part, although as a small child I was fascinated, if bemused, to hear my father tell people that his grandmother used to sit on Abraham Lincoln's lap. To me, a grandmother was an old lady, so naturally I had a mental picture of a wrinkled, white-haired woman snuggled up on Lincoln's knees and I would wonder what she was doing there. When I grew older, I learned that her father was Lincoln's law partner at the time and I was relieved to realize that she was a *child* and not indulging in some curious geriatric caper. (Her name was Mary Dunn and when I was born my father wanted to name me after her but decided "Mary Dunn Brown" didn't sound right.)

My father, Lloyd Brown, was born in Buffalo, the son of a hardware merchant. His mother, Clara Lloyd, was the daughter of a Methodist minister who came to visit us once. A stern old man with mutton chop whiskers, he thought that if the Republicans ever lost the Presidency, the United States would collapse morally as well as economically. I never saw Clara, but in her pictures she is pretty and frivolous-looking. She had yellow hair and green eyes, and she must have been a bitch. Her husband died when my father was about seven and Clara took off for London, where she put my father and his younger brother in boarding school and concentrated on having a salon, frequented by musicians like Victor Herbert and the tenor Jean de Rezke. She obviously cared nothing for her sons, who were only an embarrassment. She married Edouard Jacobowski, a composer, divorced him, and then decided to annex a title. While setting her cap for a knighted general named Maxwell, she made her sons pretend they were her nephews, forbade them to call her Mother, and further played it safe by sending my father to school in France, near Versailles. As soon as she became Lady Maxwell, she packed both boys back to Buffalo to live with their grandfather and that was the last they saw of her. My father was eleven by then, and he used to stand at the window every morning, watching for the postman, hoping to get a letter from his mother. She never wrote. (She died during World War I, was buried in London, and in 1920 my father went over there and brought her body back for burial in the family plot in Buffalo. He also brought back a few of her things for me: a zither, a writing box of satinwood inlaid with ebony and mother-of-pearl, a thick, gilt-edged guest-book bound in blue moroccan leather. My daughter now keeps this book in the Thousand Islands house, and among the more recent names inscribed therein are those of Joe Dallessandro, star of *Flesh*, *Trash* and other Andy Warhol epics, Paul Morrissey, director of same, former Warhol superstar Viva, painter Larry Poons and others similarly exotic enough to have struck the fancy of the book's original owner, I am sure.)

My father was a lonely boy, unhappy at DeVeaux Military School in Niagara Falls, never good at sports or at making friends, even though later at Syracuse University he was a member of Phi Kappa Psi and Phi Delta Phi fraternities. A handsome man—tall, slim, with black hair, gray eyes, good nose and mouth—he was all his life timid and unself-confident, not in any way effeminate, but gentle, with beautiful manners and no common sense. My gregarious, bossy mother treated him as if he didn't know enough to come in out of the rain—and perhaps he didn't. (Literally, as well as figuratively. He not only enjoyed walking in the rain but he also loved the thunderstorms that so frightened my mother. Her grandfather was killed by lightning while riding his horse and whenever she was at the Thousand Islands during a storm, she would crouch in the living room on a pile of feather pillows—supposedly insulators—howling in terror at each clap of thunder and flash of lightning, while my father stood outside on the porch, reveling in the fury of the storm that lashed the water of the St. Lawrence into angry gray-green waves fighting and crashing against our dock.)

My mother resented my father's inability to be a good mixer, a hail-fellow-well-met, and she equated masculinity with sports and rorty male pursuits. She despised his lack of interest in baseball and football—"Football builds character!" she often announced—and the fact that he was no good at golf (and certainly a washout as a locker-room one-of-the-boys), that he liked to lie in the sun but swimming bored him, that he was afraid of horses and hated riding, while as for hunting, a sanctified annual ritual in upstate New York, I think he would sooner have shot himself than a deer.

She didn't have any better luck with me. I had lessons from professionals in swimming, diving, tennis, riding, golf (she made my grandmother buy me a set of little clubs when I was ten), archery, fencing, ice-skating—and I was a dud at all of them. If she put me outside in the winter, telling me to play in the snow with my sled, I would stand by the door and cry till she let me back in the house, where all I wanted to do was sit by the fireplace and read. One ghastly year in Syracuse she marched me off to membership in a YWCA gym class where we had to swing from rings suspended from the ceiling and perform other horrible feats called calisthenics. (I was just as bad at what was called "aesthetic dancing," a class in which she determinedly enrolled me and I had to go every Saturday morning and pretend to be a wave on the beach or a daffodil in the wind.) At boarding school, to my dismay, basketball and field hockey were compulsory. I was happy to get to Vassar, where we were on our honor to atttend gym, so I could get a friend to sign in for me and in return I'd do the same for her in chapel, a less exigent pastime, as I could read a book or just sit and daydream.

My father was a chronic daydreamer. When people ask me what he did for a living, I usually answer, "He was an unsuccessful promoter." For a short time after he left Syracuse University, he was editor-publisher of the St. Lawrence *Bulletin*, a weekly publication he founded to record historical anecdotes and social chit-chat of the Thousand Islands, in those days a resort for the rich and their yachts. (People like Pullman, the railroad magnate who gave his name to sleeping cars, and George Boldt, who owned the first Waldorf-Astoria, built ostentatious castles on their islands.) Even in those days my father lived on borrowed money. He met my mother at the Thousand Islands. They married in June, 1906, when he was twenty-three and she was a black-haired, olive-skinned beauty of nineteen. I was born October 1, 1907. (When I was about twelve or thirteen, she told me that she hadn't wanted me and did everything she could to abort me—hot mustard baths, huge castor oil doses, enemas, riding horseback, skipping rope, even falling down stairs.) My grandmother supported us while my father flitted from one project to another: insurance, investment advice, advertising, the new-fangled electric light signs, a mosquito repellent he concocted from various mephitic liquids, fire extinguishers. (After his death, I found two trunks full of unused cards and stationery—for different companies—that all read: Lloyd E. Brown, President.) He borrowed money from almost everyone he met and from everyone he could locate with whom he once went to school. His longest-lasting venture was a fire extinguisher, a powder he mixed from simple ingredients like soda and salt and marketed under various names, selling stock in different companies he formed, one after the other (Lloyd E. Brown, President, of course). No one, to my knowledge, ever collected a penny in dividends, but the powder did put out fires, and he had dozens of testimonial letters. He used to travel around the country, selling it. (He also sold the sales rights in different parts of the country and had no compunction about selling the same rights to several different men.) He carried the extinguishers in cartons in his Overland touring car (which was always getting flat tires or failing to start, so he would have to get out and crank it) and one summer in New Jersey, when I was seven, he had a spectacular gimmick that involved my mother and me sitting in the front seat of the Overland, outwardly all aplomb and nonchalance, while he opened the engine, poured gasoline on it, and set fire to it with a match. As the flames shot up and onlookers gasped, he would throw a handful of his fire extinguisher powder "forcibly at the base of the flames" (as the directions said) and *poof!* the fire immediately went out. It really was good stuff, and if he ever could have gotten enough capital to manufacture and advertise it, he probably could have made a lot of money, because it was the first nonliquid fire extinguisher. At one time, Tex Rickard, the famous fight promoter, was all set to put up the cash and the contracts were drawn, but Rickard died before they were signed. That was the nearest my poor father ever came to a glimpse of solvency. What he really wanted to do was go to the South Seas, and he was always getting travel agency brochures about Tahiti and reading books like Frederick O'Brien's *White Shadows in The South Seas.*

True, at one point early in his marriage, while he was young and eager, he did get an offer to go to Egypt as manager of the Standard Oil office in Cairo. My mother refused to go. Whether or not his life would have been different is difficult to say. He was a weak man whose life was a failure. He was also not very intelligent. Mindlessly reactionary, he didn't like Jews or "foreigners," thought the Democrats were bogeymen, believed in the Yellow Peril and was afraid the Reds were always about to poison the water supply or "seize control of the public utilities."

At least, my mother wasn't that stupid. Although neither of them was at all well read or remotely intellectual, my mother was surprisingly free of racial or religious prejudice —surprising because of her LaFargeville background. She went to the village school until she was fifteen, when my grandmother sent her to finishing school at St. Agnes Episcopal School in Albany for two years and then for two years to Finch in New York, then known as Miss Finch's. Although my mother was a boarder there, my grandmother went to New York and took an apartment on Park Avenue, near the school, to keep an eye on her in the big city. My grandfather, a hay and grain merchant (the "teazle king" of upstate New York), bank director, Town Supervisor and Masonic bigwig, a large, bald man with a fierce walrus mustache, had died, leaving my grandmother not rich but what was known in those parts as "well off." Both he and my grandmother had taught in one-room schoolhouses in their teens: she after graduation from a finishing school called the Select School for Young Ladies; he, straight from the LaFargeville public school. None of my ancestors ever had the driving, gut-burning, ruthless ambition requisite for building a fortune. They were all content to be farmers, teachers, lawyers, clergymen, with here and there a minor merchant.

As a child, I felt toward my parents more curiosity than affection. When I was around them I used to watch them and wonder about them. Why was my father sobbing in the living room one day, when I was five? Why did my mother go tea-dancing with other men? Once in New York when she had no one to leave me with, she took me with her and her beau of the moment, leaving me to sit alone at the table eating dish after dish of chocolate ice cream while they tangoed or danced the turkey trot, the bunny hug, the grizzly bear ("It's a bear! It's a bear!") or the maxixe, my mother wearing kohl on her eyelids, a hobble skirt of red panne velvet and her Irene Castle tricorn hat of stiffened gold lace, trimmed with mink tails and red silk cherries. She was a born flirt, sensual, passionate, very beautiful and spoiled. She never earned a dime in her life and had no idea of thrift—when she was first married, her flat silver and her diamonds had to come from Tiffany's (my grandmother paid for them), and even in her eighties, in her last years, when she was living on Social Security payments, and what I could give her, she would say things like "But I *must* have new cocktail napkins!"

They both had many affairs and were separated long before their divorce, which came when I was in my teens. My mother divorced my father for adultery, although he could just as easily have divorced her on the same grounds. They both remarried, each choosing a mate as opposite as possible to the original one. He married the daughter of a German immigrant baker, a girl whom he first seduced when she was fifteen and working in his factory, a ramshackle building outside Syracuse where for a while he made his fire extinguishers. My mother married a rough, hard-working laborer who had become a top building construction engineer. (I went to their wedding, held in New Jersey for reasons connected with his own divorce. It was followed by a rowdy supper in a German hofbrau, with a large white paper bell hung over the table and a flossy cake with two white papier-mâché doves squatting on it. The best man, a friend of my stepfather, was a policeman who had won a watch for being the Most Popular Policeman on the force—"From Commissioner Whalen down, girlie," he told me—and he had also been written up in *The New Yorker* as "the singing cop": he had toured Europe with some opera company and then returned to rejoin New York's Finest. We all had a lot of champagne and the cop sang "Mother Machree" and my mother cried. (My mother always enjoyed a good cry. She cried every time she heard Christmas carols; and when she watched events like Princess Margaret's wedding on TV she was all choked up.)

Both remarriages, moderately happy at first, had dismal endings. My stepmother became insane, although she was not hospitalized until after my father died of pneumonia, when he was seventy-one, an endemic debtor to the end. As to the other couple, my mother's nagging and torrential nonstop chatter drove my stepfather increasingly to the refuge of drink and eventually he, too, died in a state mental hospital. My mother survived him for eight years, dying of a heart attack when she was eighty-two. My daughter was with her at the Thousand Islands, and I was living in London. I did not go to her funeral, which doubtless shocked our upstate neighbors and remaining relatives, but I felt it would be a futile gesture.

As long as they lived, I continued to see my parents, particularly my mother, attempting to understand them, to figure out their motivation, which wasn't difficult, and to be tolerant. Above all, I was sorry for them. I didn't try to avoid seeing them, but neither did I seek it. (In my mother's case it was impossible to escape, as we both lived in New York and she demanded—and got—constant attention, with special command performances on all holidays, including Easter as well as her birthday and even St. Valentine's Day.) My father was feckless, my mother was domineering, but neither one was malicious or intentionally unkind. He lacked the stamina to resist, from the beginning, her reliance on her mother's money. She probably should have married one of her richer admirers so she could have spent her life buying clothes, playing auction bridge, and going to country club dances—her idea of the good life—but she had no social guile. They were shallow people who led barren lives, although she was gayer and more vivid, with a brisk enthusiasm even for discontent. As I say, I was sorry for them both, but I could not admire or respect them—and I did not love them, possibly because I knew from the time I was two that they did not love me.

Three

SOWING THE DRAGON'S TEETH

P EOPLE DON'T BELIEVE ME WHEN I say that I am never lonely, but it is true. I suppose that books were probably the key that unlocked the door to self-sufficiency. They guided and shaped my life, with some selective inner monitor extracting from them what was needed to sustain that contemplative curiosity—at once an attitude toward life and a defense against it—from which I have derived not only pleasure but the fortunate gifts of adaptability and survival. Their work was done a long time ago, but when I look back I can recognize their early influence and also that elements of it persist, like the detritus of dreams in the subconscious. Rummaging through memories, I can pinpoint the relationship between certain events and the literary allusions with which I adorned them, ridiculous and sophomoric as this may now seem . . . At the age of nineteen, I enthusiastically spurred myself into bed to lose my virginity while thinking of a poem by Langston Hughes, the last line of which was "Youth is the time for careless weather. Later, lass, be wary."

In view of the fact that I contracted syphilis from that first tentative encounter, I probably should have picked a more meteorologically cautious poet. However, when I learned the bad news, I sat up in the hospital bed and my first thoughts were of Oswald in *Ghosts* ("The sun! The sun!") and, less loftily, of Boy Fenwick in *The Green Hat*, committing suicide on the night of his wedding to Iris March. I did not feel especially tragic, bitter or fearful. Instead, I was more fascinated at finding myself in such a melodramatic plight, not as the result of a sinful life in the gutter, but of an unpremeditated night on the town with a friend of my parents, a man I had known from childhood. I didn't even have a crush on him, but he had a sort of rakish Jazz Age charm and I was flattered by the attention of someone who to me had always been one of "the grown-ups." I suppose I ought to have hated him but I didn't, even though he knew what he had done to me but he was evidently a prime subscriber to the old adage "A stiff prick has no conscience." I even kept the French china tea set he sent me in the hospital—I had to spend Christmas there—and was still using it twenty years later. ("Just Give Me Something to Remember You By." Indeed, he did.)

I copied in my diary what Wilde wrote in *De Profundis*: "I have got to make everything that has happened to me good for me . . . the silence, the solitude, the shame—each and all of these things I have to transform into a spiritual experience . . . The important thing . . . is to absorb into my nature all that has been done to me, to make it part of me, to accept it without complaint, fear, or reluctance. . . . To regret one's own experiences is to arrest one's own development."

This might seem to some an asinine method of therapy but it helped to pull me through without despair. I even wrote to an ex-Vassar friend a blithe couplet describing my affliction as "Infection labiorum Exceeding all decorum"; and I took a jejune satisfaction in making a list of famous people

I could think of who, according to what I had read, were equally unfortunate: "Caesar, Cleopatra, Henry VIII, Nietz-sche, Ivan the Terrible, Casanova, Napoleon, Catherine the Great, Dürer, Gauguin, Van Gogh, Goethe, Goya, Keats, de Maupassant, Wilde, Schubert, probably Beethoven and possibly, in the Bible, Abraham, Job and David."

In the three following years of intensive treatment with intravenous injections of Neosalvarsan ("606") and intramus-cular injections of mercury (those were pre-penicillin days), I was completely cured and have been astonishingly healthy ever since. (I sometimes startle people by saying, truthfully, "I've never had any diseases in my life except chicken pox when I was five and syphilis when I was nineteen.") It certainly didn't put me off sex one iota, or off literature, either. When I had my first illegal abortion (irrepressibly fertile, I had three in one year alone), while the anaesthetic was being administered, scared though I was of the whole procedure, I heard the doctor talking to the nurse about taking his vacation in Haiti. I managed to struggle out of the ether daze long enough to advise him, weakly, "A book you ought to read is *Black Majesty* by John Vandercook." Just before I regained consciousness again, I thought I saw two eagles swoop out of a tangerine-colored sky to begin pecking at my vagina. I opened my eyes to see that it was the doctor, dabbing at me with cotton swabs. He and the nurse helped me to my feet and as the latter led me from the surgery, I asked groggily, "Are you the silver-footed The-tis?" "No, honey, I'm the nurse," she said, guiding me into the little room where they let you lie down for ten minutes before putting you back out onto New York's East 17th Street. I must have had a real ether jag on (in my parents' youth, the wild party set used to get high by sniffing ether) because as I lay down on the couch and closed my eyes, I murmured sadly, "I shall never see the blue pigeons of Aldabra now." "Never mind, honey," the nurse said. "Just you lie here for a few minutes and you'll be right as rain." I bet she went back and said to the doctor, "That was sure a queer one!"

Even my erotic dreams had a literary tinge. I never dreamed of Rudolph Valentino or Clark Gable. Not me. My all-time favorite is the night I dreamed that President Franklin D. Roosevelt went down on me in celebration of his having been elected for a third term. When it was over, we lay on the bed, side by side, smoking—he with a long ebony cigaret holder, I with a short ivory one—and talking, but not of sex or politics. In the dream he said to me, "What was the first book you ever read?" "*The Sunbonnet Babies*," I replied.

And so it was. I could read when I was three and in the next ten years ran the gamut from *The Bobbsey Twins at the Seashore* to *The Castle of Otranto*, going through books in the LaFargeville house and the Syracuse Public Library like a revved up termite, with a ravenous and undiscriminating passion. I enjoyed just about everything and never skipped a word, whether it was the forty-eight small green volumes in my grandmother's set of Scott's Waverly novels, all the James Fenimore Cooper books, or Jerome K. Jerome's *Three Men in a Boat*. I sobbed over *A Dog of Flanders* and shuddered at fairy tale collections of stories about death, torture, beatings, cannibals who cooked and ate little children, desperate poverty, the poor little match girl who froze to death in the snow. I loved the *Diary of Marie Bashkirtseff* and started one of my own, but I also loved *Girl of the Limberlost* and was momentarily determined to spend my life collecting moths, just as when I read *Ben Hur* I pretended I was a leper and went around moaning "Unclean! Unclean!" During my Elsie Dinsmore phase (ten volumes of that series) I read the Bible every day and dreamed of growing up to marry some elderly friend of my father's, the way Elsie married Mr. Travilla, her dear Papa's old crony.

I had a tutor until I was seven, at which age I spent nearly a year in New York with my parents, living in a hotel and attending the Ethical Culture School on Central Park West. My mother never got up until noon, but my father took me to school every morning (we stopped for breakfast of pancakes and maple syrup at Child's, where he read his newspaper and I read the funnies page) and called for me afternoons. He also took me to my first movie, *The Birth of a Nation*, when it opened in 1915, and I was so enthralled that I chewed the brim off my panama hat and then had nightmares for weeks afterward in which I was saved like Mae Marsh from a fate worse than death (it was either that or jump off the cliff) by the timely arrival of the Ku Klux Klan.

I was happy when my parents sent me back to my grandmother. She took an apartment in Syracuse, and for the next seven years I went to a private school called Goodyear-Burlingame, run by the Misses Fanny and Hattie Goodyear, two spinster sisters whose uncle invented the rubber process. The school was in the former mansion of Walter Burlingame, son of Anson Burlingame, the first accredited American minister to the Imperial Court in Peking in 1861. Anson was so popular with the Chinese that they made him *their* ambassador to Washington in 1867.

I disliked most of my teachers, especially the Misses Goodyear and their rigid discipline, but I enjoyed studying and there wasn't much they could do about my recusant attitudes—they never expelled anyone, because they needed the money—in view of the fact that I always got A-plus or 100, led the honor roll each month, and won the poetry banner every year as the "best speaker." Every commencement I recited before the assembled students, teachers and parents, usually choosing to memorize some interminable poem like "Ode on the Death of the Duke of Wellington" or "The Wonderful One Hoss Shay" that stupefied my audience by length alone.

Understandably, I wasn't exactly popular with my schoolmates. My academic prowess was not the only reason. The other girls all lived in houses. My grandmother and I lived in an apartment. The others had been born in Syracuse; their parents belonged to the same clubs and were part of the same small-city so-called "society"; their fathers were local bankers or lawyers or businessmen. I was the outsider. Furthermore, when my beautiful, dashing mother came to visit me, she smoked Murad cigarets in public, something none of their humdrum, conservative mothers would have done. ("Does your grandmother smoke cigars?" one child asked me, mockingly.) My grandmother took me to dancing school each week. The others were taken by their mothers, who sat and talked to each other while my grandmother sat alone. I was invited to the birthday parties and dances, but I never gave one, and I never had a good time at theirs. I couldn't think of anything to say to the boys. I would listen avidly to the chatter of the others, trying to get the hang of it. There was a girl named Clara who was always the belle of the ball. She wasn't pretty, but she had a "line." She would roll her eyes and recite, "I can shimmy, I can shake, till my very corsets break. On the level, I'm a devil. I'm a Glen Cove parlor snake." It was years before I learned that a Glen Cove parlor snake was not something like a water moccasin.

I accepted my lack of popularity and shed no tears. I was more at ease with my grandmother. She often took me to the movies and once a week to the theater—a stock company headed by Frank Wilcox and Minna Gombell, who put on plays like *Smilin' Through, Lilac Time, Seven Keys to Bald-pate.* We also went to see Maude Adams in *Peter Pan* ("Very silly," I commented in my diary) and the Shake-spearean actors—Walter Hampden, Robert B. Mantell, E. H. Sothern and Julia Marlowe—who brought their companies to town. We heard Paderewski play the piano (he stopped in the middle of a piece and strode angrily to the front of the stage to berate a noisy latecomer) and we saw Pavlova dance, her Dying Swan solo a miracle of transcendent beauty, even to a child. I hardly dared breathe as I watched her.

It wasn't all high-class culture, either. We had a wind-up Victrola on which I played my Mound City Blue Blowers records and other hits of the day, like *Dardanella.* "I've got-ten so I can shimmy just wonderfully," I wrote in my diary when I was twelve. I must have learned at the movies because it certainly wasn't my grandmother who taught me. She disapproved of sex and told me *Jude the Obscure* was "a dirty book" and I shouldn't be reading it. Not wanting to displease her, I read *The Sheik* by flashlight in bed, goggle-eyed when the beautiful white English aristocrat girl asks her desert captor, "Why have you brought me here?" and he replies, "Bon Dieu! Are you not woman enough to know?" . . . "The burning light of desire in her eyes turned her sick and faint." Hot spit! (as I'm afraid we used to say). I was thirteen and believed every word, unaware that the author, Mrs. E. M. Hull, had never set foot in the desert or laid eyes on an Arab sheik, but was a quiet country housewife in Derbyshire, England, whose husband, Percy, bred prize pigs.

When I went away to boarding school my appetite for the printed word was still insatiable, but my taste improved. I also had friends for the first time. The school was Bradford, now a junior college but at that time also college preparatory, thirty miles from Boston and the oldest institution in New England for the higher education of women. My best friend in my senior class was an extremely pretty blond girl named Elsbeth Thexton. She came from Oak Park, Illinois, and she, too, was an omnivorous bookworm. From her I learned about writers I had never heard of before—Dostoievsky, Tolstoi, Fielding, Smollett, Sterne—and our idea of a good time was to discuss what we read or to memorize poetry and recite it. We were drunk on words. (From my diary: "Feb. 17, 1924. Elsbeth and I read *Dr. Faustus* out loud. Then we learned passages from it. Wonderful time!" "May 13, 1924. Am reading Sophocles and Euripides with Elsbeth. Great stuff!") We must have been insufferable at sixteen. Our letters to each other, during holidays, were larded with quotations— "as Schopenhauer says . . ." "to paraphrase Baudelaire . . ." and this went on for years to come. A letter she wrote me when we were both nineteen began, "Rather late in life I have started reading Spinoza." (She threw away my letters but I kept hers. It's a trait I inherit from my mother, who was a magpie. My mother never threw away a piece of used string, an empty mayonnaise jar, a button. She kept everything, on the theory that "it might come in handy some day.")

After graduation from Bradford, Elsbeth went to Wellesley

and I to Vassar. We spent Easter vacations together at the Hotel Bristol in New York and while our classmates were dating boys, going dancing, and otherwise behaving like normal flappers of that era, Elsbeth and I spent every day in Room 315 of the New York Public Library on Fifth Avenue, from early morning till closing time, *reading*. At our respective colleges we both perused *The American Mercury* every month and assiduously made lists of books and authors praised by Mencken, Nathan and James Huneker. Armed with these lists of names—Hauptman, Sudermann, Huysmans, Stendhal, the de Gourmont brothers, Flaubert, etc.— we daily put in our requests and sat happily at the library tables, reading and making notes. Once we took time off to browse for hours in Brentano's, and there I selected the first book I ever bought, aside from school books. It was the early nineteenth-century James Hogg's *Confessions of a Justified Sinner*, that extraordinary, phantasmagoric, anti-Calvinist satire that shocked Gide. I was more excited at buying that book than I would have been with a diamond bracelet. I can remember, but never recreate, the surge of pristine rapture.

Certainly my standards were higher in those years than they've ever been since. Hazlitt believed that what people think in their youth is often wiser than what they think when they mature; and Dr. Johnson said, "It is a hard enough reflection, but a true one, that I knew almost as much at eighteen as I do now." I'll go along with them both on that ground. This is why I have enormous respect for the young people of today. I think they're brighter—and more often right—than their elders. I only fear that they, too, may choose eventually the multiple practical rewards of compromise, rewards not only in a material sense but also because it is easier to settle for less than the best, to fudge the issues, to relax one's guard against the seductive appeal of glossy mediocrity.

Four

THE DIE IS CAST

M Y FIRST APPEARANCE IN print, aside from contributions to school magazines, consisted of a series of letters I wrote my Aunt Grace, who was married to my father's younger brother. The summer I was eighteen, Elsbeth and I went to Europe together. Our hearts were young and gay all right, but our trip was more unorthodox than the genteel escapades of Cornelia Otis Skinner and Emily Kimbrough or the usual student tour.

Deeply under the influence of Dos Passos' *Manhattan Transfer*, we thought the only "real" people, the truly "swell" (the highest compliment in our vocabulary) people were sailors, truckdrivers, prizefighters, prostitutes and their ilk, so that on shipboard, instead of joining the other students in potato races, shuffleboard, dancing, necking in the lifeboats and similarly normal teen-age pastimes, we spent every evening up in the forecastle, talking and drinking beer with the Dutch crew members. They may have been slightly bewildered, but as long as we were paying for the beer they accepted us in the same comradely, friendly spirit with which we treated them. Our obvious innocence was an impenetrable shield. We were so clearly not on the make, not trying to flirt with them, that not one of them ever made even a suggestion of a pass or said an improper word. (At least, not in English.) They tried to teach us Dutch; we queried them constantly about their lives; sometimes we sat with them on their deck space, in the June night, and we all sang—translating "Yes, Sir, That's My Baby" as "*Ja, Mynheer, das ist mein meisje*"—while one of them played his guitar. We had a wonderful time: Ah, this is Life, we thought. And, of course, we wrote it all down in our diaries each day, just as, later, we described our visits to Schiedamske Dyke, the red-light district of Rotterdam, to the brothel-lined Rue Fontaine-Ruvière in the twisting, sinister alleys of the Vieux Port in Marseilles, to Paris music halls and Heidelberg beer gardens. In letters home we simply copied from our notebooks, and my Aunt Grace, without changing a word and without bothering to inform me, sold my letters under her own name, with the title "Travel Diary of a Sub-Deb," to a magazine called *College Humor*. It was the only thing she ever sold in her life, although she always described herself as a writer and for some forty years tried unsuccessfully to sell something of her own. What's more, she didn't even share the money with me or buy me a gift. Instead, she had the nerve to send me a copy of the magazine. I was more amused than annoyed. I didn't want to be a professional writer anyway, and wrote to a Vassar friend, "The idea appalls me. I'm quite sure I'll never be able to write anything. I can't make up anything—I always have to tell the truth—and if I tried to do something autobiographical I couldn't pick a starting point or choose the episodes, and if I tried to settle on any particular one, I know it would dwindle away until there was no substance in it. Then, too, I can't decide on a goal: whether I'm going to try to write for *Scribner's* or *Liberty*. So I never get beyond a few minutes of raddled thinking, which then slips into outrageous daydreams in which I miraculously write *something*, become rich and famous, win the Nobel Prize, and marry a belted earl. The trouble is, I guess, that I really have no ambition."

I felt I was wasting my grandmother's money at Vassar, taking courses in Arthurian Romance, Spanish, French and English literature—merely an extension of what I had been doing on my own—and I objected to what I called "chainstore culture," the packaging of subjects in handy containers with labels. So I made my decision not to go back, and I stayed on in Europe alone, taking a ship home when it was too late to begin my junior year. The publisher of the Syracuse *Herald* had once worked for my father on the St. Lawrence Bulletin, so my father telephoned him and asked him to see me. He did, and I was immediately hired as a reporter. Neither one of us mentioned money, so I was indeed surprised when I received my first pay envelope at the end of the week and discovered that I was getting twelve dollars. I began on December 6, 1926 (my diary reads: "Up at 6:30, downtown by 8:00. Am in the City Room. Wrote minor church notices. Not very dazzling start but atmosphere of office rather exciting"), and spent two years on the *Herald* and two on the *Journal*, the Hearst paper in town (the editor lured me away from the *Herald* by offering me forty dollars a week). I have earned more or less of a precarious living as a writer ever since.

At first, I did the usual hack stories about missing girls, couples celebrating fiftieth wedding anniversaries, mother cats who nursed orphan puppies, geriatric features (a hundred-one-year-old woman who once knew Emerson), train wrecks, car accidents, fires (I can never forget the scene of one fire in a stable of race horses: the nightmarish screaming of those horses that ran out, their flesh burning, and were shot to end their agony), political and business conventions, as well as those of groups like the Lions, Eagles, Elks, Rotary Club, American Legion, Oddfellows. I covered one news story about a husband who tried to kill his wife with an ax but, as she told me, she stopped him in the nick of time by shouting, "Great God, Gus, don't do it! Remember you're a good Oddfellow!"

I soon graduated to by-line interviews with people who came to Syracuse to lecture or perform, at least one a week, among whom were Judge Ben Lindsey, the controversial advocate of birth control and "trial marriage" or "companionate marriage" (by which he meant that couples should live together without getting wed—and this was in the mid-twenties!), who came to lecture on "The Revolt of Modern Youth" and said to me, "Why insist on a twentieth-century banking code and yet remain content with a moral code made by a small nomad tribe centuries ago to suit their particular needs?" I interviewed Jackie Coogan, then about ten and wearing what were called knickerbockers, who came to visit his grandparents, a Syracuse couple. Lindbergh, following his solo Atlantic flight (I thought him "boyish, bland and boring"). Admiral Byrd, theatrical and handsome as a matinee idol. Gar Wood, who built speedboats. Count Felix von Luckner, "the Sea Devil," who as a German sea raider in World War I sank eighteen ships with not a life lost and gained such a reputation for chivalrous conduct that when he arrived in New York to begin his lecture tour he was greeted by five thousand cheering people at the West 79th Street pier and received an official reception at City Hall. Gilda Grey, Queen of the Shimmy, a Polish girl with milk-white skin, gray eyes, a mop of yellow curls and a magnificent body. Aimee Semple McPherson, about whom I wrote a friend, "the greatest religious bunk shooter of the century, greater than Billy Sunday because her line is more patently hypocritical, more blatantly stupid, but she puts it across through sheer magnetism, and she sure has sex appeal, with her flaming hair (every man in the audiences must imagine how she would look with that glorious hair unpinned and flowing over her naked body) and a voice huskier than Lenore Ulric's, with a purring, persuasive note." I had breakfast with Red Grange, the legendary football hero; I drank with the great Walter Hagen; I interviewed Con O'Kelly, Ireland's heavyweight champion, in his dressing room. Lita

Grey Chaplin had received a million-dollar settlement on her divorce from Charlie (she was sixteen when she became his second wife and was only twenty when I interviewed her) but she was doing a vaudeville tour, certainly not just for the money. Although she could neither sing, dance nor act, she had flamboyant good looks, with curly black hair, snapping dark eyes with what then were called "beaded eye-lashes," and long, lovely legs. She chewed gum vigorously all during our interview and refused to discuss details of her marriage except to remark that Chaplin was not very funny at home. Jean Acker, the dead Valentino's first wife, also played our local vaudeville house and told me she refused an offer of five hundred dollars more salary because it was contingent on letting herself be billed as the ex-Mrs. Valentino. "There are some things people don't do for money," she said. "I have worked since I was fourteen and supported myself on my own name and I'm not going to change." She took a couple of verbal swipes at Pola Negri, Valentino's last affair, who was making the most of the publicity, and at Natacha Rambova, the official widow, who claimed publicly that Rudolph still made love to her from "the Spirit World."

I also wrote a daily column which I revoltingly called "Feminina, by Peg," a grab bag of items ranging from gossip and fashion to politics and prize fights (I was a fight fan in those days). For a while I was burlesque critic, reviewing the performances of the Step Along Burlesk Company, a job I obtained when a fellow reporter named Kenneth Sparrow, who had been both church editor and burlesque editor, decided to resign the more secular position. I had applied with alacrity to replace him, having become a burlesque buff at Vassar, when a classmate and I used to go to New York and sit entranced at the National Wintergarden Burlesk on East Houston Street, which we first learned about by reading e.e.cummings on the subject in *The Dial*.

Later, on the Hearst paper, I became the film critic, the drama critic, the art critic and an occasional substitute for the music critic, who had locomotor ataxia and couldn't always make it to a concert. I suppose the editor figured that because I had been at Vassar I must know about art and music, an erroneous assumption in the latter case, as I couldn't tell the difference between one instrument and another, or, more truthfully, the only ones I was sure of were the piano, harp and violin. I hadn't the faintest notion of what a woodwind was, or the others. I made up a patter from scraps of what Huneker had written about Brahms and bits I had gleaned from other music criticisms, and I wrote things like, "Rosa Ponselle was in fine voice last night," when for all I knew she could have had laryngitis and I couldn't have told the difference. I also reviewed concerts by Mischa Elman, Heifetz and Kreisler, and interviewed them all, as well, for feature stories, thereby adding a phrase here and there to my critical jargon.

Although never a scoop-scoop reporter, I did have an exclusive interview now and then, through no ingenuity of my own, such as the time I rode to prison on the train with Ruth St. Claire, the first woman to get life under the Baumes Law (a law making life imprisonment mandatory for a fourth felony). She had stolen two baby dresses. I felt outraged by her sentence and so was Mrs. Eleanor Roosevelt, whom I interviewed soon afterward, but apparently nothing could be done about it. I also covered the trial of six convicts involved in an Auburn prison riot, during which a guard and another convict were killed. Although usually law-abiding myself, through cowardice, not morality (my husband used to say I was a chicken-hearted mouse), I have never had much admiration for the loud Law and Order advocates or their deputies in uniform. This tendency to side with rebels was partly of literary origin. At that time I was still under the spell of *Manhattan Transfer*. (There are four books that have strongly influenced my life and my thinking: Conrad's *Victory*, *Manhattan Transfer*, Jack London's *Martin Eden*, and Edgar Snow's *Red Star over China*.) Prison conditions back in the twenties were even worse than today, so my sympathies were with the convicts who had taken part in the riot. One of them had also gotten life under the Baumes Law, for holding up a brothel; another had robbed a bank in

Buffalo; and the other four, as I wrote in my notes, "were in for what I would call petit larceny, with the exception of one in for sodomy, which after all is not a crime but a pleasure."

The three interviews that left the strongest impression were with Clarence Darrow, John Cowper Powys and Al Jolson. It was a year after the 1925 Tennessee "monkey trial" that Darrow came to Syracuse and, in a quiet, calm, easy way, he tore into cherished conventional beliefs about law, religion, education, conscience, morals. With my own views on our educational system and as a college dropout, I enjoyed it when he said, "I used to go to school. I learned a lot of things. Yes, lots. Why, I could even bound Indiana once. Not that I ever had occasion to bound Indiana. Not that I could bound Indiana now. I don't think I'd want to, in particular." He ended the interview by telling me, "Nothing in this world is absolute. Even what I'm saying isn't absolute. But it's as near it as you can get."

As for Powys, I had read *Wolf Solent* and wanted the book never to end, I loved it so much. Of course I was thrilled at the chance to interview him and to hear him lecture. The following day I ran into him on the street and we had coffee together. I thought he was wonderful-looking, with his great, gaunt body and face, the fierce eyes under heavy eyebrows, the strange, mystical manner. He was the one who turned me on to Dorothy Richardson, because at the end of his lecture he said, "If you remember nothing else of what I have said, I want every person to leave this hall, saying over and over again, 'Dorothy Richardson, Dorothy Richardson, Dorothy Richardson.'" When I asked him about her, he said that Willa Cather and other good women writers wrote "like clever men," but that Dorothy Richardson wrote "like an honest woman."

If you live long enough, everything comes around again. In 1973, a long-overdue biography was published in London: *Dorothy Richardson: The Genius They Forgot*. When I read the review, it was the first time I had seen her name in forty years, not since the mid-thirties, when Frank Crowninshield, the editor of *Vanity Fair*, wrote to her in London (where she was trying to support herself and her husband by doing translations) and bought from her, for me, six of her books I had been unable to find. She wrote thirteen in all, under the collective title *Pilgrimage*. She was the inventor of stream-of-consciousness writing—before Joyce, before anyone—but her books, intensely personal and obviously autobiographical (including a flimsily disguised revelation that she had an affair with H. G. Wells—who didn't?—that ended with a miscarriage), never caught on and were soon out of print. Powys, also long neglected, suddenly reappeared about the same time in 1973, with the critic George Steiner writing in the London *Sunday Times* of "his legendary charisma" and stating flatly that "Hardy, D.H. Lawrence and John Cowper Powys are the three great modern English novelists," comparing him, in some respects, to Shakespeare, Proust, Tolstoi and Dickens. It was certainly a year of revived memories for me. Even my first book purchase, *Confessions of a Justified Sinner* (and I had *never* heard or seen any mention of that one since I bought it) popped up in a new British edition and in a dramatized version at the Edinburgh Festival, while another old forgotten favorite of mine, George Meredith, now seems likewise due for renewed attention.

And then there was Al Jolson, to my mind unquestionably the greatest entertainer of his kind in my lifetime, far better than Sinatra ever was, better than Chevalier, better than any others of his own day, like Eddie Cantor. I don't mean the Jolson of "Mammy" or "Sonny Boy." I mean Jolson singing jazz. No one could rival him then, and no one has since. His terrific vitality, his marvelous rhythm, above all, the electrifying intensity of his personality—it all comes over still on film, but alive, on the stage, it was blazing. You can't describe it. I can't, anyway, except to say that it was overwhelming and irresistible. Last year a London television program about old movies showed a clip from the 1927 film *The Jazz Singer*, with Jolson—not in blackface—singing "Toot, Toot, Tootsie, Goodbye," snapping his fingers, rolling his eyes, swinging his hips, stopping once to shout, "Get hot!"

I was spellbound, but the interesting thing is that my son Kevin, twenty-six, watched with amazed admiration. "He's got everything!" he exclaimed. "The Mick Jagger bit—everything!" while the young TV commentator, after the scene was over, shook his head and said in an awed tone, "What a sex pot! Makes Tom Jones look like a Mother Superior."

I was very lucky to have fallen into the kind of work that was all fun and never boring. Also, save for the first few months, I was the only girl reporter both on the *Herald* and the *Journal*. Naturally, this made things even more interesting. It was a matter of pride with us never to appear to be working, never to be seen taking notes. At nineteen, I was sizzling with energy and enthusiasm, but I learned to disguise this and, as we would say today, to be cool. One of my fellow reporters said to me early on, "Don't rush around like a fart in a mitten. The idea is to do your job but never act as if you take it seriously."

I caught on quickly and, aside from a hiatus of about a month at the start of my career—I had only been working one week—when I was in the hospital with my so-called social disease (what, I wondered, would be an unsocial disease?) and the discomfort of the treatments for it, the life I managed to lead was an entertainingly dissipated caper. It was during Prohibition and we all did a lot of heavy drinking in speak-easies (a diary entry says: "Yesterday I left the office at 9 A.M., taking three of their best reporters with me, and we never came back all day. Two of the reporters are still missing. Cf. Tacitus: 'To pass an entire day and night in drinking disgraces no one.'")

I had first learned to drink when I was sixteen and visited my Bradford roommate, Kay Watson, in Manchester, New Hampshire. Kay was a small, slim girl with large brown eyes and pretty legs. She was what we called cute and peppy, no intellectual, but I was impressed by her popularity with boys and also because she shaved under her arms with her father's old-fashioned straight razor. In her home town of Manchester, she went with a crowd of kids who were right out of *Flaming Youth*. Those dear old twenties, an era we now think so adorable, were not all Joan Crawford dancing the Charleston. The darling flappers, and their boyfriends ("finale hoppers" and "lounge lizards") used to get dead drunk at country club dances and prep school proms or "hops," swigging from hip flasks in the rumble seats of cars; and there were teen-agers, as well as adults, who went blind from bad bootleg booze. When I think of some of the stuff I tossed down, not only then but in the early thirties (we gaily called it "rot gut," an adequate descriptive term), the hair-raising rides in cars with drivers so pissed they couldn't tell the street from the sidewalk, the bar brawls I witnessed, including some speak-easy shoot-outs and knife fights, I consider myself fortunate to have survived it all. I defy anyone to deny convincingly that today's harmless pot smoking is far preferable.

Of course, I didn't drink at school—too busy reading, I guess—although I do remember that when I was at Vassar, we could get bootleg gin at the Victory delicatessen on Sixth Avenue in New York simply by asking for it by the code name "one pint of square white rock." Peter Lehman and I daringly bought some there one weekend and brought it back to Vassar, where we drank it in paper cups and it all but ate through the cup bottoms to take the veneer off the table. (Peter—her name was Frances, but she was always called Peter—was a lovely-looking, intelligent, dark-haired girl, daughter of Albert Lehman of Lehman Brothers, niece of Herbert Lehman, later to be Governor, and granddaughter of Adolph Lewisohn. She was immensely rich but was so truly well bred that it never showed, and I liked her. She left Vassar, the same year I did, to marry John Loeb, the stock broker.)

My initiation in drinking preceded my participation in sex. When I was a small child, my Aunt Grace, the plagiarist-to-be, explained the mechanics of sexual intercourse to me in some detail and shocked me by assuring me that everyone did it. Worst of all, she said that Lillian Gish did it.

"*Not Lillian Gish!*" I cried in a stricken tone. She was my favorite movie actress. Watching her in *Hearts of the World*, *Broken Blossoms*, *Way Down East*, my grandmother and I would cry so hard our eyes would be red-rimmed for hours. Frankly, I didn't believe my aunt.

When I grew older, it never occurred to me that any of my acquaintances might not be as virginal as I was. There were probably several who weren't, but the first one I knew about was a frisky, baby-faced blonde named Alice. We were friends my first year at Bradford and during the summer holiday she wrote me that she was dating a boy who was evidently a mine of fascinating information. "You know those funny knobs on the nude male statues in the Boston Museum?" Alice wrote. "Well, they are called balls. Bob says they have something to do with sexual intercourse. Also, he told me that if a boy strokes the inside of a girl's thigh, it makes her feel sleepy, so then she doesn't care what he does to her." Alice didn't return to Bradford the following year but a note in my diary reads: "A letter from Alice. She says she 'went the limit.' I just can't believe it!!" I should have been prepared by her previous letter. Doubtless, she simply got too sleepy.

Recently, I've been reading and throwing away old love letters. Not counting the initial disaster, I seem to have had quite a few affairs during those newspaper years, but I never took any of them too seriously, an attitude explained in a diary entry made when I was twenty: "I can never mix for long in the fluid exchange of social life. Every once in a while I must withdraw from it and revert to watching. My mind is always standing off and criticizing, seeing myself act, hearing myself talk, even watching myself think. Sometimes I have wished that I could feel in an experience, in a relationship, the ecstasy of the moment, aureoled with an ironic consciousness of what went before and what would come after. The trouble is that I want to have that intellectual detachment and also at the same time completely to submerge myself in unself-conscious emotion, drench my ego in feeling, render it momentarily impossible for it to hover in the air, observing coldly the material me. The two states are incompatible and so, in the end, I have always settled for the role of the observer, the spy, even where my own emotional involvements are concerned."

Nevertheless, I remember my lovers fondly. I remained on friendly terms with them, even after we broke up—and I was always the one who did the leaving—and I gained something, some gift of tenderness or illumination from each. One of them, in those Syracuse newspaper days, probably loved me more deeply than any other man ever has. He was a thin, ascetic-looking man with a gift for acidic sarcasm and a dry-ice wit that seemed cold until it burned you. An Irishman born in England, he spent years in a Jesuit monastery (I just threw away a snapshot of him in cassock and biretta) before packing it in to become a newspaper reporter. He introduced me to Francis Thompson's eloquent life of Ignatius Loyola (I had only known *The Hound of Heaven*) and to Gerard Manley Hopkins. He used to quote to me from Edward Mangan's *Dark Rosaleen* ("And Spanish priests shall bring you ale across the ocean green") and send me telegrams in Latin. I quit him for another newspaperman, Fleet Phelps, who was bright, funny, and sexually inciting, even though slightly deaf, slightly lame, paunchy, more than twenty years my elder, a drunkard, with a hacking cigaret cough, and inconveniently married. He left his wife and we decided to move from Syracuse. He went to New York to become news editor of the *Morning Telegraph* in the winter of 1928–29, when an imaginative but doomed effort was made to turn the famous old racing sheet into a high-class paper. Walter Chrysler put up part of the money and Gene Fowler, hired as editor, assembled a dream staff that included Ben Hecht, Ring Lardner, Westbrook Pegler, Lois Long, Peter Arno, Whitney Bolton, Norman Hapgood. Fleet was an old friend of Fowler's and persuaded him to offer me a job, but I turned it down because my former Jesuit, who had also left his wife for me, was working on the paper, too ("I hired him because I love you," Fleet wrote me, "and feel some sort of odd responsibility for him") and I decided that working in the same City Room with the two of them could be a situation that might be described as fraught.

My most surprising sexual encounter (at least, it certainly surprised *me*) was when Rabbi Stephen Wise came to Syracuse in 1930 to deliver a sermon during Christian-Jewish Brotherhood Week. He was the most famous rabbi in America and during those Easter vacations in New York, Elsbeth and I had gone to the Free Synagogue to hear him. He was one of the most powerful orators of our time and his vigorous personality made a great impression on us. (I thought he was the most *Male* man I had ever seen.) So, when I was sent to his suite in the Hotel Syracuse to do a routine interview, I naïvely started by telling him that my friend and I had gone to the Free Synagogue to hear him and how much we had admired him. The next thing I knew, he had toppled me backward on the sofa and was making love to me, my hat knocked askew, and *with my gloves on.* Before I knew what had hit me, it was over, and not a split second too soon, either, as someone was knocking at the door and calling his name. "My God!" cried Rabbi Wise. "It's Rabbi Bienenfeld," leaping up and buttoning his fly. And so it was—not only the leading Syracuse rabbi, but with him was Mrs. Wise, who fortunately didn't have her hotel key. After some hasty introductions, Wise thrust a mimeographed copy of his speech into my hand, autographed a picture for me (I hadn't asked for one) and said he would telephone further details to the paper. He did call, later that day, and asked if he could see me again. Although still flustered, I agreed to meet him for coffee and nothing else, as the situation offered too strong an appeal to my curiosity for me to pass it up. However, it turned out that he meant coffee in his hotel room. I refused a reprise of our earlier set-to, although I was amazed by his persistence. As he was sitting on the sofa and I stood before him, he put his hands on my shoulders and tried to force me to my knees. "Kneel before me in prayerful attitude, my darling," he said. In *prayerful* attitude! I had to pay instinctive tribute to his sheer audacity in choosing that word, when he knew and I knew, and he knew that I knew, what he wanted me to do. I didn't comply—at that time, I was too sexually unsophisticated—but I did ask him how he dared risk the consequences of my blabbing to people or denouncing him. I assumed he acted the same way in every city he visited.

"At least you'll admit I have guts," he said, adding, with no undue false modesty, that he believed every dynamic man has a powerful sex drive and should make the most of it. He asked me to go to New York, as his guest, explaining not very convincingly that he wanted to show me "some of the work that is being done by the Free Synagogue." I was tempted, but of course I didn't go.

Three years later, however, when I was on the staff of *Vanity Fair*, Condé Nast wanted to have Wise photographed by Steichen for the magazine. At an editorial meeting the others were discussing how to approach him and I piped up to say, "I once interviewed him in Syracuse" (a contender for understatement of the month), so Nast asked me to arrange the studio sitting. I called Wise and to my surprise he remembered me. I made an appointment, went to the Free Synagogue to make the arrangements, and whoops! there I was on my back again, this time on the long table in his office, with Wise reciting in Hebrew: "Lift up your heads, oh ye gates; and be ye lifted up, ye everlasting doors; and the King of Glory shall come in." (I don't know Hebrew but he translated it for me when I asked.)

This time we had a chance to talk. I truly admired him for his many valiant crusades and wanted to discuss them. He had been outspokenly on the side of the women workers in the celebrated Triangle shirtwaist factory fire; he fought Tammany corruption in the days of Boss Croker; he helped draft the first child labor reform laws in Oregon; he was outstandingly active in other progressive, even radical, causes—which sometimes lost him influential members of his congregations, as many prominent Jews differed with his views.

I was frankly more interested in this aspect of his career than in his sex life. He telephoned me a few days later to say that he had borrowed a friend's apartment on Gramercy Park and I agreed to meet him there but then decided against it and failed to show up. He called to reproach me, saying ruefully that he had gone to the apartment with sandwiches and beer, and adding, "I even took a bath with perfumed soap."

The Steichen photograph turned out fine and I wrote the caption that said, in part: "Leader of America's protest against the Hitler anti-Semite campaign is Dr. Stephen Samuel Wise, perhaps the best known Jew in the country, aggressively racial, always a controversial figure. Enemies, disapproving his tactics, doubting his integrity, still are forced to admit his tremendous gusto and the power of his leadership. America's Number One rabbi was born on St. Patrick's Day in Budapest, the son of a rabbi, the grandson of a baron. . . . A born organizer, he has founded and directed hundreds of groups. . . . Physically a combination of William Jennings Bryan and Gentleman Jim Corbett, he has a leonine head, a voice of muted thunder and the strength of an ox. . . ." When the issue came out, I received a note from him thanking me and ordering five hundred copies of that page, including the caption, which he thought was delightful. We sold him the five hundred copies for the ridiculously low price of $7.25.

There was a brief epilogue to all this. In March, 1949 (by then I was a contented housewife and mother of two), Wise spoke out forcefully on some national issue. I can't remember now what it was, except that I was surprised and pleased by the stand he took. I sent him a brief note, congratulating him and mentioning that, although he wouldn't remember, I had once interviewed him long ago. I didn't say where. He answered promptly, saying that he was glad to hear from me, that he remembered me from our Syracuse interviews, and that he sent me cordial greetings. Three weeks later, he died of cancer at the age of seventy-five. Among all the newspaper editorial tributes, I cut one out to save: "He was a warrior and a magnificent one. To the causes which he championed through the years . . . he brought the formidable equipment of his resonant voice, majestic bearing, personality, integrity, intelligence and a sometimes shocking candor . . . He was a fearless man and caution was not in him." ("You can say that again!" I thought.)

By far the most important and serious event during my newspaper years was my politicalization. It was in 1929 that I became—for always—a radical, if not in my manner of life, at least in my way of thought. Until then, I had little interest in political affairs and knew less. My instinctive sympathies were with the poor and the oppressed; I had long believed that prejudice based on color, religion, race or nationality was stupid; and naturally I hated injustice. I didn't spend much time thinking about any of this and I had heard only vaguely of the labor movement. At Vassar I read Zola's *Germinal*, which put me unequivocally on the side of miners everywhere, an advocacy later strengthened by Pabst's 1931 German film *Kameradschaft*. I still believe that no pay can ever be too high for the conditions under which miners work. Also while at Vassar, I read about the British general strike and noted in my diary: "May 5, 1926. English general strike. *Tremendous* thing!!" (in my teens I was addicted to exclamation points and italics) but it never entered my head that I would ever become involved personally in the trade union movement, nor had I more than a faint idea what socialism was. When I was twenty-one, I cast my first vote for Al Smith for President. My only reason was because of the campaign against him as a Catholic. (When he lost, the current joke was that he sent the Pope a one-word cable: "Unpack.")

In the summer of 1929, I rewrote for the *Journal* an item that had appeared in the morning paper, *The Post-Standard*. The *Journal* was an evening paper, and for our first edition that was on the street in the early afternoon, most of the staff were given items from the morning paper to rephrase. This particular one reported that in a neighboring county some thirty patriotic male citizens had marched on a children's camp run by two young Communist women and had forced the two to kneel on the ground and kiss the American flag, after which the vigilante group smashed the camp's furnishings. I didn't know what a Communist was, but I was indignant at the thought of a group of men physically assaulting two girls in their early twenties and then breaking up the camp. When I rewrote the short item, I phrased it in sarcastic terms, lauding the extraordinary courage shown by thirty men in confronting and subduing two girls.

I suppose that when the local Communists read my rewrite—in a Hearst paper, of all places!—they couldn't believe their eyes. I received a visit from a girl I will call Ann, whom I had interviewed when I was on the *Herald*, writing a brief story about her then because she had hitchhiked from Arkansas, in those days a method of travel almost unheard-of for females. When the item about the vigilantes appeared, Ann came to see me and find out who had written it. She was a friendly, intelligent, warm-hearted Jewish girl who worked in a small bakery in a working-class section of town and whose parents, Russian immigrants, had been charter members of the American Communist Party. I liked her and started seeing her and her friends, among whom were some German Communists, members of the *Natur-Freinde*. The men were iron molders and steelworkers; the women either worked in factories or were servants. Weekends, they went on long hikes, and I, who never walked five blocks if I could find a taxi or drive the office car, was soon walking five miles into the countryside, part of it through woods, stumbling into mud and over fallen branches, getting hit in the eye by twigs, and finally, ending up sleeping side by side with ten young men and four girls in a hay loft. I was amazed to discover that I enjoyed it. I had never had any working-class friends before and for me it was a revelation to learn how bright, well-informed, attractive and pleasant they were. It made me happy to have them like me. Although the women were suspicious of me at first and inclined toward hostility, I won them over until even the one who disliked me the most admitted to her brother-in-law, an iron molder who fancied me, that I was "nice and kind and not stuck-up." In the daytime we swam in the lake and at night we sat around, drinking beer and talking or singing. (Several of them played the guitar, accordion or violin.) They taught me a great deal and so did the members of the Young Communist League, intent on proselytizing. It fell on fallow ground. I read the books and pamphlets they gave me, and it all made a lasting impression. I attended their discussion groups and once I even joined them in a demonstration, helping to carry a large red-and-white placard with the legend LONG LIVE THE RED ARMIES OF INDIA AND CHINA! By and large, most of those earnest young persons were honest and unselfish, with an enviable and consistent goodness, a profound morality, a principled idealism and commitment to justice. I have known many bad Communists in my time, but the finest people I have ever known have been Communists, too, and even some of the ones who later turned out to be the phoniest had their lives for a brief time touched with a certain sense of valid purpose through the experience of being part of the struggle to help their fellow men. The failures and errors and misdeeds only confirm to me that human beings are fallible and corruptible, but this does not invalidate the basic theory and the goal. As Heywood Broun once said, when accused of prejudice, "Yes, I am prejudiced. I am prejudiced in favor of truth and right and justice."

I didn't join the Party then, but I might have. In October, 1930, right after my twenty-third birthday, Ann tried to get me to hitchhike with her to Commonwealth, the Workers' College in Mena, Arkansas, founded by Red Kate O'Hare and other followers of Eugene Debs. The idea was that I would teach journalism part time and work part time, as did everyone at the college, at manual labor of some kind. Faculty and students together constructed the buildings, grew their own food and were a self-sufficient commune. I seriously considered it, but then I decided that I was simply not a type for hitchhiking and roughing it in the simple life, so instead I took a different route to a different milieu.

Djalma Desai, a handsome Hindu from Bombay, whose father had been prime minister of the native state there, drove me to New York, where with two young women I had known at Bradford I shared an apartment on East 30th Street, just off Fifth Avenue, and started looking for a job in those dreadful days of the Depression.

Five

CONDÉ NAST:
He Knew
What He Wanted

THE PRIVATE ELEVATOR LEADING
to the penthouse at 1040 Park Avenue was loaded with Vanderbilts, Astors, Whitneys and their ilk, all dressed to kill,
when two men squeezed in, just before the door closed. Once
before, I had seen them without make-up, so I recognized
them, but I doubt if the others did, because Groucho, minus
fake eyebrows, mustache and spectacles, and Harpo, minus
wig, looked ordinary to the point of anonymity. As we rode
up in dignified silence, the brothers looked us over and then
Groucho said, loud and clear, "This is a classy joint." "Yeah!"
replied Harpo, just as loudly. "You said it!" The others acted
as if they hadn't heard, eyes averted, while the two Marxes
tried to keep from laughing.

Groucho and Harpo were right. It was indeed a classy joint.
We were all guests at one of Condé Nast's famous parties,
invitations to which were considered an accolade with a

social cachet ludicrously out of tune with the era, which was that of the Depression. He had three guest lists, card-indexed: "A," which was society; "B," those prominent in the arts; "C," other celebrities, including an occasional top model or even an upper-bracket hetaera whose horizontal rise to fame had been topped (if that is the word) with a distinguished liaison. His best galas were an amalgam of the three lists, about two hundred people, and were held in his thirty-room triplex. A huge terrace surrounded the penthouse, there was a Chinese Chippendale ballroom, ornate French furniture all over the place and, for party guests, a lavish ladies' powder room where the toilet was disguised by an antique wooden throne with a piece of rare tapestry as a cover on the seat and a musical toilet-paper roll. The whole apartment had been decorated by Elsie de Wolfe, who later became Lady Mendl, renowned as an old lady who dyed her hair green, wore gloves when eating, stood on her head as a daily exercise, and received visitors in her bathroom, which was furnished with zebra-skin couches, a silver tub with silver-swan faucets, and a waterproofed white velvet rug.

For this particular party Condé had hired two orchestras, two bars were set up, and there was a slew of extra footmen and waiters. He also bought hundreds of gardenias and had them stuck, one by one, in flower boxes on the terrace. Although he told me that he had been worth $17 million on paper before the 1929 Wall Street crash ("I lost my shirt in Goldman Sachs," he said), during this period he used to complain about being broke and how he had had to borrow $4 million from Harrison Williams, who headed something called the Blue Ridge Holding Company. He had explained the whole financial set-up to me, step by step, but I never could understand the devious pecuniary maneuverings of the rich and sometimes I used to wonder if Harrison Williams, often a guest at the parties, ever took a look at all those gardenias and then said, "Hey! Don't forget you owe me $4 million."

The big parties usually began shortly before midnight, following some special event. For example, he gave a supper and dance in honor of Clare Boothe Luce on the opening night of her play *The Women*, another for Ina Claire when she starred in a Frederick Lonsdale drawing-room comedy —so-called because the characters were upper-class twits who sat around in drawing rooms and spouted brittle dialogue—and one for George and Ira Gershwin after the opening of *Porgy and Bess*. These parties lasted until four or five in the morning, sometimes later. I've forgotten what this particular one was celebrating—I went to most of them over a period of six years—but I remember that I wore a pale yellow silk-crepe evening dress with a train. It was high in front but cut to the waist in back (we often went braless in those days, too) and I had two fresh daffodils pinned in my pageboy bob. I brought extra ones with me and told the butler to put them in the icebox so that I would have replacements when the first ones began to droop. I also remember that, as usual, the guests were glittering and the conversation silly. The women talked in high, thin, cold-silk voices and used expressions like "Shall we make it Friday-ish?" . . . "Yes. Five-ish?" . . . "My dear, it's too blush-making" . . . And everything—a new book, play, opera or whatever—was either "absolutely foul, darling" or, conversely, "too, too divine." Those were the days when there were people who actually referred to themselves as "the literati" or "the intelligentsia," and they all obviously preened themselves on being a glossy elite, but I thought of them as bubble-blowers—irridescent bubbles that had no substance and burst in the air, leaving no trace. The wits were those who excelled at the malicious wisecrack: "She's the girl who married a Jew to get in the Social Register" . . . "She's kind to her inferiors." "Really? Where does she find them?" . . . "He objects to meeting her former lovers." "How does he avoid it? Is he a hermit?"

They talked incessantly about the *Vogue* editor who had found her husband in bed with the butler ("The butler! Oh, well, buggers can't be choosers."); about Mimsy Taylor, a young socialite model with an exotic Balinese face, who had gone to Quito with Ben Hecht (he later wrote a play about it, *To Quito and Back*)—"Quito? But why Quito, of all places? My dear, her family must be wild. Why couldn't he have taken her to the Riviera?"—and how her aunt, Countess Dorothy di Frasso, had taken Gary Cooper on an African safari; about the two new men in town with the curious names, my dear, of Baron Hubert Pantz and Baron Niki de Guinzberg, and how the latter, a rich young White Russian, had given *the* party of the Paris season on an island in the lake in the Bois de Boulogne, with white velvet carpeting laid from the water's edge to the entrance, for the use of guests who arrived in rowboats—"Princess Marina of Greece was there and Elsa Maxwell came as Napoleon III—my dear, it couldn't have been more amusing!"

Well, that was the way the conversation went at these affairs. I know I have it right because sometimes I took notes of the tidbits. I always felt like an anthropologist observing a strange tribal cult, even though, as a top Condé Nast editor, I was accepted as part of the whole. I certainly never felt as if I belonged, and if the others could have read my thoughts they would have shrunk from me in dismay. Still, it was entertaining to be on the inside with a good view of the show, so I could watch, for instance, George Jean Nathan, pie-eyed drunk, grab his long-time love, Lillian Gish, pale and demure in a brown monk's robe with a cord sash, and yank her unceremoniously onto the dance floor to stagger around in a foxtrot—or Barbara Hutton in the ladies' room struggling to adjust the gold coronet which kept tilting rakishly askew on her blond head. She had married in Paris the first of her seven husbands, Prince Alexis Mdivani of the "marrying Mdivanis (whose titles were suspect because they came from Georgia where, it was said, "anyone who owns ten sheep is a prince"), settling on him a trust fund of $1 million. She was a pudgy, pretty girl whose enormous wealth inspired a steady flow of gossip column reportage, such as the exhilarating news that she changed her nail polish three times a day to match her gowns. Her debut at the Ritz-Carlton cost $50,000 for the decorations alone, of

which $10,000 went to cover the walls with California euca-
lyptus trees. This was in a year when there were breadlines
and soup kitchens for the hungry unemployed, and the
"Hoovervilles" (little shacks for the homeless, built of corru-
gated cardboard and tin on the outskirts of cities) were
multiplying. By the time of Condé's most lavish parties there
were 12 million unemployed in the country, and there were
riots and hunger marches throughout the land, although not
a mention of these dreary events dimmed the luster of those
gay and amusing people dancing in the penthouse . . . May I
give you a lift in my tumbrel?

Condé was the president of Condé Nast Publications, Inc.,
and his magazines, in addition to *Vogue*, *Vanity Fair* and
House & Garden, included the *Vogue Pattern Book*, *American Golfer*, *Glamour* and, through his subsidiary French
company, *Jardin des Modes*. There was also an English
company (there were separate English, French, Italian and
American *Vogues* and, briefly, a German one, which was a
flop, as well as a South American one, started in Argentina,
which also failed) and there was the Condé Nast Press,
situated on thirty-one acres in Greenwich, Connecticut. He
was also a director of The Waldorf-Astoria Hotel and president of the Park-Lexington Corp., owners of Grand Central
Palace and adjoining properties. His clubs were the Racquet
and Tennis, Piping Rock, Tuxedo, Knickerbocker, Dutch
Treat, Riding, National Links, City, Deepdale Golf and various country clubs and beach clubs.

He was born March 26, 1874, in New York but the family
moved to St. Louis. He never talked much about his childhood. According to Edna Woolman Chase, the *grande dame*
editor of *Vogue* for so many years, Condé's father, William
Nast, was "the founder of German Methodism in America,"
but whatever that means, it doesn't sound like something
one does for a living. His mother was Catholic, of French
descent (Condé was named after her ancestor, Dr. Andre
Condé, a military surgeon who emigrated from France to
St. Louis in 1760). Condé graduated from Georgetown University in 1894 (while there, he managed athletic teams and

learned to play the flute) and received his M.A. degree there the following year. He then studied law at St. Louis University, getting his LL.B. in 1897. For a while he practiced law in St. Louis. A former Georgetown classmate, Robert Collier, asked him to go to New York as advertising manager of *Collier's Weekly* and he accepted, starting in 1900 at a salary of twelve dollars a week and rising, by 1905, to $50,000 a year, by which time he was business manager. This was his true métier. He had a passion for figures, balancing budgets, and financial organization. In 1907 he left *Collier's* to manage the Home Pattern Company, which he had started, not because he was wildly interested in female fashion but because he thought it a sound commercial enterprise. In 1909 he bought *Vogue*, a journal devoted to society and fashion, which had been founded in 1892 by fifty-six backers, including Cornelius Vanderbilt. Under Nast's ownership and the editorship of Mrs. Chase (who had started on the original *Vogue* in 1895, addressing envelopes), it became the most famous fashion magazine in the world, an arch synonym for chic.

In 1913 Nast bought a magazine called *Dress*, fearing that it might be a possible rival to *Vogue*, and decided to fill it with stuff about the theater, art, music, and other material that didn't fit *Vogue*. He paid $3000 for the name *Vanity Fair* (a defunct publication of the late nineteenth century, "sort of a refined *Police Gazette*") and he called the first issue, which came out in September, 1913, *Dress and Vanity Fair*. He then showed the acumen that was the secret of his success by asking Frank Crowninshield to edit the new magazine, which Crowninshield (shortening the name to *Vanity Fair*) brilliantly did from 1914 through February, 1936, when *Vanity Fair* merged with *Vogue*—although submerged would be a more accurate verb.

Crowninshield, known as Crowny, came from a distinguished old New England family and spent his youth in Paris (where he was born), Italy and Boston. He was assistant editor on *Munsey's*, editor of *The Century*, and publisher of *The Bookman*. He was an authority on French art;

he knew the writers of the day and had been a friend of Max Beerbohm, O'Henry, A. Conan Doyle; he played bridge at the Cavendish Club (of which he was a co-founder and president); he frequently had tea with Mrs. Astor and dined with Mrs. Hamilton McK. Twombly, granddaughter of Commodore Vanderbilt, and was therefore considered acceptable to those who were, like Miss Jean Brodie's girls, *la crème de la crème*. He was everyone's idea of a polished Edwardian gentleman of wit and urbane elegance, the perfect choice to edit and shape *Vanity Fair* into the most sophisticated magazine of its time. He was sixty when I first knew him, a slender man with neat white hair, a crisp white mustache, and the bright, hard, staring, brown eyes of a bird. Possibly a neuter, he had never been known to have any sexual relationship with man or woman. Nor had he ever touched alcohol, and he gave up smoking in 1906. He never disapproved of other people's indulgence, no matter what the vice, but took a worldly and amused interest. He was a delightful companion, despite his snobbery. Seemingly modest and self-deprecatory (these are often the biggest snobs of all) he wore humility as an occasional decoration like the carnation in his lapel buttonhole, and I sometimes thought that his more exaggerated snobbishness was also part of a practiced divertissement. For example, he never used a telephone directory and would say of someone, "How will we ever get in touch with him? He's not in the Social Register." He thought, or pretended to think, that newspapermen were uncivilized louts and once disposed of Edwin James, then managing editor of the *New York Times*, by saying airily, "Look at Edwin James! He's never asked anywhere." And when recommending a girl for a secretarial job, it didn't occur to him to mention her typing and shorthand skills, if any. Instead, I heard him say, "She's well bred and comes from a good family."

He and Nast were a strange pair (they shared an apartment for six years—"I suppose people thought we were fairies," Condé told me) but they were both smart enough to appreciate each other's exceptional talents. Condé wanted "class magazines." For *Vanity Fair* his aim was not circulation, which never rose much above 90,000, but quality and prestige, which it certainly had on both sides of the Atlantic. It never really made money, but his other enterprises did, and all through the Twenties he amassed his fortune. Despite the apparent affluence of his life, he was sometimes a tight-wad, in true millionaire tradition. In restaurants and night clubs he often gave tips so mingy that I was embarrassed. Once, at the Coq Rouge, after eating and drinking for several hours, he left a fifty-cent tip and I slipped back to our table, telling him I had forgotten my cigaret case, and put down an extra five dollars. He seldom wore a hat because he hated to tip hatcheck girls. (He wasn't stingy out of meanness. I think it was a matter of principle: he thought tips a degrading way of conning extra money, as of course they are.)

One evening he took Bill Paley (then Chairman of the Board of CBS) and Paley's first wife Dorothy and me to dinner at The Colony. I thought the check was rather reasonable, considering it was The Colony, but Condé insisted that the waiter call Gene Cavallero, the owner, to whom he said, "This check is outrageous." They took ten dollars off it. I thought then, "Boy, you sure have to be rich *and* famous to get away with something like this!" He didn't like to carry money with him, so he was always borrowing from me, a dollar for a taxi, a quarter for a doorman, and never paid it back. When I went to Havana for a holiday, he kept sending me cables asking me to come home. After I returned, he said, "I was afraid you might not come back." "I had to," I said. "I kept thinking of all that $17.25 I have invested in you." And once, when he asked me to marry him, I told him that I appreciated the honor but that if I did, everyone would think I married him for his money, whereas the true situation was that I couldn't afford him.

"You actually knew Condé Nast?!" an American woman said to me recently, in an awed tone. "He must have been a fascinating man." Condé fascinating? No, he wasn't. It isn't a term one would ever have applied to him, but when I said so, at this London dinner party, I could see that no one believed me, such is the potent glamour of a legendary name, especially one associated with the arts, high fashion, high society, high living, a man of whom a newspaper columnist wrote in the thirties, "In the mid-Victorian sense he is probably Manhattan's most perfect man-about-town." He was not brilliant, witty or erudite. No raconteur, he never contributed much to any group conversations and in public he had a stiffly formal, precise manner, rather grim-faced, not given to spontaneous laughter, with a smile that seemed, as Daniel O'Connell said of Peel's, "like a gleam of wintry sunshine on the brass handles of a coffin." Nor was he attractive in appearance, at least not in the years I knew him. He looked like a banker. He was about 5' 9," bald with a fringe of thinning gray hair at back and sides, small eyes behind rimless pince-nez glasses, a thin-lipped mouth turned down at the corners, a deeply etched line running from each side of his nose to his chin. He never slouched in public, whether at work or play, but always stood as if encased in a plaster cast from chin to toes. When seated, he didn't relax, lean back, cross his legs or put his elbows on the table. Even when playing golf there was a rigidity about him, while at parties, no matter how much he drank (champagne, whisky, lethal mixtures like stingers and sidecars), he consistently displayed the vivacity of a stuffed moosehead. That steel backbone only unbent in private. There was a time when I suppose I knew him better than most people. At least, I knew a private side to him that was incongruent with his public face. I was genuinely fond of him. How can I explain it?

He was a kind, gentle, tolerant man. He had no hubris, no dishonest tricks, no vanity, and there was nothing mean, cruel, violent, vicious or bitchy about him. He was never a poseur in any way (when named one of the Ten Best-Dressed Men, he said to me, "Shows you how silly it is. I've worn this same dinner jacket for ten years") nor was he in any way deceitful. He never lied to me, nor I to him. I could tell him anything and he never lost his temper with me, despite the fact that I must have tried his patience not only with my capriciousness but because we always disagreed politically and often editorially. He was not a snob, although most of his friends and associates were; he never behaved in a condescending or patronizing manner to anyone; and unlike, for example, his friend Bernard M. Baruch, he never basked in the flattery of toadies trying to butter him up. Above all else, he was a man who loved women. This austere-looking, sedate, fastidious, impeccably-mannered, dignified man, treated with deference by everyone, was perhaps the most deeply sensual person I have ever known. To put it bluntly, he was cunt-crazy. He loved to taste it, smell it, feel it, look at it, above all, fuck it. He didn't give a hoot for conventional discretion, a sometimes disconcerting attitude. Once, in a taxi, he suddenly lifted my skirt, removed his pince-nez glasses and, holding them aloft, proceeded to go down on me. Far from arousing any passion, all it aroused was a hysterical desire to giggle and the fervent hope that we wouldn't go over any bumps in the street.

Certainly, I've never known a man who savored sex more raptly. It was his primary interest in life and he pursued it with wholehearted, shockproof, uninhibited enthusiasm. That he appeared to be exactly the opposite probably lent a piquancy to an affair with him, because it was all so unexpected. It didn't really matter to him if women were duchesses or call girls, socialites, actresses, models, waitresses, salesclerks, manicurists or what, as long as they were good-looking. Of course, being Condé Nast, he could just about have his pick. The models and the society women always hoped to be photographed for *Vogue*; the actresses, for *Vanity Fair*. He was aware of this but he never traded on it. He was no casting-couch seducer: Be nice to me, honey, and I'll put your picture in the magazine. Although doubtless many of the beautiful women in his life let ambition spur their affection, there were also those who truly liked him for himself, not for his name or worldly position. (When he lost his money, he was deeply touched because the delectably exquisite Edwina Pru, by then married to Leo d'Erlanger of the international banking family, made a long-distance call to him as soon as she learned of his plight. "She wanted to give me back a valuable pearl necklace I'd given her years ago," he told me. "Of course I refused, but wasn't it good of her to try to help me?") I suppose his great love was Grace Moore, the opera star, a sexy soprano who came out of Jellico, a village in the Cumberland hills of Tennessee, and made it all the way to the Metropolitan Opera House. She had lemon-colored hair, flirtatious blue eyes and a bubbly, vivacious manner. She seethed with vitality.

Condé liked to tell about the time she interrupted a concert tour to join him in London. (She always traveled with her own black silk sheets—by ship or Pullman train, of course, in those years—because she had read that Nellie Melba used to travel with pink silk ones). Condé was staying at Claridge's and neglected to check Grace in, so at one point during the first night of their reunion, the hotel manager knocked on the door and discreetly informed Condé that the lady must leave. Grace was not a prima donna for nothing. She turned on the manager in fury. "I came three thousand miles to be with this man," she shouted. "Now, you just get out of here and leave us alone." And he did.

It certainly wasn't her singing that attracted Condé. Opera or any kind of classical music bored him. He once took me to *Carmen* at the Met and fell sound asleep. I woke him at intermission so we could get some champagne at Sherry's bar, where we chatted with the opera's two elderly stalwarts, Mrs. George Washington Kavanaugh, in a gold lamé gown, floor-length ermine cape, a dozen diamond bracelets, huge diamond pendant earrings, a six-inch-high diamond tiara on her dyed yellow hair, a diamond necklace and a diamond stomacher, and Mrs. Cornelius Vanderbilt, also wearing *her* diamond stomacher but more simply, if regally, clad in purple velvet, with her usual matching "headache band" on her white hair.

Apparently, I didn't appreciate good music, either, because a letter I wrote to my aunt during this period said, in part: "Condé and I went to dinner at Grace Moore's (she and her husband have rented Miriam Hopkins' house in Sutton

Place) and Gloria Swanson was there, looking young and beautiful, with magnificent blue-green eyes. When I was a little girl she was one of my favorite movie stars and I once sent a quarter for her photograph, but I didn't tell her that, as I don't suppose it would have been tactful. Ex-Ambassador Cárdenas of Spain was there and Clifton Webb and that dreadful professional party-giver, Elsa Maxwell, and after dinner the eight of us went to hear Richard Tauber sing. I really don't like any singers except Paul Robeson. Besides, the ambassador sat beside me and his stomach kept rumbling and he kept whispering to me in Spanish all through the concert and Condé was on my other side, just as bored as I was, fidgeting in his seat and making his stiff shirt crackle, so I was surrounded by a symphony of noises quite apart from the singing. I was glad when it ended and we all went to '21.' "

Grace was married to Valentin Parera, a self-effacing man who looked like John Gilbert, star of silent films, and seemed to be content to be known only as Grace's husband. The two of them and Condé and I sometimes went out together, hard to take because Grace was like an animated swizzle stick and indomitably coquettish, looking archly at the men and cooing, "Oooh, aren't you *terrible?!* Isn't he *naughty?!*" until I felt like throwing up. (Once, when Condé and I were at some night-club opening, I spotted a girl at another table who was wearing a spangled veil that gave her an alluringly mysterious look. I pointed her out to Condé, commenting, "I wish I were glamorous." "My dear Helen," he said, "you and Grace Moore are the two most glamorous women I have ever known." I knew he meant it as a great compliment, but I would have felt more flattered if he had paired me with someone other than Grace.)

When her first movie, *One Night of Love*, advertised as "the most glorious musical romance of all time," opened at Radio City Music Hall, Condé took two hundred guests to the film and afterward we all went back to his place for a midnight supper dance—lobster, champagne, and Leo Reisman's orchestra. Among the frolicsome throng were Mary

Pickford, once known as "America's Sweetheart," who had written a book called *Why Not Try God?* now that she had given up films, pinned up her corkscrew golden curls and settled down with Buddy Rogers, her third husband; Nelson Rockefeller (he used the servants' elevator, by mistake); Averell and Marie Harriman (I thought of Harriman in those days as a handsome playboy and never dreamed he would turn out to be an Elder Statesman); Jim Forrestal and his wife Josie (when drinks were poured, his weakness was so obvious that who would have thought he would some day have an aircraft carrier named after him?); Baron Alain de Rothschild, Cole Porter, Marshall Field, the Arthur Krocks and the Walter Lippmans, the Nelson Doubledays, Rudy Vallee, the Adam Gimbels, the Walter Chryslers, and the usual top-drawer "old society" names—the lot. Maurice Chevalier was there, but he knew hardly anyone, so he stood by himself, pretending to look at the books in the library until he was rescued by a strange and raffish girl named Mary Gill, the only one with nerve enough to go up to him and start talking. They soon left the party together and I daresay they had a better time than the rest of us, except possibly Harold Ross, *The New Yorker* editor, who clung to the bar like a limpet and, when the others had all left, was sprawled on the terrace at dawn. "What will I do with him?" Condé asked me. I had no suggestions, so he decided to let the butler worry about it.

Some years later, I went to a party Grace gave in her country house on one of her wedding anniversaries. The guests were seated for dinner at different tables, in groups of six. I was at Grace's table, along with Harry Luce, Mrs. Lawrence Tibbett, Stanton Griffis (later ambassador to Spain) and Gilbert Miller (who had the worst table manners I have ever seen, bar none). I could scarcely believe it when Grace stood up, made a sappy little speech about how long she had been married to Parera, and then burst into the title song from *One Night of Love*, trilling away like an estrous titmouse. I thought it so embarrassing I kept my eyes on my plate, so I don't know how the others reacted, except that everyone in the room applauded loudly when she finished. Parera, at another table, murmured his appreciation quickly, but Lawrence Tibbett stood up and sang "On the Road to Mandalay," which didn't seem to me to have much connection with the occasion. Grace at that time was in the process of being converted to Catholicism and when, during a conversation, I said that some well known girl-about-town had "a catholic taste in men," Grace looked at me angrily and said in a sharp tone, "I resent that!" There was an uncomfortable silence, and I thought she was going to send me from the table. She ignored me the rest of the evening and refused even to say good night to me when I left with the Luces, whom I was visiting. I never saw her again, a loss I endured with equanimity.

Condé's girls were usually lovely blondes and in comparison I felt like something out of *The Last of The Mohicans*, but our friendship endured, somewhat surprisingly, considering the number of times we each got sidetracked. I met him first in December, 1931. Clare Boothe Brokaw, later to become Clare Boothe Luce, but then an editor on *Vanity Fair*, had written a book of satirical essays, *Stuffed Shirts*, published by Horace Liveright, for whom Leane Zugsmith, a budding novelist, did publicity. Leane was a friend of Ramona Herdman, head of publicity for Harper & Brothers publishing house, whom I had known from our days as reporters on the Syracuse *Herald*. *Vanity Fair* at that time was edited by only three people, Crowninshield, Donald Freeman and Clare (they didn't have the proliferating mastheads of today), and they were looking for a fourth. Clare told Leane, who told Ramona, who told me. The upshot was that I received a letter from Mrs. Brokaw, dated November 28, 1931, asking me to write captions of a hundred words each about Henry L. Stimson, then Secretary of State, and William Faulkner, nominating them for *Vanity Fair*'s Hall of Fame page, and also captions to go with pictures of Greta Garbo and Will Rogers, an Oklahoma cowboy who had made good by twirling his lariat in the Ziegfeld *Follies* and then became internationally famous as a homespun philosopher-humorist. She also asked me for criticism of the magazine and any suggestions. I must have answered posthaste because her next letter was dated December 1st, signed "Cordially" (the first had been a businesslike "Sincerely"), and December 3rd she wrote again, asking me to come to the office. (I didn't really expect to get the job, but my attitude was, Well, what the hell. They can't shoot me for trying.) I found Mrs. Brokaw to be a dazzling creature with bright golden hair, who could charm a bird out of a tree and whose fragile beauty made me feel as if I looked like Abraham Lincoln. She was wearing an emerald-green dress and matching hat, she had a rippling, silvery laugh, and I was almost too dazed to open my mouth. She was then twenty-eight years old. She took me to meet Donald Freeman, also twenty-eight, the managing editor, a bald, plump-faced, Teutonic-looking man who, I later found out, didn't want me because he was hoping to give the job to the daughter of Deputy Chief Inspector of Police Valentine so he could get a police pass-card and other perks. However, a few days later, Mrs. Brokaw telephoned to ask me to come in again to be interviewed by Mr. Nast, in his impressive office. My grandmother had died a short time before and I was wearing her coat, a shapeless gray tweed with a gray fur collar (my grandmother was nearly six feet tall and I was some four inches shorter and the coat had not been shortened), and a hat and dress from Empsall's Dry Goods Store in Watertown, N.Y., an emporium not exactly celebrated for *haute couture*. I must have been an odd sight in that coven of chic, but Mr. Nast was kind and friendly ("Even if you don't get the job, perhaps we could have dinner some time," he said). He asked me if I had any samples of my Vassar themes, which struck me as pretty funny because I could scarcely imagine myself bringing in "Why the *Areopagitica* Was Banned" or my term paper on how the Parnassian School of French poetry influenced Rubén Darío, the Nicaraguan poet.

The next thing was a telegram from Mrs. Brokaw, asking me to pay another visit and meet Mr. Crowninshield. Thus I was hired, at a salary of twenty-five dollars a week. I started work January 4, 1932, and when I came into the office that first day there was a corsage of gardenias on my desk, with a card from Crowninshield on which he had written, "To wish you luck and a moderate degree of contentment." On my second day at work, Mr. Nast came from his office to mine, shook hands warmly and said he was sorry he hadn't been able to be there to welcome me the day before. It all seemed to me like a big hoax and I wrote a friend, "These people are unbelievable, and I don't know how long I can stand it, but it ought to last a month, anyway." I was twenty-four and my only previous jobs had been on the two Syracuse newspapers, working with hard-boiled *Front Page* types (at least, that's the way we all tried to act), and a four-month stint in New York as a salesgirl in a Womrath bookstore.

Since childhood I had thought of *Vanity Fair* as the *ne plus ultra* of culture and brilliance. My grandmother subscribed to it from early in 1914, and it was from its pages that I acquired my extracurricular education in the arts. There, I first learned of sculptors like Brancusi and Mestrović, of painters like Braque and Modigliani, of writers like Colette. It has been called "America's most memorable magazine" and its editors are supposed to have been the most sophisticated group this side of, say, Petronius Arbiter, as indeed they were so considered at the time by all, inclusive of themselves. I was surprised to find myself among them, but even more surprised to discover that they were by no means intellectual giants. A letter I wrote to my Vassar friend on January 12, 1932, eight days after I started work, said, in part: "You are perfectly right about my job and it is just the fact that it is such a 'splendid opportunity' that is going to be the chief reason for my flopping on it. I know that if I were ambitious and on my toes and kissed the right asses I could probably make a way for myself here, because they are not so smart after all, not the way I used to imagine them. (They make the most elemental mistakes, such as referring to Agamemnon as Helen's husband, and putting dashes before commas, and using plural subjects with singular predicates). But I simply cannot do it. I hate their kind of cleverness. It's a mechanized wit, all triviality. These people and their friends don't seem to know what is going on in the world, except in their own rarefied purlieus."

Despite my hoity-toity tone, it was undeniably a beautiful and amusing magazine. Its virtues stemmed primarily from Crowninshield. He set the tone. He had an unerring eye for recognizing new and unknown talent. (Noel Coward told me a few years ago that when he was first in New York in 1921, young and broke, it was Crowninshield who encouraged him and bought short stories from him, "thereby probably saving me from starvation.") He would climb the stairs to a Greenwich Village garret to look at paintings and tell at a glance if they had the spark that makes the bush become the burning bush. In many cases he didn't wait until people became famous. By putting them in *Vanity Fair* he *made* them famous, whether they were artists, writers or actors. He simply followed his own eclectic taste. (He was one of the first in America to appreciate African art—he had a collection of a hundred-fifty African masks and sculptures; he had one of the largest private collections of Segonzac paintings and Despiau sculpture, the most complete collection of Matisse lithographs, and he also collected Degas paintings of ballet dancers and George Bellows prize-fight lithographs.)

Condé was proud of *Vanity Fair* but he never quite understood it. He thought Crowny was insane to publish what was then called "modern art": Picasso, Rouault, Van Gogh, etc. "The advertisers think it distorted and decadent," he said. It was ironic and unfair that he was awarded the Légion d'honneur for introducing modern French art in America, when it was Crowny who was solely responsible but never received the credit. On most editorial issues I usually sided with Crowny and he with me, and the two of us waged a four-year off and on battle with Condé. I must say that Nast always listened to other people's points of view. He was never autocratic. His favorite expression was a rather plaintive, "Can't we have a meeting of the minds?"

We argued about paintings and we argued about politics. Condé hated Roosevelt and the New Deal. Once, he wanted to run as a cover a caricature ridiculing The Forgotten Man, FDR's famous phrase for the unemployed. I wrote an angry memo that began, "There is nothing remotely funny about hunger," and Nast agreed to forget the cover, although he okayed a picture of a scruffy-looking tramp, labeled The Forgotten Man, for our We Nominate for Oblivion feature, and Mrs. Brokaw wrote the caption. At Condé's instigation, George Sokolsky, an arch-reactionary, was commissioned to write articles attacking the Boulder Dam project and other "government interference in private enterprise," and we also hired Joseph Alsop, a fat, pink-faced young man, to do other political pieces for us. In March, 1932, a writer named George Slocombe wrote an article called "Adolph Hitler, Revolutionist," in which he said, "Hitler does not believe in violence, notwithstanding the daily toll of killed and wounded in street battles between Fascists and Communists." Condé disapproved of Communism almost as much as he disapproved of modern art. He told me he knew a girl named Nadja whose mother still lived in Russia and wrote her that they couldn't get any needles. For some inexplicable reason, this impressed him profoundly. He insisted that I meet Nadja and she said, "The Czar never killed anyone." I told her that I didn't suppose he did, personally, and Condé exclaimed triumphantly, "There! You see!" adding, "And they have no needles!" I realize this makes him sound like a ninny but he wasn't any worse than the rest of his crowd. If Crowny was a political innocent (he always skipped the front pages of newspapers), Condé at least knew where he stood and why. He had no social conscience and I doubt if he ever gave a thought to the poor, beyond believing that it was their own fault. As for Crowny, if he ever thought of the poor, it was to regard them on the level of India's Untouchables.

Although our staff was always small, there were members who came and went, during my four years there, among them William Harlan Hale, looking like a young eagle (he was practically fresh out of Yale and had written a book, *Challenge to Defeat*, a precociously pretentious answer to

Spengler's *Decline of the West*); Richard Sherman, out of Iowa via Harvard and *The Forum* magazine; George Davis, who had won wide critical acclaim with his first—and only— novel, *The Opening of a Door*. Mehemed Fehmy Agha, always called Dr. Agha, was art director of all the Condé Nast magazines. He was born in the Russian Ukraine, of Turkish parents, and Condé brought him to America from the defunct German *Vogue*. Then we had our regular monthly contributors: Nathan, our drama critic; Pare Lorentz, film critic; Paul Gallico, who wrote pieces for us about figures in the world of sport; Grantland Rice, sports editor; Red Newsome (later replaced by Tommy Phipps, Lady Astor's nephew), who did The Well Dressed Man pages; and Corey Ford, who, as John Riddell, did marvelously apt and funny literary parodies. Most of them fell hopelessly in love with Mrs. Brokaw, whose lilting voice and luminous gaze reduced them to tantalized worshipers at her celestial—but heat-resistant—personal shrine. The effect she had on all males made Circe look like Booth Tarkington's Alice Adams. Donald Freeman, the most abjectly stricken of her victims, was killed at the age of twenty-nine when, on October 1, 1932, he drove his car into a road stanchion. (It was my birthday and, in a fit of pique at a rebuff from the deceptively ethereal Mrs. Brokaw, he had asked me to go to dinner with him at some Long Island restaurant. I refused because I had to go to my mother's in Flatbush.) Mrs. Brokaw succeeded him as managing editor for a year, when she left us and I took her place. For a while in 1934, Crowny and Dick Sherman and I were the only editors in the office, and Crowny was so busy with his African masks and his bridge games that he let me do as I liked. In addition to getting out the magazine, I also started a book review section (which I wrote until we hired as our literary critic George Dangerfield, a young Englishman who later won a Pulitzer prize); I had succeeded Pare Lorentz as our film critic; and I wrote a monthly night-club column which I called "the doe at eve."

I started work in the office around eight-thirty in the morning and stayed till seven at night or later, when I would rush home (I lived only two blocks away), leap into evening clothes and tear out again—to dinner, the theater (I went to every opening night), and to night clubs. I often took Condé with me, to places like the Chapeau Rouge, where the owner, Pepy d'Albrew, wore a live white mouse in his buttonhole; the Place Pigalle, where Eve Symington, a stunning blonde with a deep contralto voice, was getting a thousand dollars a week as the first of what were called society torch singers (she was Stuart Symington's wife, the daughter of ex-Senator James Wadsworth, the granddaughter of Teddy Roosevelt's Secretary of State); to the Rainbow Room to see Bea Lillie; to El Morocco, of course, with its zebra stripes and cellophane palms, the flossy domain of John Perona, an Italian from Turin, former ships' bus boy on the London-Buenos Aires run, who first came to New York with the encouragement of heavyweight boxer Luis Firpo, the Wild Bull of the Pampas, and opened a small speak-easy.

We went frequently, also, to the Central Park Casino, financed by Anthony Drexel Biddle, under the civic auspices of Mayor Jimmy Walker (famous for his charm, the corruption of his regime, and the time his showgirl mistress, Betty Compton, went down to City Hall and took a shot at him). The decor at the Casino was reminiscent of a glorified Chinese chop suey restaurant, but there was a nice sylvan view through the windows and Eddie Duchin at the piano. For one month's issue we went to nineteen clubs in ten nights. God knows where we got the energy. No one took vitamins in those days and we had never heard of pep pills, yet Condé was always in his office at 8 A.M. (and I wasn't much later) even when we had been drinking and dancing most of the night. He took the subway to work and said the ride was just long enough to read Dorothy Thompson's newspaper column. He seemed to thrive on the life, but I viewed it through a different lens and even wrote in the "doe at eve" column of January, 1935, that all the frenetic merry-making was "a constant source of amazement to me . . . You watch people pay a dollar a drink and think nothing of it; you see them stand for half an hour in the foyer of clubs, waiting for a table and a chance to spend their money—and dimly you try to remember such spectres as depression and hunger and the possible imminence of war. It's a fantastic world, but if you stop to think, you're lost. It's run, run, run, little chicken—tomorrow or the next day, the axe." When the others read it, they thought I was crazy. "War? What do you mean, war?" they said.

Then, too, there was the constant round of parties, Condés own and other people's to which he took me, and the smaller affairs he gave for ten to thirty people: a dinner for Sir Alfred Beit, son of the South African diamond king (I sat on his right and almost the first thing he asked me was if I knew how to get to a celebrated Harlem *boîte*); a dinner for the Duchesse Solange d'Ayen, daughter-in-law of the Duc de Noailles; a dinner for Gordon Selfridge, his daughter—the Vicomtesse Violette de Sibour—and his mistress, a scrumptious blond French doll named Marcelle. ("He's had her ever since he had the Dolly Sisters," Count René Willaumez whispered to me, which gave me an immediate image of the department store merchant, then nearly eighty, with a Dolly on each knee. Willaumez added that in London the luscious-looking Marcelle drove around town, not inconspicuously, in a white Rolls Royce with a black chauffeur in an all-white uniform). It was at this party that a woman guest said, emphatically, "Of course I'm a Fascist! What else could people of money and position be?" Selfridge wanted to see Harlem, so Condé asked me to take them up there, as I was the only one of the party who knew my way around in that area. We went to the Savoy Ballroom and then to the Plantation Club, where the cigaret girl was hawking white fur toy kittens that squeaked when pinched. Marcelle begged Selfridge to buy her one, but the multimillionaire refused, saying, "I absolutely refuse to pay five dollars for a toy cat!" so Marcelle sulked for the next hour, while Selfridge and I fought over politics and Condé tried to change the subject. Selfridge was enjoying himself and didn't want to go home when the club closed at 4 A.M. The rest of us were dead but the old man, who had flown in from California that afternoon (and this was long before jet planes) and hadn't even had a nap, was fresh and sprightly and kept asking, "Don't you know some after-hours place?" I did, but Condé nudged me, so I kept mum.

I had early recovered from my stage fright at these gatherings of the famous because I discovered that to converse with them was not all that difficult. Early in 1933, when I had been going to parties with Condé for several months, I wrote a friend, "I feel as if I were playing make-believe and pretending to be important, or that we are all characters in a warmed-over 'anyone-for-tennis?' farce. They all keep up a pretense of being 'well-informed'—learning a few catchwords here and there, knowing first names they can throw at people—all the parrot paraphernalia that go to make up the pattern of modern so-called brilliance. Really, all you need in order to be considered a smart person is a good memory. Because all these clever people do is repeat incidents and anecdotes and statements and opinions they have either read or else heard someone else say. It is never at all necessary to make up anything of your own or, least of all, to do any *thinking* of your own. It is a whole new type of conversation for me, in which we all sit around and toss names at one another, picking at them and dashing in and out around politics, the theatre, sport, etc. like those little water bugs that go skipping over the surface of lakes."

I went to work on *Vanity Fair* in January, 1932, and it wasn't until August 11 of that year that Condé first asked me to go out with him. I had had dinner and gone to the theater with Crowninshield the evening before and we were discussing the play while lunching at the Crillon, when Condé passed our table on his way out and sat down to have coffee with us. It was a warm, sunny day, and he suddenly asked me if I'd like to go to Palisades Park with him later that afternoon. I said Yes, and we went. We had an innocently pleasant time, drinking beer and playing pinball games. Afterward, he took me to Jack and Charlie's country roadhouse for dinner. I was surprised by how much at ease

I felt with him. I was further impressed because it didn't bother him at all that I was wearing a rumpled white linen suit from Klein's on Union Square, with a red bandanna on my head, while other female diners were sleekly groomed and expensively garbed. He didn't make any passes at me. We simply enjoyed being together. Back in town, he had Ben, his chauffeur, drop him off at his place and then take me down to Greenwich Village, where I lived on West 3rd Street, practically under the "El." I don't suppose Ben had ever been there before and he must have thought I was visiting someone because he said to me, "Tell me, madam, do people actually live down here?" "I do," I said.

I wonder what Condé's servants thought of some of the goings-on. (I'm sure our pursuits were discussed at the Butlers' Balls—if you'll pardon the expression—of the thirties, which were affairs given for the servants of the rich.) Condé had a book of exercises, *The Culture of the Abdomen* (Arnold Bennett wrote a plug for the jacket blurb), and he insisted that we try the exercises, one of which consisted of rotating the stomach while holding onto the back of a chair: stomach in, up, over, out, down—as if turning like a chicken on a rotisserie spit—and while we were energetically doing this, the butler came into the room unexpectedly. His eyes almost popped out. "Don't stop," said Condé. "You'll lose the rhythm." The butler discreetly withdrew, probably wondering what perversity we were trying, and I thought of a line in a verse recited by a longshoreman I knew: " 'Gor blimey!' cried the butler. 'He has come to bugger us all.' "

In the summer we spent our weekends at the Atlantic Beach Club or the Lido Beach Club, both on Long Island. Condé loved to swim, to lie in the sun, and to dance at night on the open-air dance floor under the stars. At the Atlantic Beach Club we ate and drank and lolled around with ex-film stars like Harold Lloyd, Richard Barthelmess, and Phyllis Haver, blonde and cuddly, the former Mack Sennett bathing beauty who was married to Bill Seaman, a grocery tycoon who called her "Poopsie." I had seen these stars when I used to go to the movies with my grandmother and it seemed strange that I should be drinking with them, especially one like Barthelmess, over whom I had wept buckets when I saw him in *Broken Blossoms, Way Down East, Tol'able David,* and whose pictures I used to collect and paste in a scrapbook (I still have it today) but who was now an aging man with heavy jowls. Dancing with him one night at the Club, I was astonished when he began to wriggle his hips in a startling version of the hoochie-coochie, an odd look in his eyes. Suddenly, he left me standing on the dance floor and darted away. "Goodness!" I thought. "Could he have been seized with a sudden attack of priapism?" No. When he came back to our table he explained it: "I dropped a lighted cigaret down the front of my trousers."

A few times we went to polo matches, at one of which I sat with Norma Talmadge, then incongruously married to George Jessel. I was so intent on gawking at her that I could hardly stop when Condé brought over Jock Whitney, who wanted to meet me because I was *Vanity Fair*'s film critic and he was producing *Becky Sharpe* (starring Miriam Hopkins), the first full-length feature film in color. I also remember a weekend we spent as the guests of Harold Talbott (later to become Air Force Secretary in the Eisenhower administration) and his handsome wife Peggy in their Locust Valley house. Mrs. Talbott's own bathroom had zebras painted on the walls and a zebra-skin rug, but our bathroom had a glass floor with tropical fish swimming underneath in real water, so that every time I went to the toilet I felt like William Beebe. Saturday evening the Talbotts took us to Jones Beach to see an outdoor production of *The Student Prince.* Mrs. Talbott had never been to a public beach before, I gathered, and she was enchanted. During intermission we went to the hot dog shop. "It's the most divine food I ever tasted," she announced. She was terribly interested in everything and asked the bus boy what his hours were and how much he earned. When he said that he worked twelve hours at a stretch for thirty-five cents an hour but was only permitted to work long enough to earn nine dollars a week, she told him how lucky he was, "working out here in the fresh air, with the ocean and everything." On the way home, she said, "The only bad thing about going to a place like that is that you can't feel sorry any more for people who haven't any money, when they can go there and have a marvelous time for a dollar or two." Then she added that she was surprised she hadn't seen anyone she knew: "At a place like that you really ought to see someone who does your hair or your nails."

Despite all our gadding about, Condé and I were happiest and most at ease when we were alone. Away from other people, he could be quite playful, with a rather amiably unsophisticated humor. I often went into the office Sundays to work and so did he. Once, on a typed memo to me from Crowny that read: "Remember the possibility of photographing Jim Londos in a dresssuit" (Londos was a Greek-American wrestler who won the championship Diamond Belt), Condé had added in pencil: "Also speak to Public Enemy No. 1—presently located in his cell—if you are working this Sunday afternoon." The year I told him about my Harlem gangster friend, Bumpy, he said that if he had to lose me to anyone he was glad it was someone out of the ordinary, and when I went on a Cuban holiday, he sent a radiogram to the ship, "Oh come on back," and signed it "Bumpy and Condé." He had a good-natured disposition and he was never pretentious or embarrassed. When a fashion model saw me in the office reception room and said in a clear voice, in front of several *Vogue* editors, "Didn't I meet you and Mr. Nast in Atlantic City last weekend?" he thought it was very funny—and of course she *had* met us in Atlantic City, not the most elegant site for a rendez-vous, but we had gone there on the spur of the moment to ride in the board-walk wheelchairs, buy salt-water taffy and visit the amuse-ment arcades. Another time, we went to the Cavalier Hotel in Virginia Beach and just as we boarded the train in New York, our redcap called to the train porter, "Drawing rooms

A and B. And, Jackson, they want the connecting door unlocked." Everyone stared at us, but we kept straight faces until safely in our rooms, when we collapsed with laughter.

I continued to see him after I left the magazine in December, 1936. For that Christmas he gave me an evening bag and wrote on the card, "With a hell of a lot of love for darling Helen," and the next year on my birthday I received a Special Delivery letter at my mother's in Flatbush, where I was staying, in which he repeated his offer of marriage—"We get along together so well and I love you very much." But I could never have married a man who didn't hold the same political beliefs as my own. I could sleep with them, yes, but never live with them or marry them. And, of course, I wasn't in love with him. I have only been really in love with one man in my life—Jack Lawrenson. Also, I was spending more and more time in the trade union movement on the waterfront. One New Year's Eve I went with Condé to the Ritz (he belonged to a private club that gave what were called "Mayfair dances" and this was one of them), where we sat with people like Brenda Frazier, the first debutante "glamour girl" (and the most famous of them all, perhaps because she was the first to hire a press agent), who had jet-black hair, a dead-white skin, and used purple lipstick—and I went straight from there, shortly after midnight, to a party in Greenwich Village given by a Communist longshoreman and his wife to raise money for the radical rank-and-file movement on the docks.

I was already in love with Jack when I went to a dinner party Condé gave in the French Pavilion at the World's Fair of 1939. I sat next to George Schlee (later Garbo's steady escort). His blond wife, Valentina, an expensive and fashionable couturière, sat opposite us. (She changed her seat because she was a White Russian and couldn't bear to sit where she could see the Soviet Pavilion.) I remember telling Schlee about Jack and when I said that he was an Irishman from Dublin, Schlee shook his head disparagingly and remarked, "As my wife would put it, 'Irish no sex is.'" The opera singer Gladys Swarthout, dark and handsome, who came from Deepwater, Missouri, was seated on Schlee's other side and she spoke up in defense of the Irish but was interrupted by the late arrival of the guest of honor—for whom everyone stood up, obsequiously—Her Royal Highness the Grand Duchess Marie, granddaughter of Czar Alexander II and cousin of the executed Czar Nicholas II. Her father, the Grand Duke Cyril, had also been shot by the Bolsheviks. Her brother had helped kill Rasputin, Schlee told me, and he also related that when she married her first husband, Prince William of Sweden, she wore for the wedding ceremony the diamond crown of Catherine the Great. I was amused to think how horrified the others would have been, had they known they had a viper like me in their midst. However, I had already met the Grand Duchess when I went to her apartment to discuss with her a proposed fashion magazine, the brain child of an exotic—and erratic—Hungarian, Alexander Ince. The Grand Duchess was to be the nominal Editor, but I was to do the work and had thought up the name, *L'Elegante*, and prepared a prospectus, when the plan fell through, probably because Ince, whose idea was to get financing from stores like Bergdorf-Goodman, Hattie Carnegie, Tiffany, Cartier and the like, couldn't persuade enough people to ante up for the kitty.

After Jack and I were married, we went to several of Condé's parties, and when our first child, Johanna, was born, Condé sent roses to me in the hospital and, for the baby, a fabulous long christening dress of organdy trimmed with real Valenciennes and a pink satin bow. He himself had been married twice. In 1902 he wed Clarisse Coudert, daughter of a lawyer (his firm, Coudert Brothers, is still well known internationally). They had two children: Natica, who married Gerald Warburg (when their first child was born, Condé said to me, "With Condé Nast for grandfather and Jake Schiff for great-grandfather, how can it lose?") and Coudert, whose first wife, Charlotte, I met shortly after her divorce, when we were both guests at Harry Luce's South Carolina plantation, and whom I shall always remember for such astonishing conversational gems as "What else can you do in England at night except play bridge? It gets dark at quarter to four and you can't shoot any more."

Condé and his first wife were divorced in 1923. In 1928 he married a coolly beautiful ash blonde from Illinois, Leslie Foster, who had been working on *Vogue*. He gave her a divorce in 1932 so that she could marry Rex Benson—later knighted—a British merchant banker (a partner in Morgan Grenwell, where the Vatican kept its gold). Her daughter by Condé was formerly married to Lord St. Just. She is now the wife of Mark Bonham Carter, an ex-member of Parliament, and lives in London.

Condé died of a heart attack in September, 1942. He was sixty-eight. A eulogistic editorial in the *New York Times* referred to him as a "genius," called him "one of the most notably powerful characters of his time" and "an artist who made use of printing to gain the creative ends he sought. And his objectives, let it be understood, were nothing less than the improvement and democratization of modern civilization . . . He had broad social visions which gradually he realized to the benefit of the entire race."

I read the editorial with mixed emotions, as I'm sure Crowny did, too. Condé himself would have been astounded. He was not an artist or an idealist. He was a businessman. His "genius"—although I would call it shrewdness—lay in choosing talented editors—Crowninshield for *Vanity Fair*, Mrs. Chase for *Vogue*, Richardson Wright for *House & Garden*, with Dr. Agha as overall art director—and letting them put their own stamp on the magazines. I doubt if he would have claimed more than that, certainly not the high-faluting tribute of the *Times*.

I was among the eight hundred who attended his funeral in the R.C. Church of St. Ignatius Loyola on Park Avenue, an illustrious gathering worthy of his final party. Baruch, Averell Harriman and Henry Luce were among the honorary pall bearers. I went alone because my husband, who was vice-president of the National Maritime Union, went that day to the funeral of an old friend and trade union associate, a black merchant seaman named Percy Jenkins, whose last rites were conducted with a minimum of ceremony. We met later and sat at the Sevilla bar in Greenwich Village, comparing funerals and feeling that sadness tinged with fear that affects us all when someone we have long known has gone, irrevocably. "Poor old Condé," I said, lifting my beer. "Poor old Percy!" my husband said, lifting his.

Six

"THERE IS A FAIR KEPT, CALLED VANITY FAIR"

Pilgrims Progress

URING THE FOUR YEARS I was on *Vanity Fair*, 1932 through 1935, just about everyone who was anyone in art, music, literature, politics, sports, the theater, films or the public eye sooner or later came to our offices or our photographic studios. J. P. Morgan, Garbo, Yeats, Babe Ruth, Chaplin, Churchill, Eugene O'Neill, Jack Dempsey, Pirandello, Lily Pons, H. G. Wells, Sinclair Lewis were among those who were happy to sit for their pictures. Dr. Ditmars of the Bronx Zoo brought a fifteen-foot python in a metal trunk; the celebrated circus clown Emmett Kelly came in full regalia, carrying a performing pig; Ruth Slenczynski, a chubby, sad-faced tot of eight, whom the critic Olin Downes called "the greatest piano genius since Mozart" and who was taking over the American concert tour of Paderewski, ill in Poland, sat at a rented piano in our studio while Lusha Nelson clicked his camera. Steichen photographed

Thomas Mann when the latter came to New York in 1934; and he posed Gerhardt Hauptmann against a prop background of night sky and stars. No one ever turned us down, to my knowledge, except Spencer Tracy, who went on a drunken binge and never showed up, and Barbara Stanwyck, whom we wanted to take by herself because she was a big Hollywood star but who refused to be photographed without her husband Frank Fay, an alcoholic who was trying to make a comeback on the stage and Barbara, always an intensely loyal woman, had walked out on her own career to come to New York and serve as a deliberately subordinate assistant to Fay in his act. (Before she ever went to Hollywood, when she was Ruby Stevens of Brooklyn, she once worked in the Condé Nast mail room but was fired when Mrs. Chase caught her turning cartwheels in the corridor.)

Steichen was the top banana on our photographic staff. The *Vogue* ladies fawningly called him "Colonel Steichen," which I thought ridiculous because World War I, when he was given the rank of Lt. Colonel in the photographic division, had been over since 1918. He managed to give the impression that a photographic session in his Beaux Arts studio was the equivalent of an investiture at Buckingham Palace. Editors tiptoed reverently, speaking in whispers, if they dared speak at all, and I found this the-Master-is-creating atmosphere repellent. Besides, I didn't like the way he treated other photographers as if they were inferior serfs. He was good, but not that good. No one is. He had none of the simplicity and humility of Alfred Stieglitz, whom Crowninshield called "the camera's almost legendary saint" and "a great apostle of honest photography," and whose portraits and landscapes were in the Metropolitan and other museums. When Steichen first went to New York from Michigan (he was born in Luxembourg but came to America as a child), Stieglitz helped him. Together they opened a photographic gallery, which Steichen left to join Condé Nast. His subsequent manner, adopted after his success and celebrity, alienated Stieglitz as well as others. For example, he treated Lusha Nelson like an errand boy. Nelson was a young Russian who also became a staff photographer, an unassuming man whose work was as good as Steichen's but he lacked the other's talent for self-aggrandizement and therefore gained neither the fame nor the money.

We were every photographer's Mecca because our reproduction was so good. Few magazines before or since have surpassed it and we had the best color in the country. We also attracted clever caricaturists and artists from all over: Raymond Bret-Koch, a Frenchman with dark, convex eyes like Anna Held's; Marcel Vertès, Budapest born, who left Hungary for Paris during the Bela Kun revolution and came to us in 1935; our own Bill Steig; Paolo Garretto from Italy; Eduardo Benito from Spain; the almost impossibly handsome Bolín from Buenos Aires, whose drawings we were the first to publish, as we were also the first to publish those of the enormously talented Mexican, Miguel Covarrubias, who came to New York at the age of eighteen, self-taught, knowing no one, and, like many others, was discovered by Crowninshield.

Georg Grosz's brutally vitriolic satirizing of monopoly capitalism and its spawn of incipient Nazis made it expedient for him to leave Germany in 1932. It was natural that he would be invited to work for us, although it was riveting to see the expression on his face when Crowny said to him, "Why don't you do us some drawings of the chic, fashionable life in Moscow, dear boy? You know, society people going to the opera and ballet and all that." Another radical artist whose politics were similar to mine (his drawings appeared in the *New Masses* and the *Daily Worker*) was William Gropper, whom I abetted in a page that nearly caused an international incident when it appeared in August, 1935. I wrote the title "Not on Your Tintype," with a caption "Five highly unlikely historical situations by one who is sick of the same old headlines," and a line under each drawing: "Huey Long enters a monastery," "J. P. Morgan becomes a soapbox orator" (Gropper drew Morgan orating behind a sign that read "DOWN WITH CAPITALISM"), and so on. The one that caused the ruckus was a caricature of Hirohito dragging a coolie cart with a beribboned scroll in it. My caption said, "Japan's Emperor gets the Nobel Peace Prize." (Japan had already conquered Manchuria and sent troops into China proper, and Mao began the Long March.) The issue was barred from Japan, the Japanese ambassador in Washington protested to the State Department, Westbrook Pegler and Heywood Broun wrote columns about it, and a diplomat named Kuriyama was sent from the Japanese Embassy to see Crowny and persuade him to write a letter of apology to Ambassador Saito, which was done. (There was an apocryphal story that when Mr. Kuriyama and his aide came to our office, Crowny mistook them for some Japanese acrobats he wanted photographed and suggested that they show us their tumbling feats.) Gropper and I did a sequel that November, confining ourselves to situations that included "Barbara Hutton succeeds Frances Perkins as Secretary of Labor" and Hamilton Fish, William Randolph Hearst and Matthew Woll singing the Internationale, with a sign, "VOTE COMMUNIST."

In addition to our regular monthly writers, we published contributions from people like John Maynard Keynes, Lord Dunsany, Paul Morand, Ferenc Molnar, Antoine de Saint-Exupèry, Joseph Hergesheimer, Erskine Caldwell, Somerset Maugham, John Gunther, William Saroyan. (We rejected Saroyan's first manuscripts, including *The Daring Young Man on the Flying Trapeze*, but then, long before I ever worked there, *Vanity Fair* also turned down Saki.) John O'Hara used to send me stories and I kept rejecting them until finally I bought one in the summer of 1933 for which I paid him fifty dollars. He wrote me from Pittsburgh, where he lived at the William Penn Hotel, "Oh, you Kiddo: I will take fifty and like it. Secret of my whole success is keeping everlastingly at it. So now you can expect to see at least three pieces a week from me. Now I must plan to go out and buy something. If I were in New York I would like to buy you. Oh, you can be had, and I don't mean the whole fifty dollars, either. By the way, since the point has come up, what *are* the latest quotations on a tall handsome girl with pretty teeth, a gay and

amusing and deep voice, and a wonderful record at Bradford
Academy? I may want to come in out of the rain some night
in New York and I like to know the umbrella fee in advance.
Devotedly, Mr. O'Hara." I guess I didn't answer, because his
next letter complained of my silence. I never liked him. I
met him through his first wife, Petie—Helen Pettit—who
had been a friend of Elsbeth Thexton's at Wellesley. When
O'Hara died, I thought it odd that not one of his obituaries
mentioned Petie, or even that he had been married more
than once. She was a lovely, slender, bright, gay, rather fey
girl who wanted to be an actress but never got much further
than going to audition for *Green Pastures*, having heard that
it was by Marc Connelly but not realizing that it called for
an all-Negro cast. O'Hara treated her abominably and made
passes at all her friends. He was an ugly drunk. He got
Wolcott Gibbs of *The New Yorker*, one of the Very Smart
Young Men, as a blind date for me one night. The four of us
started drinking at the O'Haras' apartment, moved on to a
restaurant, and ended at the Algonquin, where John and
Wolcott played Ping-Pong for five dollars a game while Petie
and I sat and drank brandy. The more he drank, the nastier
John got—to every one of us—and he and Gibbs got in a
fight, throwing money at each other until finally Gibbs got
up and went out. We thought he had gone to the men's
room. When he didn't return, John went to look for him and
discovered he had left the hotel. John and Petie took me
home and I kept thinking, "I bet if I looked like Ruby
Keeler, he wouldn't have walked out on me." The O'Haras
separated shortly afterward. John went to Paris, from where
he sent me a story that I turned down. He followed it with
another and a letter that began, "Here is a piece which
cannot possibly offend, for not once do I use the transitive
verb to fuck."

Even after he became successful, I still thought he was a
second-rate imitation of Scott Fitzgerald, plagued by an envi-
ous preoccupation with the rich and their world of fashionable prep schools and Ivy League universities to which he
yearned to have belonged. Not that I was enthusiastic about

Fitzgerald, whom I peremptorily dismissed in a theme written at Vassar in 1925, which began: "Not so very many years ago, John Dos Passos was being lauded as one of the literary sensations of the year, along with two other precocious youngsters, F. Scott Fitzgerald and Stephen Vincent Benét. All three enjoyed an extraordinary popularity and then, like so many authors whose first books are successes, they fell flat. Fitzgerald went smugly on in his own collegiate, shoddy style; Benét degenerated into writing rather tawdry stories for *Cosmopolitan* magazine; and Dos Passos, whose first book, *The Three Soldiers*, had been the finest of the three offerings, lost himself in a fog of mediocre essays and the almost unbelievably bad Imagist poetry of *A Pushcart at the Curb*. But in all his work there was evident the same spirit that made *The Three Soldiers* a better book than *This Side of Paradise* or *Young People's Pride*: the spirit of finding out the truth about things and telling it as effectively as possible. This spirit has splendidly fashioned his latest book, *Manhattan Transfer.* . . ." I then went on to discuss this book, ending with the qualification, "The book is not, of course, anywhere near a great book . . . but it accomplishes its purpose, which is to give with clarity and insight the picture of a city. And even in the midst of ugliness, there will be a bit like this, delicate and lovely: 'The trees in the square were tangled in blue cobwebs' . . ." (At that time, I had yet to read *The Great Gatsby*, which came out that same year, nor could I foresee that Dos Passos would become eventually a nagging reactionary, with a consequential deterioration in his work. But nothing has altered my evaluation of O'Hara.)

I am reasonably sure there has never been another office like the *Vanity Fair* one. It certainly spoiled me for ever working in any normal place. The informality was due to Crowny's personality. It is impossible to imagine him ever cracking the whip or talking about a "chain of command" or maintaining any semblance of the authoritarian discipline to which many magazine editors were, and still are, addicted. He was too much the humorous dilettante. Dorothy Parker,

Robert Benchley and Robert Sherwood all left the magazine before my time. According to Crowny they were an obstreperous lot who sat around making wisecracks and never did anything on time. He told one story about Benchley, whose arrival at work became later and later, until Crowny felt obliged to suggest that he mend his ways. The next morning he came in even tardier than usual and when Crowny mildly inquired the reason, Benchley said, "I'm going to tell you the truth. I set my alarm and I got up early, but on my way here I was attacked by five lions."

Under Donald Freeman the hilarity was subdued, but after his death the atmosphere became decidedly relaxed, especially at our weekly office lunches, with food sent up from the Savarin restaurant in the building. We would invite honored guests, among them Thomas Wolfe, 6' 7", towering over everybody, serious, awkwardly uncommunicative, and justifiably suspicious of our frivolity. *Look Homeward, Angel*, that beautiful book, had been only a moderate success and he was trying to earn money to tide him over while he worked on *Of Time and the River*, for which his $5000 advance was being doled out to him at the niggardly rate of $250 a month. During lunch, Crowny entertained him in his customary anecdotal way. "Have you seen the Brancusi exhibition, dear boy? I took this terrifyingly respectable elderly lady, and you know his Mlle. X? No? Well, it's a faithful reproduction of the—er—female private parts. That's all it is, the whole sculpture, and this dear old lady just stood and stared at it. I tried to hurry her on, but she kept saying, 'Now, what *does* that remind me of?' 'Oh, there's the famous Bird over there!' I said, *trying* to draw her away, but she was muttering, 'This reminds me of *something*, but I can't think what it is.' Then her face suddenly lit up and she said, 'Oh, I know! Raw liver!'"

Aldous Huxley came a few times. He was then nearly blind and Crowny kept passing small-print galley proofs, saying, "Do take a look at this, old boy," even though poor Huxley had to bring each galley right up to his eyes, brushing his thick glasses, in order to try to make it out, until he finally said, "Most writing today is pure cat piss," at which Crowny murmured gently, "Quite right, dear boy."

Occasionally, our guest was Condé himself, or Mrs. Chase of *Vogue* explaining her own editorial policy. "Remember, we're not appealing to the little $49.50 woman," she said. The *Vogue* people looked askance at our levity and thought we were all dotty, while on our part we were bored by their devotion to fashion, except when they unintentionally amused us, like the time they featured pictures of black straw hats with the caption "Why not spend your summer under a black sailor?"

The level of our humor was not always exalted. Crowny and Agha and I loved burlesque. The three of us went together to the Irving Place Burlesk, Agha with his opera glasses. This was sometimes reflected in our luncheon meetings, as when Agha turned to a guest and asked, "Do you know William Fox's wife?" "No." "Well, he does," at which we all fell about laughing; or when we amused ourselves with a game we called New Definitions. (Samples: adulation means whipping people for fun; morons live in Salt Lake City and have a lot of wives; a moratorium is where they put dead people.) Crowny could write with his feet and he sometimes took off his shoes, grasped a pencil with his toes, and demonstrated. He could also bark like a seal, stand on his head, throw peanuts up in the air and catch them in his mouth. He showed Agha how to thumb his nose and how to make a spoon jump off the table and into a glass. Condé could imitate barnyard animals and fowl but it took a lot of coaxing to get him to do it. I showed them how I learned at Vassar to take my thumb apart and crack my nose.

We became even more rambunctious after Mrs. Brokaw left. We irritated our neighboring toilers at *Vogue* and *House & Garden* to such a degree that we were banished to another floor. When Frank Soule, business manager for all our magazines, took us to inspect our new premises, the walls were covered with plaster dust and Crowny wrote with his finger, "Frank Soule is a big stiff," which Soule didn't seem to think as funny as we did. At one time, we had a running crap game going, and in 1935, when the chain letter epidemic hit the country, we, the supposedly sophisticated and disdainful, fell for it. We made complicated charts tracing the course of each letter, wrote inspiring memos to lethargic weak links in the chain, and initiated a follow-up campaign that would not have disgraced the Northwest Mounties. At first we were afraid to approach Dr. Agha, but when finally asked if he was interested, he replied, "Hell, yes!" The writer Tess Slesinger was heard to say that she joined our chain because its list of names was so chic she thought it might help her socially. The dollar bills rolled in—I received a hundred-fifty—and it was a wonder we managed to get out the issue.

You can bet your boots Henry Luce never ran his magazines like that. It was never dull, whether it was Crowny bringing in his magician friends like Fred Keating or John Mulholland to entertain us with their tricks, or just Crowny alone, looking at a photograph of a female nude, full frontal view, and saying, "Charming. Charming. What is it?" or telling us about the time he had Isadora Duncan photographed outdoors in the country, wearing nothing but filmy scarves, and the photographer—Genthe, I think he said—made Crowny tie thread to Isadora's nipples and then climb a tree and perch there, holding the thread ends taut so that her breasts wouldn't droop. "You can't imagine how nervous I was. One inadvertent tug and I could have maimed her for life."

I think that in the long run most brilliant conversationalists are boring if you spend much time with them. They tend to be always "on," with no respite from their anecdotes (was it about Bonar Law or Lord Birkenhead that one or the other said, "Yes, his conversation is brilliant, but it lacks the proper terminus facilities"?), like David Niven today or Alexander King, when he was alive. King, who did a piece or two for *Vanity Fair*, although he was never on the staff, as he later claimed, was an exuberant, verbose little man who was not the best raconteur of his time but was indisputably the most persistent, to the point where, frankly, when we saw him coming, we would groan, "Oh God, look who's here!" I have known several dazzling conversationalists: Herbert Bayard Swope, former editor of the New York *World*, witty, lucid, erudite; Dr. Foster Kennedy, a prominent neurologist of the thirties, noted for a pyrotechnical flow of words, every other phrase an epigram; Jonathan Miller today, exhaustively sparkling and well-informed. Of them all, I think Crowny was the funniest, the most relaxed, the only one I could find consistently entertaining, day in and day out. I cannot imagine having to listen to any of the others for more than an occasional hour. Crowny used to tell about a fellow speaker and lecturer who asked him, "Doesn't it bother you when the audience start looking at their watches?" and his reply, "No. It only bothers me when they start shaking them." (I once said to Peter Sellers, "Most people are either stupid or phoney," and Sellers said, "Most people are both." One could almost say the same about the run-of-the-mill raconteur.)

Crowny was so much the courteous gentleman that he never wanted to hurt anyone's feelings. His efforts to avoid doing so became minor classics of tergiversation. When someone brought in a story or some drawings to show him, he never permitted himself a disparaging word. Instead, he would exclaim, "Marvelous! Wonderful! Superb! Have you tried *Collier's*?" He could not bring himself to dismiss anyone. A typical example was when he fired Richard Sherman, who described it to me. "He took me into a corner of the terrace, ostensibly to show me the orchids, and then he said, 'Do you have a moment to spare, dear boy?' We sat down and he said, 'I have a feeling that you're not entirely happy here.' I knew what was coming but I wasn't going to make it easy for him, so I said, 'Oh, but I'm very happy here, Mr. Crowninshield.' 'Ah, yes, but you should be free to devote yourself to your writing. You have such talent, dear boy.' I said, 'That's very kind of you, but I like working here and I can write at home nights and weekends.'" This went on until Crowny, in desperation, told Dick that he was going to advance him a certain sum of money—"Oh yes, dear boy, I insist"—and in return Dick was to stay home and write. The implication was that he should never come back, which he didn't.

When I was hired to work on *Vanity Fair* I was living in a dump on East 13th Street with my first husband, Heinz Norden, who was playing his guitar in Romany Marie's in the Village and teaching German two nights a week at the Jumble Shop, another Village restaurant. At the time I met him the year before, through my ubiquitous Aunt Grace, he was an advertising copywriter and later worked for the *Book of Knowledge*, but during the Depression days people took what jobs they could hustle.

Heinz was a German Jew who was born in London. I was twenty-three when we were married and he was twenty-five, tall, attractive, pedantic. I never really even thought I was in love with him. To be frank, I married him because I was several months pregnant. Then I had an abortion, anyway, because my mother kept sputtering, "What will your Uncle Roscoe think?" Almost from the moment of the ceremony, I realized that it was a mistake, and I'm afraid I gave Heinz a rather hard time, although we parted on friendly terms. I got a divorce in Syracuse in 1932, and he took me to the train and met me when I came back. He wanted to go with me but he had to stay home to empty the pan under the refrigerator and feed the cat. He now lives in London with his third wife and occasionally telephones or drops in to see me.

During our marriage Heinz introduced me to Buckminster Fuller, who had recently designed the Dymaxion House, and Isamu Noguchi, just beginning to gain renown as a sculptor. We saw them a few times, although I saw more of them after Heinz and I were divorced and I was sharing a West 3rd Street flat with Irene Kittle, a Condé Nast receptionist. Once, the two of them came to dinner and spent the evening reading *Alice in Wonderland* out loud to Irene and me, and Noguchi drew pictures of Abelard, my cat.

The first time I went out with Noguchi I wrote my Vassar friend: "He took me to a Japanese restaurant where he ordered in Japanese, so I couldn't interfere as I would have done if I had known it would turn out to be raw octopus. I felt quite sick afterward and couldn't think of much to say, but he chattered away and that gave me a chance to admire his face, which is beautiful and delicate beyond words. We went to the opening night of a peace propaganda film and on the way there I tried to be intellectual and talk to him about the Russian picture *The Road to Life*. 'Well, I'll tell you,' he said. 'Every once in a while I think I ought to go see a German or Russian movie, so I start for one, but I always end up at a burlesque show.' That put me right at my ease, and we got along fine. After the movie he took me to his studio and played Japanese music on the victrola and told me his ambition is to be a good tango dancer. He hates all the art patrons who paw him and coo at him, especially the *Vanity Fair* types. Just as we left the studio, he said, 'Well, Heinz is certainly lucky to have such a beautiful wife' and right then he tripped over a box in the hall and fell flat. 'Oh dear!' he said. 'I have been making up that speech all evening and just as I get to say it, I fall on my face. I can never do anything right.' He brought me home on top of a bus."

I put his picture on our Hall of Fame page. Most of my social life had some connection with my work: taking someone like T. R. Smith, the publisher, head of Boni & Liveright, to the theater (Sean O'Casey's *Within the Gates*, with Lillian Gish, in this case); going for dinner with fellow editor William Harlan Hale to the Fifth Avenue penthouse of William C. White to meet Adam Clayton Powell of Harlem; dining at the Crillon with Crowny and Amelia Earhart, the aviatrix, as we called her, whom we decided to photograph for the magazine; attending a tea for Maurice Chevalier on board the French Line ship, the *Paris*. I described the last event in a letter dated November 19, 1932: "There were about sixty people there and, as I expected, I didn't even get a look-in at Maurice at first. So I drank a quart of champagne, instead, and finally lurked around corners and peeked at him as he talked to a few people he had met before. Someone at last introduced me to him but I just choked and said nothing. Later, we all adjourned to the dining room for the eats. I was seated with some newspaper people and Chevalier was across the room at a table for four, with his manager and the Paramount publicity man. The chair next to him was empty. I had started to eat when the Paramount guy came over to my table and asked if he could speak to me for a moment, away from the table. I got up, and he then asked if he could take my coat. I thought, "My God, am I being put off the boat?" but I went with him. When we were away from the table, he said, 'Mr. Chevalier would like you to sit with him. He told me to ask you if you would.' So I tottered across the room, with everyone staring at me, and plumped myself down in the empty chair. I was so stunned that first I did not have as good a time as I would have if I had been more than semi-conscious. He said I was the first natural person he had met and that he hated Americans who kept coming up to him and trying to speak French because he never could understand them. So I told him, 'Go ahead and relax. You don't have to entertain me. I don't know you and you don't know me, and I can't think of anything to say to you, anyway.' He liked that, and then we began to laugh and talk. When his manager told him it was time to leave, he said, 'When I was bored and wanted to leave, you wouldn't let me. Now I am happy and having a good time, you want to make me go. I think not.' But finally he did have to go and he shook my hand vigorously and said, 'I can honestly and truthfully say that you are one person I am very glad I met.' " I arranged to have Steichen photograph him, took him to the sitting, and wrote a flattering caption for the picture. It didn't do me any good, because Mrs. Brokaw took him over and came into the office with a gold combination pen and cigaret lighter from Cartier which she said he had given her "for putting his picture in the magazine." She made the most of any opportunity, whereas I made the least.

Often, I wasn't enthusiastic about the celebrities I met. The darlings of the *Vogue-Vanity Fair* set were Noel and Cecil and Tallulah and Cole and Mona. They were all cut

from the same cloth. I thought at the time they were super-
ficial—slick and glib and tinselly—and I still do. I cannot
wallow in today's indiscriminate nostalgia for the thirties. I
enjoyed Cole Porter's chic Manhattan madrigals but I didn't
get ecstatic about them when he first wrote them and I can't
now. I never was crazy about Noel Coward, elegantly epicene, looking like a slit-eyed bonze, always with a supercili-
ous expression, to whom everyone kowtowed then and who
is now described as a genius, another example of the canoni-
zation of the old or the dead, in arts as well as in politics.
(Like Herbert Hoover who, alive, was denigrated, with even
someone like Baruch contemptuously referring to him as
"Old Cheese Face," but no sooner dead than apotheosized
into a Great Statesman.) Looking through my bound volumes of *Vanity Fair* I am happy to see that I was not
entirely alone in my opinion of Coward. George Jean Nathan
didn't think much of him, either. He wrote a pulverizing
criticism of *Design for Living* (revived on the London stage
last year to rapturous reviews) when it first opened on
Broadway in 1933. Of *Conversation Piece*, in 1935, he wrote
that it was "as smart and polished as a Mayfair butler, and
as conversationally and musically stimulating."

Mrs. Harrison Williams, the adored Mona, was a member
of that Inner Circle of Chi-Chi not because of any success
in the arts but because she was beautiful, with eyes like a
Bengal tiger, her husband was very rich, she was named The
Best Dressed Woman in The World, and she did such
"amusing" things, like having her Christmas tree made
entirely of ermine tails. (Later, during World War II, she
patriotically had her famous aquamarine jewelry reset in the
shape of bombing planes.) As for Tallulah, she excelled at
the type of rude and unkind personal remarks that passed
for humor, as did the overrated, incessantly quoted Dorothy
Parker, who had only to try to take a horse into a speak-easy,
ha ha, to be adulated around town as the sharpest wit since
Swift. Yes, she said many funny things, but let's not go
overboard.

Although at times I made an effort to play the sort of

dashing, exaggerated masquerade that the scene called for, I more often displayed a talent for self-effacement. I made friends with the secretaries and mail-room boys and sometimes, even after I was managing editor, I would take my friend Irene's place at the reception desk while she went to the ladies room. Once, a singer named Frances Williams came to keep an appointment I had made for her to be photographed. Seeing her standing irresolutely in the corridor, I went out to her and asked if I could help her, only to be told haughtily, "No, thank you. I have an appointment with Mrs. Helen Brown Norden." I hastily said that I'd get her and went to my office, where I told my secretary Miss Gramercy to tell her I was in conference and to take care of her.

My secretary became a celebrity herself after I left the magazine, when Robert Irwin, called by the press "the mad sculptor," murdered her mother, her sister (and raped them *after* they were dead) and their male lodger, all for love of her. It came out then that her original name was Ethel Gideon and she had recently married a young man named Kudner. She chose the name Gramercy from the telephone exchange when she came to work for me. I thought of her as an eager, devoted, pleasant girl, but certainly not as a *femme fatale*. Irwin used to call her at the office and when she wasn't at her desk, I would take his messages for her. Her marriage to Kudner enraged him. He planned to kill her. He went to her mother's home, expecting that because it was Easter Sunday, Ethel would pay a visit there. As it happened, she didn't. Hiding in the apartment, waiting for her, he slaughtered her mother in a particularly gruesome way, slew the unfortunate male lodger, and then, when she arrived home from her job as a hatcheck girl, Ethel's pretty sister Veronica.

The case was a sensation. During the country-wide manhunt for the murderer, Ethel was repeatedly interviewed and photographed for all the papers. During that period I took her to lunch. I was carefully avoiding any mention of the ghastly tragedy, but she brought it up herself, asking me if I thought she ought not to wear her glasses for the news photographs and telling me that when she went to the beach people asked for her autograph. Irwin had not yet been caught and I was stunned when she said to me, "You know what I think? I think he's just sick and tired of the whole business." I managed to comment that I imagined he'd be even sicker before it was all over. "Did you notice in my pictures that I'm carrying the handbag you gave me?" she asked. As a matter of fact, I had. I had said to my mother, with whom I was staying, "That looks like the bag I gave Ethel but it can't be, because that was two Christmases ago," I repeated this to Ethel and she said, "I was saving it for something special."

Irwin was finally arrested, tried and convicted; and Ethel sold her story to one of the tabloids. Afterward, Clare Luce went around claiming that she had been *her* secretary, which annoyed Ethel when I told her. "She's got a nerve claiming me!" she said, indignantly. "She never even used to say 'Good morning' to me when she came in the office." Crowny was especially shaken by the murders because the daughter of one of his Stockbridge friends had been boarding with the Gideons, on his recommendation. It was probably only because she went home to her family for the Easter weekend that she escaped being another victim.

Long before this incident, while I was still working on the magazine, Crowny came into the office one day with a woman friend who, he told us, was a wizard at palmistry, although she never did it professionally. We crowded around her, holding our hands out, eager to have them read. She did so for several of us, including me, and we all thought she was terrific. Then Ethel Gramercy held out her hand. The woman took it and looked at it. "I'm so sorry," she said, "but I just can't do any more. It's a gift that comes and goes." She left with Crowny. Later, he called me into his office and closed the door. He then said that the woman told him that the reason she wouldn't read Ethel's palm was because "I saw violent death in it." "Of course, it's all non-sense," Crowny said to me, "but don't mention it to Ethel or anyone. It might upset her."

Throughout the years after I'd left *Vanity Fair*, Crowny continued to send me affectionately humorous notes and telegrams. When I took a suite at the Alrae on East 64th Street, I gave him as a reference and received from him a wire that said: "Have spoken to the hotel. Told them you are a combination Joan of Arc Cleopatra Hetty Green and Eleanor Roosevelt." Right after *Vanity Fair* merged with *Vogue*, he went to Boca Grande in Florida and sent me a rather sad little handwritten note: "I came here for a six weeks rest after 45 years of the publishing business. We had fun, didn't we, despite the worries and fears? Oh, *why* don't you write? You have a definite flair for it. Some day you will show the world what a witty, imaginative, shrewd writer you are. I shall always treasure your friendship. We must help each other, dear."

He always gave me credit for my work, which was more than many of the others did, and in an article he wrote for *Vogue* about the *Vanity Fair* days he devoted several flattering paragraphs to me, calling me "the dark and flashing Helen Brown Norden, an avowedly revolutionary spirit, a satirist of a bold, even Rabelaisian order, and the master of a highly personalized prose style. Unfortunately, she had so strong a distaste for writing that she rarely lifted her pen save under the direst compulsion."

My husband Jack Lawrenson was mad about Rousseau's paintings, especially one called "The Woman with the Serpent," which he saw reproduced in an art magazine. I tried every museum and gallery in town to try to get a print for him. Finally, I wrote Crowny. This was in October, 1947, when he was fatally ill with cancer, although I didn't know it. He answered my appeal immediately. "Dear Helen: A serpent figured in two or three of Rousseau's paintings. Will you try to describe the background, size, color, etc.? Fondly, admiringly, and ever rememberingly, your old beau, employer and slave. Gene Autry." Four days later, I received another letter: "I am sorry, but I am afraid there is no commercial print of this Rousseau jungle, which has long been in the Louvre in Paris. (Otherwise, I would buy it for you.) Apparently, the young lady in your picture exercises precisely the same effect on boa constrictors that you always had on me: the power, that is, first to lure, then to enslave, and (finally) to devour. Believe me, my oft-remembered Helen, your loving (and only too willing) python. George Raft." In November he sent me his own framed reproduction of Rousseau's "Passion in the Desert," or "Sleeping Gypsy." It shows a dark girl asleep in the desert and a lion staring at her. With the picture, Crowny enclosed a letter, "Dear Madame: I thought this might be of interest to you, as a Rousseau collector. I happen to be the editor who arranged the sitting, chose the moon, the model, the ukelele and the feminine accessories. The scene is the Ladies Rest Room in the Condé Nast Publications. The recumbent lady is Helen Brown Norden. The male lion figure is Francis W. Crowninshield, a great admirer of this amorous passion in the desert. The picture shows the predatory old editor enthralled and intoxicated by the sleeping siren. Always admiringly, Crowny. P.S. The editor's interest is indicated by his waving tail."

He was already in the hospital, in great pain, and within a month he was dead. I could never have disliked him, no matter what his limitations. He was the best of that mannerist group during the *Vanity Fair* days, but I am afraid that was simply not enough. It was not an era in which to keep on joking or dancing. That wasn't music in the air. It was the ominous beat of war drums. Hirohito's soldiers were in China, Mussolini's in Ethiopia, and Hitler came to power in Germany. In Washington, MacArthur led troops in an attack on World War I veterans who were asking for a bonus; and in the American midwest hungry women with their children went from door to door, begging for food. The Ivory Tower as a functional form of mental architecture was on its way out.

Seven

THE DELICATE MONSTER: An American Success Saga

W

HEN I FIRST SAW HER I didn't like her. Few women do. I can think of no one who has aroused so much venom in members of her own sex. Much of it is envy, of course. But not all. Other more talented women, other successful women, have disliked her intensely. Some years ago, when a magazine published an article entitled "The Many Faces of Clare Boothe Luce," the most frequent comment of her peers was "I thought she had only two."

As I grew to know her better and as I learned from various personal sources something of her early life and background, I became, if not unreservedly fond of her, at least sympathetic. She made real friendship impossible, perhaps because she seemed to trust no one, love no one, remaining inaccessible deep in the malistic concept that rankled under her shield of opaque, steely self-assurance. Oddly, I was sorry for her, because I believed that despite the ineluctable procession of her triumphs, she was unhappy, never satisfied, never content. Yet she was the glittering lodestar of a generation, or at least of those parts of it susceptible to the skittish canons of publicity. As such, she became a target for a certain amount of hyperdulia, with attendant accolades, some less awesome than others. In 1947 she came second to Mrs. Eleanor Roosevelt in a national poll to determine "the American woman you most admire"; in 1953, according to a Gallup poll, she was one of "the ten most admired women in the world," surpassed only by Mrs. Roosevelt, Queen Elizabeth II and Mamie Eisenhower; during her tenure as our ambassador in Italy, freshmen girls at Italian universities voted her "the ideal woman." (Gina Lollabrigida came second.) From a skimpily educated but clever girl, so ambitious that it hurt, to her present dwindling status as Elder Stateswoman Emeritus, she parlayed a nimble, mousetrap mind, apodictic nerve, and a will as tough as *lignum vitae* beneath an exquisitely angelic façade into one of the most strategically calculated and fascinating success stories of the century. Her technique was simple: aim for the top.

Through the years she developed an extraordinary facility for picking up pointers from men who were specialists in their own various worlds: society, publishing, literature, theater, films, journalism, military tactics, politics, finance, religion or whatever. She then skillfully incorporated these acquired tidbits, with an often magnificently flip disregard for accuracy, into what can only be described as a sort of conversational legerdemain in which, through seductive tricks of voice and glance, of phrase and timing, she sparkingly disguised any sterility of content with fertility of form. She always memorized enough of the technical jargon in each particular field to lend her remarks an impressive air of streamlined expertise. For example, during World War II she would interlard her conversation with words like *logistics*, the *deploying* of troops, the disposition of *materiel*, using them with such knowing inflection that her listeners were almost ready to imagine that she could have served as military advisor to every warrior of note from Bismarck on down. The effectiveness of this was enormously buttressed by her habit of referring to the Allied commanders by their first names, as indeed she was entitled to do, since in whatever realm she invaded she hobnobbed only with the upper-crust hierarchy thereof.

Early in her career she perfected a technique for making all other women in any gathering feel eligible for the booby prize. Sometimes she completely ignored them. Condé told me of a formal dinner to which he took her when she was in her twenties and a caption writer on *Vogue*. Those were still the days when at the end of a dinner the ladies left the room, while the men remained for brandy and cigars. At this dinner, however, Clare blandly stayed on with the men, while the other women, banished to the drawing room, fumed helplessly. Her own dinners, later in her career, tended to resemble seminars relentlessly conducted by the hostess. She would bone up ahead of time on some relatively obscure subject like the works of Pareto and then introduce it at table, where she naturally had the floor to herself, meanwhile transfixing the most important male present with the lambent gaze of those blue-gray eyes that could make strong men collapse in a state of hypnosis. She would ripple on and on in her musical, crystalline voice, brooking no interruption, contradiction or even auxiliary comment, and making the most ordinary phrase sound like a delicious witticism, while the females in her captive audience bitterly tried to keep their yawns at bay, especially when her topic was something as stimulating as farm parity, about which she could be sure they knew next to nothing and cared less. The men present might be in the same boat, but they were invariably left dazed and bewitched, although much of this was due to the shock value of hearing such a weighty lecture from the lips of a creature who looked as fragile and frivolous as those pink swirls of spun sugar candy you get at the circus. On the other hand, when confronted with a man she recognized as an authority on some subject, she devoted to him such a flatteringly grave attention that he was forthwith inspired with a desire to take her under his wing in order to sponsor and instruct this talented, appealing, delightful seraph.

When I went to work on *Vanity Fair*, Clare was associate editor. My desk was next to hers, so that I had plenty of opportunity to observe her. She was the person most responsible for my getting the job and I appreciated this, although I wished that she wouldn't call me "Brownie," which made me feel like a cocker spaniel. (She was the only one who did and she kept it up for years.) Her attitude toward me was friendly, encouraging, scrupulously fair. Yet I was wary. A letter I wrote during my third week on the magazine described my initial feeling: "Mrs. Brokaw comes sweeping into the office around 10 or 11 in the morning, looking beautiful and expensive, her perfume leaving people on her route practically in an olfactory swoon. She lives in a penthouse on Beekman Place with four servants, including a personal ladies maid to draw her bath and help her dress, just like a movie star. I had to go there one day to pick up some manuscripts. The top of her long dining-room table is all one big mirror, which must have quite a dizzy effect when you see everyone eating and chewing reflected in it . . . After she divorced her multimillionaire husband, she met Condé at a dinner and asked him for a job because she was bored. She went to work on *Vogue*, writing captions and helping out at photographic sessions, for $20 a week. Then Donald Freeman, our managing editor, fell madly in love with her and brought her over to *Vanity Fair* at $40 a week. The two of them squabble a lot. Sometimes he gets so furious he rushes out to the elevator corridor and calls her on the pay telephone there, so his secretary won't hear him, but I can hear Mrs. B. yelling back at him. She treats him like a faithful old dog that gets on her nerves. I have a feeling she has other fish to fry. Raymond Bret-Koch, a French artist who works for us, asked me out when I had only been here one week. He took out Mrs. Brokaw a few times before I came and he says men are overcome by her but that he has the feeling she's not *real*. He says, 'It's a beautiful façade, well constructed but without central heating.' Everyone else is bowled over by her, especially men. She just snows them under with charm. There is no question about her having it. An appraisal of her mind is another matter. She's clever and quick-witted. If we need a title, a caption, a word, an idea, she can think of one right off the bat. She's not a profound thinker but she's one of the fastest, trigger-quick. It's the kind of 'cleverness' I mistrust. It's difficult to explain just why I dislike her. And it is honest dislike, not just envy. I really feel superior."

Sitting next to her as I did, I was unavoidably a witness to the way she operated in those days when she was still on her way up. For example, she would telephone some fairly important man and say that in her capacity as associate editor she had been sent complimentary tickets to the opening night of a play and she would like to have him go with her. Then she would call her ticket broker and order two tickets. Sometimes it was a man she scarcely knew. George Oppenheimer, the publisher, told my friend Elsbeth that he was astonished to get a call from Clare, inviting him to the theater. He had only been briefly introduced to her at some cocktail party where the sole words they exchanged were "How do you do?" When her invitation came out of the blue he accepted, mostly from surprise and curiosity, but he reported that he never did figure out why she asked him. She had another way of meeting celebrities she didn't know. She would call, for example, Constance Bennett, getting the telephone number from our files or a friend, and say, "This is Clare Boothe Brokaw of *Vanity Fair*. I'm giving a little party for Maurice Chevalier and he suggested that I ask you." Then she would call Chevalier at his hotel and go through the same routine: "I'm giving a little party for Connie Bennett and she suggested that I ask you." It usually worked.

I've known few men who could resist her spell, once she set her mind to it and had them face to face. Even those who, before meeting her, were critical and scornful—John O'Hara, John Mason Brown, to name two I knew personally —succumbed to an extent. When George Jean Nathan's

contract was up, I suggested that we try Brown as a replace-
ment drama critic for a few months. Because I had met him,
through my Aunt Grace—who else?—I went to his apartment and we discussed the arrangements. But it was Clare
who then took over, getting herself invited for drinks, leaving her jeweled cigaret case there, intentionally or not, so
that he telephoned to tell her he had it and to suggest
another meeting. And when I told Pare Lorentz, while drinking with him at Chatham Walk, that Clare was thinking of
marrying Luce and was sailing for Europe that afternoon to
mull it over, he was so upset that he wanted to rush to the
boat and stop her. I had all I could do to dissuade him.
When she didn't know someone, she sometimes gave the
impression that she did, which was not far out of line,
because she soon would. I remember one afternoon when
she returned to the office and said, "I've been lunching with
Willie Maugham at the Waldorf." This was accurate in an
oblique way. A friend of mine who also lunched that day at
the Waldorf related that Clare was there and so was Somerset Maugham, but not together. They were at different tables.
Inevitably, however, the day came when she telephoned
me to say, "I'm giving a little dinner for Willie Maugham
and I'd like you to come."

When I was discussing her recently with Don Erickson,
Esquire's editor, he said, "I don't want to be too personal,
but was there competition between you and Clare?" I was
genuinely amazed. Competition? Other women didn't com-
pete with Clare. There was no contest. *Nolo contendere.*
She could enter a room where there were other women more
beautiful, better dressed, with better figures, and they faded
into the background, foils for her radiance. Her figure wasn't
particularly good; her features were far from classic beauty.
(She had her nose done over, but I liked her old nose better.
It was slightly longer, gave more character to her face, I
thought, and balanced her prominent jaw.) Although she
was named five times as one of the World's Best Dressed
Women, she was never really chic, never anywhere near
approaching the clothes sense and style of someone like, say,

Jacqueline de Ribes or Babe Paley. She was always too fond of ruffles, bows, frills, dowdy hats, too many jewels at one time, ill-fitting clothes, fussiness. In some of her news pictures during the forties she looks like snapshots and home movies of Eva Braun. I've only seen one photograph that caught the essential quality of her beauty in those earlier years—the quality of luminosity. Her skin was flawless, apparently not a pore in it, with a curious kind of pearl-like translucence. Her eyes were not large, but there was a magical loveliness in her gaze, level, disquieting, spell-binding. Most articles and books about her repeat the story that Cecil Beaton once called her "drenchingly beautiful." It never occurred to me to doubt it, but not long ago I telephoned him at his London house to check the date. He told me, and I quote exactly, "I never said it about her. I said it about someone else and Clare pinched it." However, even though not intended for her, the phrase fitted her.

The first time I saw her socially, outside office hours, was when she asked me to go on a double date with her and a recent addition to our editorial staff, William Harlan Hale, then in his early twenties and, of course, smitten with her. He was bringing along another young man named Bingham, son of a Connecticut politician, who disapproved of Clare but was curious about her. "Don't bother to dress," Clare told me. So I didn't. I wore the plain white linen suit I wore on my first date with Condé, with the same red gypsy bandanna on my head. Clare showed up in a long white satin evening dress, cut low in front, blazing with diamonds—bracelets galore, necklace, earrings, brooch, rings—an altogether breathtaking vision. We had dinner at Jim Moriarity's House of Lords speak-easy on East 54th Street, an expensive saloon with glass pillars, green velvet chairs, a high, arched, golden ceiling. Tommy Smith, the Boni & Liveright publisher, was there with another party and he told a mutual friend that I looked stunning and Clare just looked "like an overdressed blonde," but he was a cynical, brilliant man who, as a friend of Donald Freeman, had witnessed the havoc wrought by her charms and presumably was inoculated. Our two young

escorts were staggered by her. Her effect on young Bingham was similar to that had by Henry James' Princess
Casamassima on the young and radical Hyacinth Donegan
when she summons him to her opera box: "He had no sense
of anything but the woman who sat there, close to him . . .
with a fragrance in her garments and a light about her . . .
She was fair, shining, slender . . ." Like the Princess, Clare
"was covering the young man steadily with her beautiful
deep eyes." I might just as well have been one of the waiters.

It was over coffee that she gave him the *coup de grace*. "Let
me read your palm," she said, taking his hand, gently running her fingers over it, murmuring softly, and finally, when
he was in a state fast approaching levitation, pressing his
palm for a brief moment against the bare, pearly skin just
above where her dress began. He was a gone goose. In our
taxi afterward, he was still mesmerized. (Clare and Hale
had gone on to some party in her car.) "She's so feminine,"
he kept saying to me. "I never dreamed she'd be so feminine." A few years later, when I described the evening to
Irwin Shaw, his comment was "Feminine as a meat ax."

Yet he, too, was not entirely immune to her appeal. He was
then twenty-four and just beginning to be known. Clare
asked me to bring him to meet her. When we arrived, she
was waiting for us at a table in the Waldorf Grill, reading
a copy of his one-act antiwar play, *Bury the Dead*. I never
saw her dressed so simply: a tailored dark dress, no jewelry
except a wedding ring. Her manner was friendly, but also
respectful. She asked him to autograph the book; she asked
him the right questions about his work and ideas and aims.
Only once did she make a wrong move. After we left her,
Irwin said, "She's quite a girl. But she's no friend of yours.
When you went to the can, she said, 'Brownie's an old
man's darling.'" He knew about Baruch, so I just laughed
and said, "Well, he's more her old man than mine."

She usually held her fire where I was concerned. She knew
I was no threat to her and I think she realized that we
wanted different things from life. We got along well together
at work, day after day, a fair test. When Freeman was killed

in the car accident, she was shocked but not shattered. She took his place and moved into his big office, adjoining ours. She was an excellent managing editor, alert, industrious, resourceful, brimming with ideas, easy to work for, always serene and cheerful, although Crowny later described her in his *Vogue* article as "a creature combining the various capacities of a super-fortress, a battleship and a tank."

It was another step on her way to the top. She was becoming a celebrity in her own right. Even so, she still engaged in tactical maneuvers, such as leaving a standing order with a florist for one gardenia a day and then pretending she didn't know who sent it. Because I was on friendly terms with Archy, her secretary, as I was with the others, who accepted me and chatted with me as they wouldn't have dreamed of doing with any of the other editors, I knew that the florist's bill came to Clare. One day, she received a package that contained a handsome leather desk set. "Now *who* could have sent me this? There's no card." The set included a picture frame, into which she inserted a photograph of her daughter Ann. "Look! It just fits!" she exclaimed, with a pretty show of delighted surprise. "Of course it fits," Archy said later. "She had me measure it with a ruler before she bought the set." I think the purpose was to put across the idea that she was someone to whom gifts were an appropriate tribute. In LaFargeville we would have described her actions as priming the pump.

She left the magazine in the winter of 1933. For a few months in 1934 she wrote a syndicated column for the Hearst papers but was fired because they wanted something light and gay, and she insisted on writing about politics. She already had the bug. When she visited our office during this period, our copy editor suggested to her, jokingly, "Maybe you'll end up in the White House." Clare gave her one of those cool, devastating looks of hers and said, unsmiling, "Stranger things could happen." Before I ever met her, she had been introduced to the political world by her admirer, champion, and mentor, Bernard M. Baruch, whom she met through Nast. Baruch took her with him to the 1932 Democratic convention in Chicago, a train journey he described to me in indiscreet detail when I was visiting him in Austria four summers later. By that time she was married to Luce, although she remained Baruch's political protégée, despite the fact that he was a lifelong Democrat and she was a Republican.

She knew that I was seeing Baruch, too, and one evening, during a party in the Luces' apartment, she suddenly came over to me and knelt on the floor in front of my chair. "I wonder if you have to listen to half as much about me as I do about you," she said. I knew she meant Baruch. I certainly did have to listen. If not his favorite subject—that, after all, was how much better he could run the country if only he were in charge—she was a close runner-up. He often referred to her as "the poor little kid," a designation it was not easy to accept with a straight face. Every year, when he went to Europe, he brought back gifts for various women friends, including Mrs. Roosevelt and me, but Clare had first pick. "She's just like a little kid. She wants them all," he told me. "Poor little kid. It's hard to refuse her anything." His favorite gifts were antique gold snuff boxes and Clare practically cornered the market. I had three, but she had about two dozen, and after she was married to Luce she kept them on display in their Connecticut mansion, all laid out in a glass-topped museum-type showcase in the drawing room.

In his biography of her, Stephen Shadegg, once Barry Goldwater's campaign manager, wrote that Arthur Krock, the political commentator and old friend of Baruch, said that Bernie wanted to marry her but that Clare did not want to marry him. I disagree. I think she would have married him without hesitating a moment, but he would not have asked her while his wife was alive. He may well have wanted to marry her, but I know for certain that he would never have even considered a divorce. By the time Mrs. Baruch died, it was too late. Clare was already Mrs. Luce. In January, 1938, I took Irwin Shaw to visit her at the Luces' plantation near Charleston, South Carolina. As we were having breakfast on the train, the conductor came through and told the passengers that Mrs. Baruch had died in New York. (In that part of the country, everyone knew of the Baruch family and was interested in them.) The news had apparently reached Clare before our arrival. When we entered the main house, she was sitting on a sofa in front of the picture window, facing us. She didn't say "Hello" or "Welcome to Mepkin" or "Did you have a good trip?" Instead, she looked directly at me and her first words were "Why don't *you* marry him, Brownie?" So then I knew that she had been sitting there thinking about Baruch.

Years later, when Harry asked her for a divorce because he wanted to marry Lady Jean Campbell, Beaverbrook's granddaughter, Bernie told me that Clare came to him for advice. "The poor little kid asked me what she should do. I told her, 'Don't you budge for less than $17 million.'" (She didn't, and Lady Jean married Norman Mailer instead of Luce. I guess it made an interesting change.) "I have nothing to offer her now. I'm too old," Bernie said. Still, he always remained ready and eager to help her in every way. In 1944, when she ran for reelection to Congress, President Roosevelt, the CIO, and other Democratic groups sent their big guns into Connecticut to campaign against her. At the Republican state convention she warned against what she chose to call "Communist strangulation by underground American forces spawned, nurtured and encouraged by the Roosevelt New Deal misrepresentation." Orson Welles, Dorothy Thompson, Rex Stout, Sidney Hillman were among those who endorsed her opponent, Margaret Connors, a twenty-nine-year-old former Civil Liberties Union lawyer, and spoke at rallies in her support. Dorothy Parker went to Bridgeport to speak against Clare; Quentin Reynolds attacked her for having charged that "FDR lied us into war"; Clifton Fadiman, more cruel than correct, claimed that "No woman of our time has gone further with less mental equipment"; and FDR not only sent Henry Wallace to support Miss Connors but himself denounced Clare and stated, "Her defeat would be a good thing for this country."

After all the philliloo, she squeaked through by 102,043

votes to 100,030. "She was in real trouble," Baruch told me. "I had to go in there at the last moment and help the poor little kid out." I don't remember all the details, except that according to him it involved a deal with Jasper McLevey, the Socialist mayor of Bridgeport, to split the liberal vote. If I understood him correctly, it also was not entirely unaligned with financial expenditure. Bernie would always go to bat for her. From the start, he encouraged her. "I used to call her my little fighting game-cock," he told me proudly. "When I first knew her she wasn't always sure of herself. I'd tell her, 'Before you go to this function, you just stand in front of the mirror and you tell yourself, 'I'm the smartest. I'm the best-looking. I can't fail.' She followed my advice and it worked. When I introduced her to Churchill, he said to me afterward, 'She's the tops!' "

There have been several books about Clare and many magazine profiles. In no two of them do details of her childhood and family background tally. The labyrinth of contradictions is a researcher's nightmare. Only one date is constant: she was born, possibly in New York, on April 10, 1903. As far as I know, she has never lied about her age. Aside from that, though, the chronology gets pretty chaotic. Shadegg's biography, published in 1970, has Clare at the age of nine living in Nashville, Tennessee, with her brother, mother and father—the latter the owner of a soft-drink bottling factory—and attending the fashionable Ward Belmont School "for a year or so." On the same page, the family are living in Chicago, where Clare attends the Chicago Latin School and her father is a violinist in the Chicago grandopera orchestra. Clare remains nine. The father deserts the family for another woman and the mother takes the two children to Hoboken, where they live with the mother's parents. This all happens in one year, 1912, when Clare of course is still nine. That autumn, the grandfather dies and the mother and children move to "a dingy flat on Columbus Avenue in New York City." Not just a peripatetic child but an omnipresent one. Shadegg also writes that "she remembers that her father started her on Gibbons' *Decline and Fall* when she was nine." This is all the more remarkable a feat of memory because, in a tape-recorded interview published in 1973 in the *New York Times* Sunday magazine section, she says: "I was about seven when my father left us, and my mother had to struggle for a bare existence."

The discrepancies multiply like rabbits on a diet of Spanish fly. An article in *Scribners* said her father owned a soft-drink factory but this time it was in Memphis. A *New Yorker* profile said he was an executive of the Boothe Piano Company in New York but deserted his family, when Clare was eight, to become a wandering violinist, getting occasional gigs in music halls or restaurants as Billy Booth, The Irish Fiddler. Shadegg says the Boothe Piano Company was in Philadelphia and that Clare's father worked there for three months in 1896. In a *Look* article he was an unsuccessful violinist and the family lived in grim poverty, moving with him from one small town to another across the country. And so it goes.

According to Shadegg, when Clare was ten, she spent a year with her mother in Europe, where they "led the frugal lives of impoverished gentlewomen," returning to America in 1914 on "a blacked-out liner," with U-boats lurking in the ocean because of World War I. (But even the *Lusitania*, torpedoed in 1915, wasn't "blacked out" because the submarines did not begin operating until that year.) Clare referred to this trip in a letter she wrote me in 1968 in which she said that she couldn't imagine my liking London and added that she had never recovered from her emotional reaction to what she called her Dickensian childhood chilblains received "one ghastly winter when I was ten, living in a cheap London hotel with my mother." Yet we also learn, from various articles about her, that when she was ten she failed a screen test with Viola Dana at the Biograph Studios in Fort Lee, New Jersey; that in 1913 she understudied Mary Pickford on the New York stage in the David Belasco production of *A Good Little Devil*; that in 1914 she had a small part with Ernest Truex in *The Dummy*. (Gretta

Palmer wrote in *Look* that when Clare was seven she acted in a stock company, but this is not mentioned anywhere else.) Whatever the true facts, her childhood was not a rosy one. In a copyrighted column in 1955, Bob Considine wrote that Perle Mesta and her sister Marguerite Tyson knew Clare when they were all very young and they described her childhood as having been "in conditions so unappetizing that Marguerite added, 'I can't ever blame Clare for anything she does.'" I myself learned something of that background from different people, among them a Condé Nast receptionist named Alice Hait, who when a child lived in the same town, Greenwich, N.Y., although she said she and her schoolmates were not permitted by their parents to play with Clare. A friend of my mother's, Mrs. Maude Kilsheimer, lived in the same rooming house on Columbus Avenue with Clare and her mother. Then there was my Aunt Grace. My Aunt Grace should have worked for Walter Winchell. She knew everybody and all the gossip about them. I don't know how she did it because she wasn't rich, famous, social, or talented, but there was no doubt about her contacts. She collected celebrities the way other women collect cranberry glass or Meissen china. She took me to Tommy Smith's for dinner and to Arthur Krock's for cocktails. She knew Marilyn Miller for years, was her confidante, and called her by her childhood nickname "Lumpy." She had tea with Mary Pickford; she called Burgess Meredith "Buzz" and he often telephoned her; she was an old friend of Cornelius Vanderbilt, Jr.; when she went to call on the Chaplins, she complained of the chill in their living room and reported that Oona said to her, "Charlie likes it this way." When I mentioned meeting Mark Sullivan, she said, "Oh yes, he broke his back in Herbert Hoover's bathtub." Once, she said, "Poor Lewis Browne fell off a camel. Well, you know how difficult they are to ride." I said I didn't know, and she asked, in a surprised tone, "Didn't you ever ride a camel?" I told her there weren't many camels in LaFargeville.

And she knew a man named Yves de Villers. He was an

older man who lived in a terraced penthouse at 485 Madison Avenue, where he gave lavish parties for people like Gloria Swanson and other celebrities. Aunt Grace took me there and afterward I saw him frequently. It seemed that when Clare was a teen-ager, he was an intimate friend of her mother, a beautiful woman with violet eyes, glossy brown hair and a voluptuous figure. I met her once or twice, when she was older, but according to Yves she must have had in younger days the same effect on men that her daughter would later display. Her parents were Bavarian immigrants who ran a livery stable in Hoboken. The circumstances under which Yves met her must remain vague and a subject for conjecture, but there was no doubt that he knew her well. He had a contempt for convention and he told of a society ball to which, in defiance of his outraged friends, he took Clare's mother. A prize was to be given for the best-dressed woman. "She found out, God knows how, who the judges would be, and she made a point of talking to each in turn, weaving her spell. The result was that they awarded her the prize, to the indignation of all the other women present."

Yves told us what he knew about Clare's childhood, including the time, when Clare was sixteen, that her mother woke him in the middle of the night and asked him to marry Clare because she was worried about her and thought she was running wild. "Of course I told her it was an insane idea," he said. Clare certainly couldn't have forgotten him, but when I deliberately mentioned his name one morning when I was sitting on her bed in the Luce house in Greenwich, Conn., she never batted an eyelash and her face was expressionless. She was still in bed and we had been chatting. I said, "My Aunt Grace feels she knows you because she's a friend of Yves de Villers." She didn't even say "Who?" She just looked me straight in the eye and said calmly, "Do you feel like going for a swim?" For a moment I wondered if she might be considering drowning me in the pool. I wouldn't have blamed her.

Of course, it is possible that she has a memory like a

sieve. It is more likely, however, that she understandably chooses not to remember unpleasant details of the seminal background from which came her resilient toughness of inner strength, her tenacity and determined ambition, as well as her pessimism and lack of compassion. It was a hard, rough road. No one can deny that she has always had courage, a chilling courage, in the furtherance of her own aims. She has never flinched under attack.

When she was about seventeen she worked for a while in a factory making paper flowers, and she may or may not have gone to business school to learn typing and shorthand. The story has often been told that her first break came when in her late teens she met Mrs. Oliver H. P. Belmont on board the ship *Olympia* returning from Europe, although the year varies, depending on which book or magazine you read. Condé told me that Willie Vanderbilt, Mrs. Belmont's son by her first marriage, describing the meeting on shipboard, said, "You wouldn't believe it in this day and age, but she actually dropped her handkerchief in front of me." Anyway, she did meet Mrs. Belmont, one way or another, and subsequently went to work for her in the women's rights movement. Through her she met George Brokaw, son of Isaac Brokaw of the clothing firm, and they were married when Clare was twenty and he was forty-three. (At that time, her name was either Anna Clara Booth, like her mother's, or Ann Clare Booth. It was Donald Freeman on *Vanity Fair* who persuaded her to drop her first name, add an "e" to Booth, and become Clare Boothe Brokaw.) The marriage was a miserable one. Brokaw was an alcoholic who abused Clare physically. In addition, she was snubbed by his family and Social Registerite friends. She stuck it out six years and then divorced him in Reno. She was given custody of their only child, Ann, for six months each year.

There is some confusion about when and where she first met Henry Luce. I may have met him before she did. A letter I wrote to my mother in November, 1932, said: "Last night I went for dinner to the house of Paul Cravath, a lawyer, philanthropist, and Otto Kahn's successor as head of the

Metropolitan Opera Productions Board. Ruth Page, a dancer from Chicago whom I met through Noguchi, the sculptor, is visiting Cravath and she invited me. Noguchi was there and so was Mrs. Benjamin Harrison, widow of President Harrison. She is 84 and full of wit and gaiety. Goes to all the new plays and art exhibits. A marvelous old lady who drank a cocktail with us, had wine with dinner, and smoked cigarets delicately through an ivory holder. After dinner, we all went to see Martha Graham dance and then we went for drinks to the gorgeous apartment of Henry Luce, who owns *Time* and *Fortune*."

I met him again in 1934 when I was seated on his right at a dinner given by Condé. I was then *Vanity Fair*'s film critic and I remember that during the meal Luce plied me with questions about the movies, shooting them at me in that machine-gun rapid-fire style he had developed to control his stutter. I rather liked him. He was a serious man who never wasted time on small talk. I found his abrupt, penetrating, intelligent interrogation a welcome change from the usual artificial conversation at these affairs. In fact, I *always* liked him. One might not agree with him, but there was no bull-shit about him.

I met him a few times at other parties, occasionally dancing with him, an activity at which he definitely did not excell. Then came the widely publicized Elsa Maxwell supper dance for Cole Porter at the Waldorf's Starlight Roof, a gathering of top-billing names in the New York society circus, from the Grand Duchess Marie to Mrs. William Randolph Hearst. Prior to the ball, I attended a dinner at Condé's, where I sat between the Prince de Polignac and Crowninshield's brother Eddie, a n'er-do-well who took dope, sort of an early but elderly hippie. Crowny was slated to be my escort to the Maxwell party. As we went to our car, Clare came up to us and asked, "Can I go with you? I'm all alone." We took her with us, but after we arrived at the ball I didn't see her again for hours. I sat with Baruch and his wife and Joe Kennedy, dancing a few times with Joe, gossiping with Mrs. Baruch. Around two in the morning I went to a pay phone and woke up George Dangerfield, the young Englishman who was our literary critic on *Vanity Fair*, telling him that I wanted him to take me to Tony Codo's Foursquare Bar, a sailors' dive on Sand Street in Brooklyn.

As I was dashing through the downstairs Waldorf lobby, I passed Clare and Luce, who were walking up and down and talking earnestly. She called out to me, asking me where I was going. "Come and talk to us. Stay with us," she pleaded, but I shook my head and rushed out to get a taxi. Later, I learned that he had taken her down to the lobby to tell her that he had decided to marry her. They had met only once before and hadn't hit it off. At the Maxwell party he was on his way to his wife, carrying two glasses of champagne, when Clare intercepted him, saying something like, "Could one of those be for me, Mr. Luce?" She said she only meant to tantalize him, but the next thing she knew, he insisted that they go down to the lobby, where, to her astonishment, he announced his marital intentions. I believe the story. It fits in with everything I know about him: his quick decisions, his directness, his no-nonsense manner.

The next day I stayed home with a hangover. I had gone slightly berserk on Sand Street, doing an exhibition solo in my best imitation of a burlesque cooch dancer, while the sailors threw money at me. I was such a hit that Codo, the Sicilian owner, offered me a job dancing there. I had to turn it down because I couldn't figure out how I could work days as *Vanity Fair*'s managing editor and dance all night as a sailors' delight. The following afternoon, when I languished in bed with a mild attack of remorse and nausea, Condé telephoned me. "For God's sake, where did you disappear to last night?" he demanded. I told him, mentioning Clare and Luce in the lobby. "I know," he said. "I got stuck for hours with Mrs. Luce."

For Luce it was the *coup de foudre*. There was no doubt that he was crazy about Clare. She fled to Havana and he followed. In June, his wife went to Reno. They had been married twelve years. According to the newspapers, she got a settlement of $2 million and custody of their sons, aged ten and six. Meanwhile, Clare went to Europe to think things over. (Baruch told me that Baruch offered to buy *Vanity Fair* for her.) She wrote me a long, rambling letter from Badgastein in which she said that she would like to tell me about her romance but that she surmised that everybody in New York knew more about it than she did. When she came home she took me to lunch at "21" and said she was going to marry Harry. "I always thought you would marry someone old and wise and rich and famous," I said, tactlessly. Tears came to her eyes. She didn't strike me as deliriously happy at the prospect of her impending nuptials. They were married in November, 1935. I sent her a pewter and glass condiment castor that had been in my family for a hundred years. She wrote me that I was a fool to give away anything as useful and amusing and valuable as the castor. She said it proved that people like me with really improvident, careless ways, who give away everything good they've got and only cling to a lot of "worthless things like books by Karl Marx" deserve to have absolutely *nothing* but a good time.

Vanity Fair was soon to merge with *Vogue*. "Now, for heaven's sake, Helen, don't go around saying you were fired," Condé said to me. I don't know what else it could be called. "You wouldn't work out on *Vogue*," he went on. "You'd be just another staff member. Besides, you and the *Vogue* people aren't very compatible." (True, although I wrote articles for *Vogue* during the next ten years.) At Clare's prompting, Harry offered me a job as film critic for *Time*. He was also considering a new magazine to be called *Letters*, the contents to be selected from the deluge of correspondence from *Time* readers. He asked me if I would like to be the editor. I thought it was a boring idea. Besides, I had my heart set on Havana. Clare sent a cable to Mrs. Grant Mason, now Mrs. Arnold Gingrich, a friend of hers who lived there. In the cable she said that I was going to Havana, and she asked Mrs. Mason to take me under her wing because she loved me dearly and thought that Mrs. Mason would, too.

While I was leading my lotus-eater's life in Cuba, Clare

was a one-woman beehive back home. I sometimes thought of what Harry said to me when just the three of us were dining at "21," after their marriage: "I guess I'm old-fashioned. I think a woman's place is in the home." Poor Harry. Of all Clare's many-faceted talents, that of homebody was not among them. Success was her goal and always she restlessly sought new fields, new challenges. Nothing was ever enough. Harry was a strong-willed, puritanical man with a powerful, galvanic mind. He began his career as a sixteen-dollar-a-week leg man for Ben Hecht on the Chicago *Daily News* and went on to build the greatest publishing empire in history. "Does 'um have a dreat big publishing empire?" she once teased him in front of me, to his embarrassment. She was more than a match for him.

Her first play, *Abide with Me*, about a sadistic alcoholic and his young wife, opened two days before their marriage and was savaged by the critics. I didn't think it was that bad. I've seen far worse plays that received better reviews. The calamitous reception failed to faze her. In the next three seasons she had three hits on Broadway—*The Women*, *Kiss the Boys Goodbye*, *Margin for Error*—although the critics remained unenthusiastic. Brooks Atkinson called *The Women* "a kettle of venom" and Heywood Broun, although not a drama critic, was so incensed by the play that he devoted a column to it in which he said that she had committed the sin against the spirit: "she has attempted to degrade the human race." Milton Mackaye wrote of "her undeviating malice" and said, "Her wisecracks seem to indicate that she has contempt and hatred for not merely the group she professes to satirize but for the whole human race." True to form, she confounded critics with her annoying habit of success. Long before its revival on Broadway in 1973, *The Women* had earned her more than $2 million, was translated into twelve languages, performed in twenty-five countries, twice filmed (the first time with Joan Crawford, Rosalind Russell, Norma Shearer, Paulette Goddard) and made into a TV spectacular. It didn't make her ill-wishers any happier to learn that she wrote the first draft of the play in three days, sitting up in bed at the Waldorf, glamorous in a frilly bed jacket, with a blue satin bow in her hair.

Her capacity for work was prodigious. She could write a whole new act in the middle of the night and appear for rehearsals the next day looking fresh, rested, clear-eyed, while everyone else was haggard with worry. I never knew her to dawdle or loll around. She made every moment count. If listening to people talk, she did needlepoint. If in the bath or on the john, she was always making notes, thinking, planning. The speed of her thought and output was legendary. Margaret Case Harriman told of two women who found themselves with a half-hour to kill after lunch. "What can we do in half an hour?" one asked, to which the other replied, "Well, if we were Clare Boothe, we could write a play."

While I was still living in Havana I received a cable from Condé, in which he said that he was plugging me for a job on the forthcoming Luce picture magazine and a letter from Ralph Ingersoll saying he wanted to discuss the new magazine with me. I didn't want to work on anything, but it turned out I had to return to New York for family reasons, so I called Luce. He made an appointment for me to talk with Dan Longwell, the first executive editor of *Life*. I went to their offices and Harry introduced me to Longwell and we had a chat. The idea was that I would be the entertainment editor: theater, films, art, etc. I would have been the only woman editor. All the other women on the magazine were researchers or secretaries. The offices seemed to me filled with young, eager-beaver men, charging around purposefully, determined to forge ahead. I wanted to forge backward. I went home to the Alrae, where I was staying, and wrote Harry, saying that my doctor said I was anaemic and must not do a thing except rest. Harry sent me three dozen American Beauty roses, with a card on which he had written that he hoped I would get well soon so that I would be ready to start work on the magazine. I went to Europe that summer, instead. Sometimes I have thought that if only I had taken the job I could have become rich, like the other original *Life* editors, who all owned shares in the magazine, were paid enormous salaries and bonuses, could afford big houses in Westchester or Connecticut. They all had ulcers, too. I never could have stood the atmosphere. I would either have quit or been fired. I'm sure.

In February, 1940, Clare toured Europe alone, talking to statesmen and generals. (In France, General Gamelin personally took her to the Maginot Line, where the soldiers presented her with a bunch of red roses.) She returned to New York in June and wrote a book, *Europe in the Spring*, in five weeks. Dorothy Parker called her review "All Clare on the Western Front." It sold 22,500 copies in less than two months. She read almost half of the book out loud to me and my husband, Jack Lawrenson, whom I had married the preceding year. Jack and I continued to see the Luces, despite the difference in our worlds and our beliefs. We never made any secret of our politics and often argued with Harry and Clare during weekends at their Connecticut house, visits that afforded us some interesting glimpses of the home life of the mighty, such as the time Harry came out on the terrace and asked Jack, "What does it mean when I call a number and the telephone goes bup-bup-bup-bup?" "It means the line is busy," Jack said. (I guess someone else always put Harry's calls through for him—a secretary, an assistant, a man servant.) On one evening Harry decided after dinner that we would listen to music. They had an elaborate hi-fi system and hundreds of records, although neither of them was at all musical. "What would you like, darling?" Clare asked him. "Tchaikovsky or Beethoven?" As it turned out, we heard nothing. The record player didn't work. So the four of us sat there, solemnly watching a television program about llamas in Peru. When at last we were in our bedroom, Jack said, "Do you suppose this is the way they spend their evenings or were they just trying to entertain us?"

We also visited them at Mepkin, their seven-thousand-acre plantation at Monck's Corner, South Carolina, with deer, ducks, wild turkey blinds, dove-shooting, quail. Nothing could have persuaded us to join in the sport. I can't stand hunters who kill creatures for the fun of it, and neither could Jack. Clare was an excellent shot, but then, she did everything well: riding, shooting, swimming, tennis, needlepoint, chess, skin-diving, backgammon, games like Monopoly. At everything she played to win or to surpass, and she usually did. I made about seven visits to Mepkin, the last two with Jack in 1941 and 1947. Clare's brother David was sometimes there. They were the most ill-matched siblings I've ever seen. It seemed incredible that they could have had the same parents. There wasn't the slightest trace of resemblance between them. He could have been a black Irishman: swarthy skin, rugged features, black hair, dark eyes, husky build, handsome in a tough, virile way, with a hard-boiled manner that suited his appearance. He looked like, and had been, a fighting Marine. Once, when he was blasting his sister's Social Register friends, she said impatiently, "David, I've told you over and over again that I can get you into the Social Register!" "Oh yeah?" he said. "That's a laugh. Everyone else with a string of clubs after their names, Racquet and Tennis, Yale Club, Union League or something, and then it'll say, 'David Booth. U.S. Marines.'"

I liked him. However, he often must have been quite a trial to Clare. He refused to add the "e" to his name; he went out of his way to avoid any social pretense; his speech was in rough contrast to her polished, careful diction; he was a heavy drinker; his friends were more apt to resemble Damon Runyan characters than those in the upper bracket circles in which Clare moved. She told people that he was older than she was, but once he commented wryly, "I can remember when I was your younger brother." Another time, she was tinkling sweetly on in one of her oneiric flights about childhood days: "When we lived in Chicago we all used to go to church every Sunday and my mother and I always wore white kid gloves. Remember, David?" His answer was a strange one. He said, bluntly, harshly, "No, I don't. I was in military school in Wisconsin. I don't know where you were." She quickly changed the subject. In 1948 David, by then her only remaining blood relative, rented a

Grandmother and me

My father in 1914, at thirty-one   *My mother in 1914 when she was*
twenty-eight

Helen Lawrenson in Syracuse, age twelve

The house at LaFargeville

*As a newspaperwoman,
at twenty, in Syracuse*

UPI

The author with Condé Nast in 1937

LIFE

Helen Lawrenson with Bernard Baruch and James Farley
at a theater opening in 1939

*Clare Luce, Jack Lawrenson and Helen
at Mepkin in 1947*

*Bernard Baruch
and Helen Lawrenson in
Badgastein, Austria,
1936*

*With Colonel
Ricardo Astudillo
in 1938*

*Jack Lawrenson, Mike Quill and Joe Curran at the 1943
National Maritime Union Convention*

Jack Lawrenson in 1947 at the National Maritime Union

small plane in California, flew out alone over the Pacific, straight out, until he crashed into the sea. His body was never found.

It was in 1940 that Clare made her spectacular debut on the political scene. Wendell Willkie, president of the Commonwealth & Southern Utility system, was the surprise Republican presidential candidate, backed by Luce. Clare made forty speeches in his behalf, including her somewhat less than epic oratorical battles with Dorothy Thompson, at one time the most redoubtable woman political pundit in the country. The two girls staged a running series of exhibitions that were livelier than a bag of cats and aroused almost more public interest than the candidates themselves. These spendidly silly debates made Clare nationally known, and although her boy lost the election she herself swept onward and upward, her acidic tongue and glistening beauty a diverting novelty in an arena where most women participants were on the frowsty side.

In 1942 she ran for Congress. She wanted Jack to manage her campaign on the trade union side. He was in Detroit, organizing seamen on the Great Lakes. A letter he wrote me in July, 1942, said, "Now about Clare. I haven't wired her because it would be difficult to set forth what she needs. As far as a man to handle her campaign, that's out! I think you should call her and tell her I'll be home the last week in July, and we could discuss the whole matter then. As far as the trade union movement is concerned, she has a million strikes against her. First, aside from its anti-labor policies (this week's issue slaps the steelworkers on the editorial page), *Life* is printed in an open shop, labor-fighting set-up in Chicago. The union involved is the typographical workers, A.F.of L. This would be used against her. Further, I don't see how she can sidestep being Luce's wife. Bridgeport is a strong union town. Nearly all the surrounding country where there are factories is organized. She would have to take a stand on wage increases, the union shop issue, genuine price-fixing and rent-freezing. Housing for war workers would be a major issue. Then there is the tax program, you know, the little matter of making those with large fortunes cough up. So all in all I don't think a letter or even a telephone talk would do much good. If she were to adopt a progressive position on these issues she wouldn't need a manager. She could appear before the local city labor councils, and even the state bodies, receive their endorsement and be on her way."

She was elected anyway, without our advice, by seven thousand votes, and was appointed to the important House Military Affairs Committee. In her maiden speech she attacked Henry Wallace, who was advocating postwar freedom of the skies. She coined the word "globaloney" to describe his views. In 1943 she wrote me an extraordinary letter, during the Congressional summer recess. In it she suggested that Washington was cancerous; she compared men to cockroaches and ants; she said she was revolted by her own bird-dropping liberalism, which she seemed to think meant less than nothing. The letter was a weird paean of disgust, filled with rambling pessimism about life and human beings. It went on and on, ten hand-written pages, with strange references to wiping dried blood from corpses, washing pus from the eye sockets of a blind beggar plucked of his eyeballs. She must have been in a black mood indeed when she penned it. It was a cry of hopelessness, as if she looked on the world and herself with something very akin to loathing. It ended by advising me to teach my four-year-old daughter to struggle, struggle, struggle, and teach her early, for in life there was nothing else. It was a revealing letter and a sad one.

In 1944 Clare delivered the keynote speech at the Republican national convention in Chicago, just twelve years after Baruch had taken her to the same city as his guest at her initial political convention. She was the first woman ever chosen to make the keynote speech at a national convention of any party. She delivered a scorching assault on Roosevelt who, she claimed, had promised never to send America's sons to die in foreign wars. She invented the symbolic character of "G.I. Jim, the dead buddy of G.I. Joe," charging that

Roosevelt's "promises lie as dead as young Jim lies now." It was a morbid masterpiece of necrophilia which struck many people as in shocking taste. It was also seized upon by the isolationist elements who took it as a sensational defense of their position.

Jack and I were staying at the Luce house. She returned from the heat and hurly burly of the convention, looking pure and serene, fresh as morning dew, as if she had just spent a month at a health farm. She was very pleased with herself. We stayed up half the night, arguing about the speech. She was veering more to the Right, and from 1944 on, her anti-Communist obsession began to dominate her public life as she grew closer to the Vatican, a route that began with family tragedy. In January of that year her daughter Ann, nineteen, was killed in an automobile accident while returning to Leland Stanford University from a visit with Clare. Annie was an attractive girl with blue eyes, chestnut hair, and an appealingly natural, unspoiled simplicity. Although as a child she didn't see a great deal of her mother, they appeared to have a closer relationship after Clare entered politics. Following the accident, Clare was reported near collapse. Six years earlier, her mother had also been killed in a car accident, near Miami. But it was the effect of Ann's death that led Clare to Catholicism. She took instruction from Fulton Sheen, then a Monsignor, and was baptized by him in February, 1946, in St. Patrick's Cathedral. Like her other major steps, this was not conducted under any cloak of anonymity. Her conversion was widely publicized. She wrote a series of articles on "Why I Became a Catholic"; she gave interviews on the subject; she delivered lectures on the meaning of the Mass and kindred topics; she wrote a movie, *Come to the Stable*, about a group of lovable nuns. (It starred Loretta Young, received a 1949 Oscar nomination, and still pops up on British television.) Her most spectacular gesture was to give Mepkin, her South Carolina plantation, to the Trappists for a monastery, visiting them occasionally to see how they were getting along.

I had friends, quietly devout Catholics all their lives, who took a decidedly qualified view of all the hoop-la. As in the other areas of her activities, Clare moved among the top echelons. Cardinal Spellman became her friend and they often dined together. She visited the Pope at his summer residence, Castel Gandolfo. She conferred with the Rev. John Courtney Murray, one of the world's leading Jesuit theologians and a frequent visitor at the Luce country house. She took to wearing a floor-length crimson cape, hung a glittering crucifix over her bed (my first impression was that it was covered with sequins but I must have been mistaken), stacked her bookshelves with works on theology and lives of saints, and systematically went about converting her friends, including Mme. Wellington Koo, wife of the former Chinese ambassador.

The first my husband and I knew that we were slated for inclusion in this campaign was one evening when Clare invited us to dinner. We arrived at the Luce apartment just as Harry was leaving. He shook hands and said he was sorry he wouldn't be with us but he had a prior engagement. After he left, Clare said, "I've invited another man. I hope you don't mind." It turned out to be Monsignor Sheen. We made a commendable effort to conceal our surprise and embarrassment. The four of us had dinner and then Clare took me into her bedroom, ostensibly to show me some new clothes she had bought but really to give the magnetic Monsignor a chance to go to work on Jack. "He gives me the creeps," Jack said, when we finally made our escape after an hour or more. Our next encounter came when Jack was mugged and several bones broken in his foot. With no advance tip-off, our doorbell rang one afternoon and there was Sheen, come to call on the invalid. During his visit, he informed us that he had converted Dutch Schultz on his deathbed, doubtless meant as an encouraging note. The next week he sent Jack a foot-high statue of the Madonna (irreverently referred to by our innocently secular children as "Papa's doll"), a rosary, and copies of Sheen's writings. A line appeared in Winchell's column to the effect that Mrs. Henry Luce was trying to convert "Earl Browder, the top

Communist," an obvious mix-up in rumor, as she didn't know Browder but Jack, as a top left-wing trade union official, would have been newsworthy. However, shortly afterward, due to a fiercely fought internal battle in the National Maritime Union, Jack was out of the union and therefore no longer a national figure. Sheen dropped him like a hot potato, never mind his immortal soul. Clare didn't give up. Father McCarthy, the Jesuit priest from St. Francis Xavier's, came to see me, saying, when I opened the door, "I was told to say, 'Clare sent me.'" He had never met her—still hasn't, as far as I know—but she had indicated to her superiors that she wished to have a priest assigned to us. He became a good friend and I still correspond with him, despite my unavailability as a convert.

If Clare's conversion made many of her friends uncomfortable, the effect on Harry was more dire. The Catholic church recognizes first marriages among non-Catholics, even civil ceremonies, and regards them as binding until death. Because Harry's first wife was still alive, his marriage to Clare was not valid in the eyes of the church and they were deemed to be living together in sin. The doctrinal solution, Clare told me, would be that they live together as brother and sister.

There was nothing of the philanderer or playboy about Harry. He was still in love with Clare. The result was that he was driven to other women, surely against his strict Calvinist morality, as well as his personal preference. He had been put in an untenable position as a husband, in addition to the blow to his male pride. For a man of his dominant ego, it must have been galling to realize that his marital relations with his wife were regarded as sinful, to be repented in the confessional. I don't imagine this enhanced the rapture of their union.

A lady who was a friend of Harry's for twenty years, a close but platonic relationship, wrote me that "Harry talked endlessly about her [Clare] to me. I didn't feel he was ever talking about a human being, so I suggested we find a 'cover name' for her. He suggested 'Guardian Angel,' which we reduced to 'G.A.' I think the reason I found 'G.A.' so easy to use is because in a sense she has that asexual quality of angels—fallen and otherwise. She is like some kind of mythological creature—including a unicorn!"

Meanwhile, Clare continued her political climb, campaigning for Dewey in 1946 and again, indefatigably, for Eisenhower in 1952. During one period she skirted dangerously close to urging what she called "preventive war," a curious, insane semantic exercise meaning "Let's start a war in order to prevent a war." Her support of Eisenhower was rewarded in 1953 when he named her ambassador to Italy, the first woman ever to be appointed to a top U.S. embassy. There she continued her anti-Communist campaign by passing out crucifixes to peasants and was accused of interfering in internal affairs when in her first ambassadorial speech in Milan, five weeks after her arrival and ten days before the Italian elections, she urged Italians to vote against the Communists. A French conservative paper called it "an unbelievable blunder, perhaps without precedent in diplomatic history." Harry, dubbed The Consort by Italian papers, spent several months of the year in Rome. Once, when asked what he did at Clare's diplomatic parties, he replied, "I pass the cookies." Home on a holiday, Clare telephoned me and I asked her, "How did you settle Trieste?" I was kidding but she answered solemnly, "By hard work, night and day, day and night." That summer, after she returned to Rome, the children and I spent a month in the guest cottage on the Luce estate in Ridgefield, Conn. Harry asked me to a dinner he gave for Governor John Lodge. Another guest was Russell Davenport, who told me, "When the butler called to invite me, he said, 'It will be very informal. Mrs. Luce took all the glasses with her to Rome.'" She also took two van loads of paintings and furniture.

She resigned her post in November, 1956, because of illness, and spent the following year accepting awards: the first recipient of the Mary MacArthur Memorial Award "for outstanding contributions to the theater as well as selfless devotion to humanitarian efforts at home and abroad"; the

Gimbel Award, the citation for which called her "the bright star by which generations of American women yet to be will set their course in the search for means to serve humanity"; the Freedom Award "for distinguished leadership in combating Communism," presented by the Order of LaFayette and also received by John Wayne and Norman Vincent Peale; the Gold Medal of the National Institute of Social Sciences, presented for "distinguished service to humanity" (Billy Graham got one at the same time); the Laetare Medal, highest honor of the University of Notre Dame (announcing the award, the President of Notre Dame said, "Because few American women, indeed, few women anywhere, can approach her genius"); the U.S. Chamber of Commerce "Great Living American" award, along with Cecil B. DeMille and a man from North Brookfield, Mass., breeder of "the hen of the year."

She also delivered commencement addresses at universities and received honorary degrees. She seemed destined for even greater roles. Her critics watched her triumphal progress dourly, hoping she'd come a cropper. Eventually, she did. She made just one wisecrack too many. It ruined her career.

In April, 1959, Eisenhower named Clare as ambassador to Brazil. The Senate confirmed the appointment by a vote of 79 to 11, despite a bitter attack led by Wayne Morse of Oregon who, in a three-and-a-half-hour speech, claimed that she had proved herself unqualified to be a diplomat. "The role for which I believe she is well qualified" he said, "is that of political hatchetman; she does very well at making inflammatory and demagogic political speeches." Within hours of her confirmation she quipped to the press, "My difficulty, of course, goes some years back and began when Senator Wayne Morse was kicked in the head by a horse." In 1951, Morse had indeed suffered just such an accident. Fellow Senators, regardless of political affiliations, were outraged by her personal insult to one of their own. Several who had voted to confirm her rose to state that if given a second chance they would vote against her. Her remark was denounced as violating "every precept of propriety." Doris Fleeson, respected Washington commentator, described the Senate reaction as "a tense and emotional scene which veterans say has not been duplicated in that historic chamber." On the advice of her husband—and probably others—Clare tendered her resignation. "She had her cards and stationery already engraved," Baruch told me. "She closed two houses and fired nine servants. Her stuff was crated and on the docks, waiting to be shipped to Brazil." She had obviously been confident well ahead of time that she would get the post. With that one unkind, unfunny gibe, she destroyed the career that had been so carefully plotted and built up over the long years. She probably could have gone on to be a Senator, a Cabinet member. She had even been mentioned as possibly a future candidate for nomination as the first woman Vice-president.

She didn't disappear from public view. From her new house in Phoenix, Arizona, she continued to endorse right-wing policies but without the attention she formerly received. She sponsored Vietnam's dragon lady, the unspeakable Mme. Nhu, when the latter made her 1963 American tour and referred jeeringly to the self-immolation of Buddhist priests as "barbecues." In 1964, Clare made one of the seconding speeches for Barry Goldwater's presidential nomination. She has remained a friend and ardent supporter of Richard Nixon.

I haven't seen her for twenty-five years. I haven't talked to her by telephone for nearly that long. We've written occasionally. She wrote me when my husband died, and I wrote her when Harry died in 1967. In her reply, she said that she was totally free, with no living relatives, and that she found this total freedom could be frightening and a burden. In the event, she built a luxurious house in Hawaii. I have several friends who either live in Hawaii or visit there frequently. According to them, Clare is *the* hostess of Honolulu, giving dinners and parties constantly, as if she couldn't bear to be alone. Apparently, she still has to be the center of attention in any gathering and has no difficulty in achieving this. Last year I met a man who had just been to Honolulu, where he was invited to a dinner Clare gave for twenty-six guests. He thought she was fabulous. He described the evening: the pathway to her house was lined with orchids, twinkling lights hidden among them, and the house itself was sybaritic in splendor. After the party, a few of the guests stayed on, drinking and talking with Clare by the pool. At three in the morning she disappeared, returning shortly afterward in a bathing suit and cap. She made a perfect dive and swam several lengths of the huge pool. She was then seventy years old.

Many years ago, in 1937, a friend wrote me: "I have seen *The Women* and I think Mrs. Luce is wonderful to have thought it up. But then, I think God is wonderful to have thought up Mrs. Luce."

Eight

THE ORACLE OF THE OBVIOUS

FROM THE THIRTY YEARS I KNEW Bernard M. Baruch there is one revelatory incident that stands out, perhaps above others, in my memory of him. It occurred during a dinner in his Fifth Avenue mansion sometime in 1937.

Baruch, surrounded at table by his thanes—various congressmen, Senators and political appointees known as "Bernie's boys"—was reminiscing about a Nevada gold mine for the development of which he had put up $1 million early in the century, on the advice of his mining expert, a man named George Wingfield. Wingfield was an ex-roulette dealer, ex-jockey, ex-cowboy, who became a mining prospector, financed by Baruch. "He was a real tough cookie," Bernie said, admiringly. "Always carried five revolvers on him. He sure knew how to handle labor agitators. The I.W.W.—the Wobblies—tried to organize this gold mine of ours. You see, the gold was discovered by different prospectors who didn't have the capital to work the mines. George was slick enough to persuade them to sell to him and Senator George Nixon, so then they were working as our employees on what had been their own claims. Well, sometimes they got a little greedy, so George and his strong-arm boys used to strip them naked every night after they finished work and make them jump over a bar, so if they'd swiped any nuggets and hid them under their arms or between their legs, they'd fall to the ground." (*Laughter*) "They didn't like this and these I.W.W. organizers tried to call a strike. You should have seen George go into action on those babies! He went in there with all his guns and his Pinkerton men with guns and clubs and he broke that strike in a jiffy and ran the Wobblies out. We had no more labor trouble."

His dinner guests greeted this anecdote with sage nods of approval and cries of "That's the way to do it, Chief!" and "That's the stuff, Boss!" The conversation became more general, but Bernie wasn't listening. He was still back in the Good Old Days. I was sitting next to him, at his right, and I heard him say, musingly, as if to himself alone, "You know we took a hundred million dollars out of that mine."

At the time, I thought the sum was an exaggeration. I was more amazed that he seemed oblivious to any connection between the strike-breaking and the profits or at least to any moral implication. Twenty-two years later, an obituary of George Wingfield in the *New York Times* confirmed the story, including the defeat of the I.W.W. organizers and the fact that the property "eventually produced about $100,000,000 in ore."

A second and, I think, correlative incident—or remark—that haunts me was when my husband and I were visiting Baruch in 1947 at Hobcaw Barony, his South Carolina plantation. One evening after dinner the three of us were sitting in the living room, amicably arguing about politics, when Baruch suddenly exclaimed, with uncharacteristic passion, "I'd rather be strong and be hated than be weak and be loved!" "That's a noble philosophy," I commented. Jack just stared at him.

This was Baruch the Great Patriot, Elder Statesman, Advisor to Presidents, Sage of the Ages, the man of whom it was generally believed that every time he opened his mouth pearls of wisdom fell out, the man who was always right. You better believe it. He certainly did. Never one to run out of breath when blowing his own trumpet, he saw himself as an iconic father figure to the nation. Why stop there? The world, maybe. Called by one of his biographers (not only authorized but, in some cases, instigated and subsidized by Baruch himself) "the greatest living American legend, perhaps the greatest in all our history who has not held office," he was the possessor of a superb talent for mythopoeia woven around his own persona. It worked. As the New York *Herald Tribune* once said of him, "No private citizen in this country enjoys the prestige both here and abroad that is Mr. Baruch's." How come?

He died in 1965, two months before his ninety-fifth birthday, and the ensuing litany of panegyrics might puzzle anyone today who tried to pinpoint what accomplishments prompted it. He was never elected to any office; he occupied no Cabinet post; he held less than a half-dozen government appointments, from his chairmanship of the War Industries Board during World War I through his brief tenure as U. S. representative on the United Nations Atomic Commission in 1946. He wasn't responsible for the development of any inventions that changed society, like Edison or Bell or even Henry Ford; he didn't control any empires of oil or steel; he discovered neither penicillin nor quasar nor a military use for spiders' webs; he had no real interest in the arts; and his fame certainly didn't stem from his wealth, because his pile didn't begin to compare with that of the Rockefellers or Duponts or dozens of others in America alone. (His fortune was once estimated at $40 million, but however dazzling that amount might look to the rest of us, it was a piddling sum for the multimillionaire category.) He was always referred to, and still is, as a presidential advisor, yet in one of his moments of private candor he said to me, "They call me the 'Advisor to seven Presidents,' almost none of whom ever took my advice." It has been widely printed that Franklin D. Roosevelt offered him the post of Secretary of the Treasury and that he turned it down. "Roosevelt never offered me anything," he told me. "I don't think he ever forgave me for not backing him at the [Democratic] convention in 1932. I stayed neutral. He thought I wanted Ritchie [Governor of Maryland] and maybe I did, but I kept my trap shut."

Nevertheless, his influence was felt in most administrations through the men whose careers he furthered, a larger group than just the Southern politicians who were said to be in his pocket. Foreign statesmen, domestic office-holders, scientists, economists, college presidents, newspaper publishers, financiers and industrial tycoons were among those who sought his guidance. They were often his front men, through whom he spoke. He was an obsessive conniver and manipulator who liked to be described as a mysterious Richelieu-like figure behind the scenes, a secret string-puller. There has been no more widely publicized secret string-puller in our history. That this is so was partly due to his own knack for self-promotion. As a flower turns toward the sun, so Baruch sought the limelight. Even now, a magic glint still clings to his name.

I was introduced to him by Condé Nast in late August, 1935, at the Sands Point Country Club on Long Island. Condé sent his car to pick up me and one of the *Vogue* staff. En route, the car broke down. Ben, the chauffeur, fiddled with the engine for an hour and then set out to walk to a garage, leaving us to wait in the hot sun. As the hours went by, our make-up began to run, our frocks to wilt. Meanwhile, Nast and Baruch were expecting us for lunch and began to think they were stood up. We finally arrived, tired, hungry, irritable, disheveled, sweaty, a mess. After sandwiches and tea we all rode back to New York. As we dropped Baruch off at his house, he asked if we would like to come in for a drink. I said, "No. I just want to use your bathroom." I was in and out of the house with no time wasted on pleasantries. I certainly didn't care if I never laid eyes on him again, but he must have thought my indifference an intriguing change from the sycophantic veneration to which he was accustomed, because he telephoned Condé and asked that I be seated next to him at a forthcoming dinner party in Condé's penthouse, to which we were both invited. All I remember about that dinner is that Baruch and I kept up a lively argument throughout the meal. I was in one of my soapbox moods and when he mentioned Andrew Mellon, I've forgotten in what connection, I told him that Balzac wrote, "Behind every great fortune there lies a crime." I then stated categorically that I thought Andrew Mellon was a bastard, adding, "And you're probably just as big a one."

You wouldn't have thought this an auspicious beginning, but the next day I received two dozen American Beauty roses, with Baruch's card, on which he had written that he was leaving for South Carolina but he hoped to see me again. He added that he hoped that in the meantime I would not try to save the world. A month or so later, he sent me a brace of quail, feathers and all. I didn't know what to do with them, so I threw them in the incinerator. I suppose he had shot them on his plantation and I also suppose he thought that like most of his acquaintances I lived in a house, or a large apartment, and had a cook. I didn't. I lived in a two-room flat with a kitchenette. I usually was invited out for dinner, so the extent of my cooking was to heat up a can of soup once in a while, get my own breakfast, and, on occasion, graciously serve to a paramour who had spent the night a collation of burned toast and some coffee in which, as the saying goes, you could float an ax.

That December I sailed for my favorite city in all the world, Havana, where I spent five months. When I returned to New York, I had dinner with Baruch and Condé at Dinty Moore's. (Condé confessed that Baruch had prodded him into arranging it.) After we took Bernie home, Condé remarked cheerfully, "Poor Bernie. He's getting old." I nodded, forbearing to mention that when we were in the restaurant Bernie had said, when Condé went to the men's room, "Condé's beginning to show his age, don't you think?"

Of the two, Baruch was by far the more interesting conversationalist because of his knowledge of, and involvement in, the world of power and politics, but Condé was the nicer human being. Bernie, however, was the better-looking: 6′ 4″, with erect carriage and proud bearing, thick white hair, a strong, aquiline nose, crafty blue eyes. At the time, he was always the most distinguished-looking man in any group, and when all gussied up in white tie, tails and a high silk hat, he was splendidly impressive. He had a deep voice and a flattering grace of manner, his courtly old-school Southern gentleman pose. Deaf in his left ear from a baseball-bat blow in boyhood, he was for years too vain to wear a hearing aid. Even when he gave in and bought one, he would whisk it off and hide it whenever an attractive female appeared on the scene. About to sit down beside him once, I was startled by a cry of "Jesus! Don't sit on my battery!" as he retrieved it from beneath a shawl where he had thrust it. Women were always attracted to him, although it must be admitted that power is an aphrodisiac, as I believe Henry Kissinger once remarked, knowledgeably. There is something irresistible about feeling privy to the inside political chicanery of our leaders and watching the wheels go round in the corridors of power, sometimes from the vantage point of the bedrooms of those who spin them. It's heady stuff.

Women were forever finagling introductions to him and one wily young creature went so far as to throw herself at his feet, literally, on a road in Vichy, where he was taking the waters. She sprained her ankle but it was worth it because of the subsequent visits of the gallant Baruch, bearing gifts of flowers, fruit and trinkets. His solicitude ripened into a more frolicsome relationship in which he called her "Toots" and she called him "Butch." He took her back with him to New York, where their idyll eventually ended when she vamoosed, leaving him with large bills she had run up at Bergdorf-Goodman and similar places where he had opened accounts for her. He wryly admitted to me that she also took him for $25,000 and it turned out, he said, that she was part of an international blackmail ring and badger game set-up.

At the time I met him, he had been married for thirty-eight years and had three grown children. He always treated his wife, Anne, with great courtesy, but they didn't spend a lot of time together. I suppose it was different when they were younger, but when I knew him I only saw her at their Fifth Avenue house, never with him in Europe, Saratoga, Washington. She was not interested in politics or world affairs and seemed content to let him go his own way. Although I knew her little more than a year before she died of pneumonia, I liked her and I know she liked me. I was her favorite "extra woman" dinner guest and she encouraged my arguments with Bernie. "You're good for him because you talk back to him," she once said. Our own conversations were more apt to deal with matters of less national import, such as whether I should or should not try false eyelashes. She found out for me where I could get them, as they were not at that time generally available. One evening she invited my mother and me to dine with her and Bernie at their house, an occasion that must have bored him stiff, as we three women chattered happily about fashion, food, society gossip. He couldn't get a word in edgewise about the capital gains tax or the gold standard.

Although a philanderer, Baruch was not a passionate man. Sexually, he was surprisingly naïve. His affairs were fleeting, with two notable exceptions. One of these was an opera singer, although, like Condé, he was no music lover. What seemed to have been her chief attraction, aside from beauty, was her devotion, straight out of Fannie Hurst's *Back Street*. "Every year when I went to Saratoga," he told me, "I took a small house for her there, on an inconspicuous street, and she never went out, except for walks by herself. She would just wait there in the house for the times I could get away and go to see her."

Despite occasional sanctimonious tributes to true-love-and-marriage, his own basic attitudes in this area were mainly cynical. One night at dinner in the late thirties, he mentioned the remarriage of Ruth, the ex-wife of Raoul Fleischman (yeast and *The New Yorker*). "She's married a nobody," he said contemptuously. "I don't suppose he makes over $10,000 a year." "Maybe she loves him," I said. He looked at me sternly and snorted. "*Love!*" he said, in a tone of ineffable contempt.

He liked women of spunk and talent, provided they were pretty, and he fancied himself in the role of mentor to their careers. Housewifely virtues did not appeal to him. He preferred a woman who could make a keynote speech at a political convention to one who could bake an apple pie. He was always encouraging young girls to write, sing, paint, act, go into politics, although he judged their merit by the money they made. He boasted incessantly of his part in getting Max Gordon to produce *The Women*. He went to see it a dozen times, bought tickets for everyone from politicians to elevator boys, and proudly wore on his watch chain the gold charm in the shape of a tiny typewriter which Clare had made for him. His own literary tastes were more abysmal. His favorite book was an obscure novel about farm life, by E. P. Roe, a Methodist minister. It was published in 1886, was entitled *He Fell in Love with His Wife*, and was written in a folksy "Lands sakes! How's the crops?" dialect. Bernie tried in vain for years to persuade his theater world friends like Max Gordon, John Golden, Walter Huston, to get it dramatized. He goaded me into making a quarter-hearted stab at it, but I gave up almost immediately, despite a series of handwritten rah-rah pep talk letters. ("Dear Stupid: Forget about being sick with colds and forget about your beaux and get busy. Not that it matters, but why not succeed? You are lazy but you can do the trick but you got to hustle, hustle, hustle. Stop thinking about anybody or anything but your work. Good work gets paid. Bum work, no pay. Now get busy and give it to 'em with both barrels. Remember, I am different from the others. (More nutty.) Devotedly, Bernie.") I did write *Latins Are Lousy Lovers* to amuse him, and when it came out in book form, he wrote me, "I've been going in and out of book stores, trying to create a demand." He not only bought copies by the score and sent them to friends, including dozens of, no doubt, baffled members of

Congress, but he also insisted on reading passages out loud to helpless guests in his home.

The Latins piece was the first free-lance effort I ever sold. Just after I mailed it hopefully to *Esquire* (it was entirely unsolicited on their part), I accepted an offer from Carmel Snow, then editor of *Harper's Bazaar*, to succeed Beatrice Kaufman, playwright George Kaufman's wife, as their literary editor. I was due to start work July 19, 1936, but on July 16 I received a cable from Bernie, who was in Badgastein with a bad gout attack, asking me to join him at the Kaiserhof Hotel.

Europe versus a job in an office? I moved like greased lightning. Condé got me an emergency passport that same day; Joe Linder, head of travel advertising for the Nast magazines, wangled me the only available passage on such short notice in the summer season—tourist class on the Italian ship, the *Rex*, sharing a cabin with a schoolteacher; and, equipped with *The Theory of The Leisure Class* and R. Palme Dutt's *World Politics* for shipboard reading, I sailed on the day I was supposed to report at *Harper's Bazaar*. Instead, I sent them a radiogram from the ship: "Sorry cannot accept job Father ill in Rome," thus blithely tossing my bonnet over the windmill. The job of literary editor went to my friend George Davis, who later married Lotte Lenya.

We were scheduled to stop at Gibraltar but the Spanish Civil War had begun on July 18, so we sailed straight to Naples, where I took a train via Rome to Innsbruck. When I learned it was nine hours more by train from there to Badgastein, I hired a taxi for fifty dollars and enjoyed an exhilaratingly fast and vertiginous drive through the Alps, arriving shortly before midnight on the date I had cabled Bernie I would be there. He had gone to bed but he left a welcoming note in my room. The Kaiserhof was one of those old-time luxury hotels of pre-World War II Europe. My room was heated by a beautiful enameled pot-bellied stove, stoked by an equally pot-bellied chambermaid. From my window there was a fantastically lovely view of a pale blue shining glacier. The other hotel guests were mostly elderly American millionaires, about the only ones who could afford the prices: Max Steuer, the famous New York trial lawyer, was there, passing a stone in his kidney; old Carl Laemmle, the founder of Universal Pictures, was there for the mineral baths; so were Robert Lincoln O'Brien, Chairman of the U.S. Tariff Commission, and a couple of eminent judges, one of whom regaled us with ribald tales of his close friend, the head of I.T.&T., who at that time was a man with a memorable name of Sosthenes Behn. At sixty-five, Bernie was easily the youngest of the lot, so the pace was not what you might call feverish. We took walks; we sat in the sunshine, covered with lap robes; the over-sixties went for their mineral baths ("If I weren't so rich, I wouldn't be sick," Bernie said to me); and in the evening, after dinner, we all had coffee in the Palm Court, to the accompaniment of chamber music played by a trio as elderly as the guests and sounding even more decrepit. It certainly was restful.

After two weeks I left and went to the Lido in Venice. I saw Bernie again briefly in Paris, where I was staying at the George V. He had been shocked that I came over tourist class on the *Rex*, although I was the one paying for it, so in Paris he gave me a first-class ticket from Cherbourg to Montreal on the *Empress of Britain* and admonished me. "Don't try to save money by turning it in and going back on a cattle boat." He was going on to England to see Churchill, whom I loathed, and would board the ship at Southampton.

As it turned out, we were both poor sailors and were seasick part of the voyage, but when we were able to emerge from our staterooms we were a focal point for curious stares and, I'm sure, gossip, but we couldn't have cared less. At dinner the two of us had our own table and we would sit there, Bernie elegant in his evening clothes and me in my Lucien Lelong finery (I didn't dare admit to him that I had paid reduced prices for the gowns because they were not made to order but had been worn by the models), talking so intently that we were often the last to leave. Mostly, he talked and I listened: his life story, his financial and political coups, his philosophy. Among other things he taught me that whenever I heard anything I should ask myself three questions—Is it possible? Is it probable? Is it true? I doubt if he expected me to apply it to his own conversation, although whenever I did, I usually discovered, sometimes years later, that he had told the truth. Woodrow Wilson was his idol. He called him "the most Christ-like man I ever knew." His own mother and Wilson were the top sacred totems of his life, with Robert E. Lee a close runner-up. After all, it was Wilson who appointed him chairman of the War Industries Board in World War I, the only post in which he had the overt power for which he lusted. For him, it was the mountain peak and he was to glorify and magnify it for the rest of his life, even though he served less than a year. He was appointed in March, 1918, and the war ended that November. His achievements were debatable. One critic called the Board's work "a shambles." Only 196 planes were delivered to General Pershing and they were observation-type planes, actually dangerous to fly, nicknamed "flaming coffins." The tax payers paid one and a half billion dollars for planes for the war effort, the money appropriated by Congress. A Department of Justice inquiry in 1921–22 into aircraft monopoly revealed that a report by Otto Kahn, the famous New York banker, of a private investigation he made in February, 1918, disclosed that no combat planes or bombing planes or pursuit planes would be delivered to our forces in France during that year and that our aircraft program was chaotic. Kahn blamed Sir Basil Zaharoff, the mysterious "merchant of death," the Munitions King, originator of the cartel system, who made a fortune of at least one billion dollars. As director of the European Arms Trust, he didn't want American planes bombing any munitions plants. His aim, according to Kahn and quoted by Emile Gauvreau in his book *The Wild Blue Yonder*, was to prolong the war in order to increase the dividends of stockholders in the armaments companies. General Pétain, later to be a Nazi collaborator, was said to be under Zaharoff's influence.

I do not like to believe that Baruch was aware of this corruption and sabotage. I would think that his own pride in his position and his vanity in doing his job well would have caused him to fight it. Yet the fact remains that only the few unreliable observation planes reached Pershing. If Baruch was as smart as he was supposed to be, he ought to have probed into the background. For a while he did control the entire industrial establishment of America, and thousands of new millionaires were created by his government-spending. In 1914 there were 7,500 millionaires in the country. In 1918 there were 25,000. Profits of up to 3000 percent were made by some leading corporations. E. I. Du Pont de Nemours & Co. cleared a net profit of $255,500,000 during the war years. At least in later years Baruch repeatedly, although vainly, urged measures to take the profiteering out of war. Wilson took him with him as his economic advisor to the Versailles peace conference, where Baruch warned against imposing too heavy reparations on Germany, but nobody listened (the result was to help pave the way for the rise of the Nazis) and about the only lasting plum he plucked from the conference was Billy Rose, then a teen-age shorthand champion, serving in a secretarial capacity. Scarcely a monumental trophy, but they became lifelong friends. The combination of the Sage of the Ages and the revolting little hustler-showman caused my husband, when he met them together, to murmur, "How oxymoronic can you get?"

My passport was in the name of López-Méndez, a previous husband from whom I was divorced. He was a Venezuelan whom I met in Havana, a friend of Hemingway and Dos Passos, with whom he went deep-sea fishing. I don't suppose I lived with him more than a month. It's all so unimportant to me that I can't even remember the dates, except that he divorced me for desertion in 1935. He went back to Venezuela, became Minister of Culture in the government there, was at one time Venezuelan consul in Paris and, the last I heard, a Senator in Caracas. It never occurs to me to mention him because I don't feel that I've ever been married to anyone except Jack Lawrenson. The others just don't count.

However, the point is that during the period with Baruch, I was continually addressed as Mme. López-Méndez, my legal name at the time, but Bernie called me Mme. Fathead, in appreciation of my vigorous attacks on the capitalism he held dear (and rightly so, because it certainly had been good to him). Other passengers on the ship often must have wondered what we were shouting about (I had to shout because he refused to wear a hearing aid, and he shouted back) at dinner, in our deck chairs, taking our walks. "Society," he said at one point, "can only progress if men's labors show a profit." Yes, Boss, but profit for whom? He was telling me that he had made money out of every depression and panic —1901, 1907, 1929—by anticipating each one. "I am a speculator," he said. "The word comes from the Latin *speculare*, meaning 'to observe.' I am a man who observes the future and acts before it occurs." This was one of his favorite little set speeches and I was to hear it monotonously repeated over and over again during the ensuing years, together with the ancillary comment, "I have a talent for making money, the way Fritz Kreisler has a talent for playing the violin and Jesse Owens has a talent for running. I buy when stocks go down. I sell when they go up. When prices go up, production increases, consumption decreases, and prices then fall. When prices go down, it's vice versa. I got rich, Mme. Fathead, by remembering those words." And maybe with a little help from his friends? Old Joe Kennedy, whom I met through Bernie, once told me, "Bernie operates strictly on a you-scratch-my-back-and-I'll-scratch-yours principle." Bernie and the Guggenheims were forever giving one another a leg up, according to his stories. "When they were backing the Utah Copper Company," he said, "the shares started to fall, so I gave the company half a million in cash, and then I went right smack into the market and bought at low rates. In the next thirty years Utah Copper paid out over $250 million in dividends." "No wonder they shot Joe Hill," I said.

He didn't always talk of the past. It was during this voyage that he conceived the idea of the "ever-normal granary," a plan to store surplus food to relieve shortages. "I got to thinking last night of Joseph in Egypt and the way he stored grain against a time of famine, and I thought, 'That's it!'" He later outlined the plan to Henry Wallace, then Roosevelt's Secretary of Agriculture, who put it into effect.

Most of his ideas made sense, but he was not a particularly original thinker. He was the oracle of the obvious. Senator Carter Glass of Virginia (he came from a town with the infelicitous name of Lynchburg), one of Bernie's old-time Southern pals, said of him, "Bernie is dogmatic as hell about two and two making four," a remark Baruch was forever quoting until the end of his days, along with such simplistic maxims of his own as "To reach the top you have to take the bitter with the sweet"; "You can't repeal human nature by an Act of Congress"; "Communism arises from poverty. End poverty and you end Communism." His courtiers, no matter how many times they may have heard them, always greeted these gnomic gems with gasps of admiration. He would come out with some intellectual blockbuster on the level of "A new broom sweeps clean" and they would cry, "Chief, how do you do it?!"

I think that my deepest disillusionment with him was because he refused to stand up in public for things he believed in private, unless he was sure of the applause. He was too cagey to risk any diminution of his safely popular image. Spain was one example. From the beginning of the Civil War, Bernie was against Franco and on the side of the Republican government. "It's a democratically elected government, the only constitutionally elected government in Spain's history." But he never once said so publicly. Behind the scenes, he tried unsuccessfully to block the passage in Congress of the bill forbidding the sale of arms to the Spanish government. "They've got the money in gold right over here to pay for them." Within minutes after Congress passed the bill, a Coast Guard speedboat rushed out and caught the *Mar Cantabrico*, laden with purchased arms, just before she reached the safety of the twelve-mile limit. Later in the war, Bernie confided to me that Roosevelt asked him how he could lift the embargo. "But he won't do it," Bernie said. "He's afraid of the Catholic vote." No one seemed to remember that the Spanish Republicans were also Catholic, and that it was Hitler's elite Condor planes that practiced their saturation bombing on Guernica, the holy Catholic Basque city. I talked myself blue in the face, trying to persuade Bernie to make some public declaration. He wouldn't. I was visiting him in South Carolina when the news came over the radio, on March 28, 1939, that Franco had entered Madrid. I burst into tears and ran from the room.

I had friends who fought in the Abraham Lincoln Brigade, the American division of the International Brigade, which was composed of 45,000 politically committed men from fifty-two different countries. There has never been a crusade like theirs, when men with no military training, men who had never fired a gun, defied their governments to risk their lives in Spain for no pay, no pensions, with no bands playing. They did it because they recognized in Franco's rebellion, supported by Hitler and Mussolini, the simple clarity of the charted Fascist-Nazi blueprint rehearsal for World War II. Illegally and secretly, the American Brigade volunteers had gone to France, where they were led at night by a nine-year-old girl to the passage they were to make on foot through the Pyrenees into Spain. After Franco's victory, the survivors who escaped back into France were stranded, many of them wounded. In America their friends raised money to bring them home. I collected $11,060 from Bernie and $250 each from Clare and Harry Luce. "Cardinal Spellman has rebuked me for giving that money," Bernie told me, years later, chuckling as he pointed to the framed photograph of Spellman on his desk, inscribed in slyly humble terms of gratitude by that scheming ecclesiastical satrap who within two decades was to let himself be photographed behind a machine gun in Vietnam, a curious newspaper pose for a man of God. "Yes, he really told me off," Bernie went on, "but I made it up to him." He did, indeed. It was Baruch, at Clare's request, who enabled Spellman to meet Churchill. The latter's American visits ordinarily would not have included hobnobbing with the Catholic hierarchy, but the two men had a series of strictly hush-hush meetings prior to Churchill's famous Iron Curtain speech in 1946 in Fulton, Missouri, the kick-off for the Cold War.

Baruch was always proud of his close relationship with Churchill. I think he felt flattered by it, but he was often privately critical of him. I was probably one of the few people, if not the only one, to whom he freely expressed these criticisms. He knew that I considered Churchill an evil and immoral man. Throughout his life he was consistently on the side of the most appallingly reactionary policies, from the time he went to Cuba at the age of twenty-one to fight with the Spanish against the Cubans who were struggling for independence, through his disastrous conduct in World War I, when he wanted to use poison gas at Gallipolli, advice rejected by the commander there. Then, as First Lord of the Admiralty, he didn't warn the *Lusitania* of German U-boats he knew were lying in wait off the Irish coast, nor did he send the usual convoy to escort her, with a resultant loss of 1,195 lives. He advocated the use of troops against striking workers and sent them in 1910 against South Wales miners. In 1926, he again called for troops to be sent against the miners but was reprimanded by King George V, who refused. When Belgian miners went on strike, Churchill sent word, "Shoot them." The Belgian government failed to heed him. He was also the first on the Allied side to advocate bombing towns, which of course meant bombing civilians. No one in history has a more overrated reputation nor one more based on disregard for the facts.

"You know," Bernie said to me one afternoon during World War II, when I was having tea alone with him, "Churchill is paranoiac about the Russians. When they had their revolution he was the only one who wanted intervention on a massive scale. Of course we all sent armies of intervention, but he wanted to march on Moscow and he wanted to use German troops! He said that by fighting the Bolshies they could atone for World War I. Lloyd George, he was against intervention, but Churchill kept pushing it and the British Foreign Office was all for it, but they turned down Churchill's idea of using German soldiers. It's his dream that England and Germany unite to crush Soviet Russia. He's not one of your anti-Fascists, my dear. He admires Mussolini and, between you and me and the lamppost, if Hitler had stopped at just killing Commies and Jews, I don't think Winston, like a lot of other people, would have had any quarrel with him."

He was right. Before the outbreak of the war, Churchill had publicly thanked God "for men like Adolph Hitler." He also, in 1927, said that he was "charmed by Mussolini's gentle and simple bearing" and that if he had been Italian he would have been wholeheartedly with Il Duce in his "triumphant struggle against the bestial appetites of Communism." The most startling revelation, though, was after Rudolph Hess made his flight to Britain on May 10, 1941, six weeks before Germany invaded the USSR. The official Soviet version claimed that the Hess flight was made in response to a secret invitation from Churchill. This has always been denied. Instead, it is said, Hess went to see the Duke of Hamilton, uninvited, on the theory that the Duke would be pro-German. Whatever the truth, the RAF was ordered to let his plane fly in, unhampered.

His proposal was that Britain and Germany sign a separate peace in order to pursue "the right war" together, i.e., against the Soviet Union. The Duke of Hamilton immediately drove to the country house of Ronald Tree, where Churchill was among the guests at a party. According to several accounts, he was in high spirits because the House of Commons had been hit by incendiary bombs the night before, which might seem slight cause for exhilaration but Churchill, not only according to Baruch but also to subsequent commentators and historians, loved war and became excited by heavy air raids. All reports agree that when the Duke told him about Hess and his mission, Churchill's only comment was, "Well, Hess or no Hess, I am going to see the Marx Brothers," and he went into the cinema screening-room. Hess was imprisoned briefly, his mission discredited as the fantasy of a madman, even by Hitler, although Baruch believed, as have others, that he certainly never made his flight without Hitler's knowledge nor without some hint, from someone authoritative in Britain, that he and his proposal would be welcome.

The hitherto unpublicized fact I want to make clear is that Bernie, swearing me to secrecy, said: "Roosevelt called me to the White House and told me to telephone Churchill and convince him that the first job is to defeat Hitler and after that, we can worry about Stalin. I did it, but we had a helluva argument. He's all for letting the Germans and the Russkies fight it out together. Now, don't you spill the beans." I didn't. I can't believe that if he told me, he didn't tell a few others. Perhaps not. Naturally, I didn't expect him to reveal this publicly, but I was bitterly disappointed when he later failed to endorse the opening of a Second Front in France, before we invaded Sicily, to help take the strain off the Red Army, who were battling the cream of the Nazi troops on the Eastern Front. Some of our own generals, including George Marshall, wanted to open a Second Front in 1942 in southern France, but Churchill opposed the plan so adamantly that even Baruch couldn't budge him, so it was delayed as long as possible without losing face (or the war). Churchill's hope that in the meantime the Germans would smash Russia was not fulfilled. Baruch said to me, "You know, I was wrong when I told you that if the German army ever invaded Russia they'd go through it like a hot knife through butter. When it comes time to talk peace terms, all Joe Stalin's got to say will be one word: 'Stalingrad!'"

Another issue on which he refrained from any public airing of his private views, until after we entered the war, was Hitler's treatment of the Jews. He told me that he thought American Jews should keep quiet because if they didn't, "they'll only make things worse for Jews over there," a view allegedly shared by Pope Pius XII, but to which the obvious answer was, "For Christ's sake, how much *worse* could they be?!" "We can't interfere in the internal affairs of another nation," Bernie said, a laughable stance in one whose hero, Woodrow Wilson, had sent the Marines to Vera Cruz and General "Black Jack" Pershing, with 12,000 troops, to Durango. He wasn't ignorant of the history of meddling, so I had to conclude that his attitude was one of expedient hypocrisy. He did approach Roosevelt quietly in 1939 with a plan to settle Jewish refugees in the interior of Africa. He said he would give $5 million and guaranteed to get $1 million from each of the Guggenheims (there was a gaggle of Guggenheims around at the time). I told this African plan to Irwin Shaw and Irwin said, "Yeah—50 percent Jews and 50 percent lions."

Baruch's father had emigrated as a boy from a village near Posen, now Posnán, Poland, to Camden, South Carolina, where Bernie was born August 19, 1870. His father was a surgeon in the Confederate Army and a member of the Ku Klux Klan. Although the family moved to New York when Bernie was eleven, he always played to the hilt the role of old-time Southern plantation owner—the magnolias-and-the-pickaninnies-are-in-bloom—and he practiced a benign paternalism at Hobcaw Barony, the South Carolina estate he bought in 1905 and of which he was so proud. It once consisted of 24,000 acres, with nine Negro villages on it. The original house burned down and was replaced by a colonial-type red brick mansion with six white two-story columns supporting the front portico, ten bedrooms, each with its own fireplace and bathroom, and quiet, beautiful grounds thick with cypress, pine, azaleas, magnolias and, particularly, the great live oaks festooned with gray and ghostly Spanish moss.

I was a frequent house guest there, and one of the quaint customs was to entertain visitors by taking them Saturday nights to watch the plantation blacks dancing in their little frame schoolhouse. We white folks, of course, sat strictly apart, amused observers of the dutifully picturesque performance. I found it unbearably embarrassing and never went after the first time. Bernie thought of "his" Negroes as "simple, lovable, irresponsible." He instructed William, a man he called "my trusted retainer," to spend a couple of days driving me around to visit blacks on the Baruch estate and also in the dilapidated tar-paper, tin-roofed shacks in which others lived throughout the countryside. William (who later left Hobcaw, thus angering Bernie, who couldn't forgive those who deserted the plantation) and I both thought this a humiliating exercise, so we soon abandoned the farce of my chatting about the "conditions" and simply distributed the largesse of a dollar at each shack, as Bernie had ordered. When my supposedly educational survey was over, Bernie said to me, "Now you see how silly you are to go around beating your breast. They're happy the way they are. No sense in stirring them up." It was useless to argue with him. He even refused to attend Condé's big party after the opening of the Gershwin *Porgy and Bess* because a few top members of the black cast were also invited. As he said to me, "I couldn't sit down in the same room with them or meet them on a social level and I don't want to embarrass Condé so I just won't go."

His sympathies for the downtrodden were limited. In a pencil-written letter from a luxury hotel in Vichy, he wrote me: "Very great crowds of people. Not much elegance. The masses are on the trek. I suppose you have never heard of Karl Marx. He is the other Marx Brother, only they don't recognize him. Nobody knows whether he is funnier or only as funny as they because no one understands him. I will give you a prize if you can explain him. I read read read & can't understand. Then I light a pipe (and try to look like a pundit—another name for a gazoodle) and don't shave for several days and don't wear a hat, hair disheveled, don't wash and smell awful. Then read again and even then can't understand. When I try to be intellectual which means talking a lot of hooey I just flop. I guess I am as stupid as you and baby that is going some. Affectionately, Bernie." His prose style was certainly no challenge to Pater. His speeches and printed articles or books were worked over by professionals like Herbert Swope or Marquis James. His humor, too, was pretty puerile, and he told the same jokes over and over. (Sample: Man goes to doctor and says, "Doctor, I need a woman in the worst possible way." Doctor replies, "Well, the worst possible way I can think of is standing up in a hammock.")

He was always generous to the deserving rich. One of his friends was Morton Schwartz, a financier from Louisville, Kentucky, who told me that he made his first million before he was twenty-one. At one time, with Clarence Dillon, he bought the Dodge Brothers motor car business for $150 million. I was therefore surprised when Bernie said to me, "Poor Morton. Don't tell anyone, but he's dead broke." "Broke!" I exclaimed. "What did he do with all his money?" "Spent it." We were driving home after having dined with Morton and his wife at their home, an excellent meal served by a butler in opulent surroundings. I was puzzled. "How do they live?" I asked Bernie. "Oh, I loaned him $250,000," he said, "but that's all gone now and he hasn't a cent." "What are they going to do?" "Well, they've taken a house at Saratoga for the racing reason, and I lent him some more money."

Such charitable acts were commonplace to him. The wife of a wealthy British Tory Member of Parliament left her husband and child in London during the blitz to seek sanctuary for herself in America and found it under Bernie's wing. He not only installed her in a luxurious apartment but he bestowed upon her such tokens of his esteem as a floor-length ermine evening coat, sundry jewels and, perhaps as a compensatory gesture, a $10,000 ambulance donated in her name to the British forces. (A somewhat similar instance was when President Roosevelt gave Crown Princess Martha of Norway a submarine. She was visiting America and FDR was so taken with her that he had her move into the White House. "She's a pip!" said Bernie. Forced to spend ten weeks in bed with the gout, practically immobilized, he said jokingly, "I'm going to ask Roosevelt how he does it.")

I would have been hopeless as a gold-digger, so it's just as well I was proudly independent. Besides, the rich only give to the rich. To a young girl who was living in a cold-water walk-up flat in Greenwich Village, Bernie gave the less than munificent sum of twenty dollars, telling her to buy herself a "nice dress." True, he did give me the *Encyclopaedia Britannica* for Christmas one year but, as God is my judge, he said, "I think you can pick one up second-hand." I told him

I didn't have time to run around looking for bargains, so he broke down and gave me the cash for a new set. I bought it and gave him back the change, which amounted to a couple of hundred dollars. He took it. I should have remembered a story he told me one time when we were at Saratoga, about Bet-A-Million Gates, a financial promoter who got his nickname when he placed a $1-million bet in a private baccarat game at the Waldorf-Astoria. According to Bernie, Gates left a thousand-dollar bill under his plate in the dining room of his Saratoga hotel. His Negro waiter ran after him and said, "You left this by mistake, sir." Gates took the money and handed it to another waiter standing nearby. "Here, boy," he said. "This is a present for you." Then he turned back to his own waiter and snapped, "That'll teach you to hang on to what you get." Bernie considered this an amusing anecdote.

Whenever he did something for anyone, he didn't believe in keeping it a secret. Thus I heard all about how he paid the hospital bills for Harry Hopkins' first wife, the wedding party he gave when Hopkins married Louise Macy, the money he gave a nurse in Austria—"My! She was so grateful!" —the money he loaned Condé's ex-wife when she came to America during the war, and so on. The most amusing one was the case of my mother's rheumatism, when for a few months she had to walk with a cane. At the time, Bernie was being treated for gout by an immunologist named Dr. Ramirez, and when I mentioned my mother's slight rheumatism, he insisted that she go to see Ramirez at the clinic he conducted at the French Hospital. That was the extent of it. She went twice a week to the clinic, waited hours for her turn, paid the clinic fee, and that was it. It did help her and the rheumatism eventually went away. "That was a wonderful thing I did for your mother, wasn't it?" Bernie would say, always in front of guests. "Yes, Bernie." "Poor woman was a hopeless cripple," he would explain to the guests. My mother was furious when I told her, and I didn't blame her.

He was my daughter's godfather. This came about because

when Jack and I were visiting Clare at Mepkin after Johanna's birth, Clare asked us if she could be the baby's godmother. We hadn't even thought of having her christened, but it seemed churlish to refuse. Jack had been born a Catholic in Dublin but hadn't been to church since he was thirteen. I was an Episcopalian. I arranged to have the christening at The Little Church around the Corner. With Clare as a godmother, we had to get a godfather to match. I called Baruch and he said he'd be delighted. A few days later, he called me back. "I'm pleased that you asked me," he said. "I'm honored and all that. But, you know, I'm Jewish." "Yes, Bernie. I know you're Jewish." "Well, I don't think they'll let me be godfather." I said it hadn't occurred to me, but I'd find out. I telephoned the Rev. Randolph Ray, the snobbish Episcopalian clergyman then at the church. I reminded him of the date of the christening and then asked if it would be all right to have a Jewish godfather. When he said that it certainly wouldn't, I told him, "I'm glad I asked, because the godfather in question is Mr. Bernard M. Baruch and I wouldn't want him to be embarrassed." There was a brief silence. Very brief. Then Dr. Ray said, "Oh well, in that case, it will be all right." Bernie arrived for the ceremony, impressive in striped trousers, morning coat, high silk hat. They wouldn't let him hold the baby, but aside from that it went off all right. After it was over, Dr. Ray sidled up to Clare and said, unctuously, "You and Mr. Luce should really come to services here," to which she replied, clearly and crisply, "Except that I am a Lutheran and my husband is a Presbyterian."

Johanna has never benefited in any way from either of her grandiose godparents. The sole gift she received from Bernie was a copy of his autobiography, *Baruch, My Own Story*, in which he wrote: "To Johanna, my lovely godchild, with affectionate good wishes, B. M. Baruch. June 1958." He had five or six other godchildren but she was the only one whose christening he attended in person. She was also the only one to whom he left nothing in his will. I still think that a secretary or whoever typed the document must have omitted her name, as I cannot believe that he said, "Cross her name off." I had received a note from him a few months before he died, in which he said, "Give my regards to my god-daughter Johanna." As for Clare, whose idea the christening was, Johanna didn't hear from her for twenty years. In 1973 Clare invited her to visit her in Hawaii but then rescinded the invitation.

Bernie never pretended to care for children. He told me that his secretary, Miss Mary Boyle, who served him devotedly for something like forty years, once wanted to adopt a baby but that he persuaded her not to do so. "What does she want with a *baby?*" he asked me, in a tone that would not have been amiss if she had proposed to adopt a boa constrictor. When I held a small black baby in my arms during a visit to Hobcaw, he said, "Put it down, Helen. It might have fleas." His own children remained in the penumbra of his legend, leading a sort of Son of Tarzan existence. His only son was called Mr. Junior even when he was in his fifties. ("Has Mr. Junior come in yet?" Bernie would ask the butler) although away from his father I found him an intelligent and likeable man. Bernie settled money on his children, as he did on his three brothers, the only one of whom I knew was Herman Baruch, a handsome man with a goatee, who said I was the only woman he ever met who had heard of *Brann the Iconoclast.* I said I'd only read excerpts, so he sent me his own two volumes. He was a lot more erudite than Bernie but he, too, lived in the shadow, although Bernie got him named ambassador to Portugal by Roosevelt and ambassador to the Netherlands by Truman.

Of course, it wasn't too difficult to be more versed in literature, music or art than Bernie was. His valet, Lacey, was a far more cultured man, with a sense of humor. I was having breakfast with Bernie in his apartment in the Waldorf Towers one morning, when the telephone rang. "If that's Mr. Nast," Bernie instructed, "don't mention that Mme. López-Méndez is here." "Of course, sir, that would be the first thing I would say," Lacey said, with a straight face. He had been with Baruch since 1909, and *his* memoirs would have made more interesting reading than did Baruch's own. He also would have been a more literate writer. I remember one time when Bernie came across a reference to *Cranford.* "Cranford? What's Cranford?" Before I could answer, Lacey said quietly, "It's a book, sir, written in 1851 by an English lady, Mrs. Gaskell."

Was there no basis for his extraordinary reputation as a wise man? Yes, there was. He blocked FDR's "work-or-fight" law by warning against the drafting of labor "so long as men and women work for private employers who make a profit from their labor." He was the father of price-fixing, repeatedly calling for "a floor under wages and a ceiling over prices" and insisting that you cannot freeze wages without also freezing prices. His advice went unheeded, first by FDR during World War II (and not until prices soared was rationing introduced, a measure Baruch had been urging) and, later, by Truman. Bernie would telephone me to ask me how much I paid for butter, for my children's snowsuits, and so on, and he would talk, sometimes for an hour or more, about his ignored proposals to curb the rising cost of living. I think he used me as a sounding-board for some of his ideas. He kept harping on the need for overall price controls until finally Congress gave Truman the powers, but they were not used until, once again, prices had spiraled upward. One time, Bernie and I made a list of policies he had advocated to various Presidents who ignored them at the time, although some of them were later adopted; some, never. It was a long list and included, among other snubbed proposals, the following: In 1937 he advised FDR to quarantine Japan ("Don't buy gold from her and don't sell her steel or scrap iron"—ignored until after Pearl Harbor); after World War II he advised setting up an Advisory Peace Council to correlate all the nation's resources in case of another emergency (idea shelved); he opposed the reduction of the excess profits tax ("If those taxes had not been reduced, there would be no budget deficit today," he said later); in May, 1950, he said, speaking on the extension of the draft: "To me there is something immoral in offering human sacrifices on the altar of patriotism and interfering with the lives of our youth, without first setting up complete plans for the mobilization of industry, capital, materials, transportation, profits, prices and wages." (Ignored by Truman.) His quarrel with Truman was well known. In his memoirs, the latter wrote: "Most Presidents have received more advice than they could possibly use. But Baruch is the only man to my knowledge who has built a reputation on a self-assumed unofficial status as 'advisor.' " Baruch's comment to me was "As Jimmy Byrnes [former Secretary of State] says, 'Never get in a peeing match with a skunk.' "

He did have influence, if more qualified than was popularly supposed. We had a personal demonstration in my own family circle. My stepfather, Al Taylor, a tough Scots-Irishman from Nova Scotia, was a construction engineer. He had been in charge of building the New School for Social Research in New York, Park Avenue apartment houses, and buildings throughout the state, but his trade was badly hit by the Depression. He was finally hired as construction superintendent for the building of Floyd Bennett Airport, a WPA project. A stickler for honesty, Al objected too vigorously when he discovered the fiddling that went on, as I suppose it does in all government-contracted projects, and he was fired. I told Bernie, who said, "I'll get in touch with Harry Hopkins right away." Hopkins was the head of the WPA. Months went by, with telegrams to me from Bernie ("Hopkins here at Hobcaw assures me matter will be alright") and calls to Washington by him, with no results. Finally, he went directly to FDR, who called in McIntyre, the presidential secretary, and gave orders that Al was to be reinstated. Still no action. When we had about given up hope ("I don't think he could get a guy a job as dogcatcher," Al said), the President telephoned Bernie to say that Al was to start work the next week, adding, "I hope this is the end of this business because I've got other things on my mind besides Al from Brooklyn." Thus, at last, due to the combined efforts of Bernard M. Baruch, Harry Hopkins and President Franklin D. Roosevelt, my stepfather Al was hired back by the WPA at a lower position than he previously had and at a dollar less a week. One thing, it proved we certainly don't live under a dictatorship, at least not in those days.

Baruch was always loyal. When Joe Curran's goons tried to smash their way into our flat, it was Bernie I called. It happened in February, 1950, during the internecine battle in the National Maritime Union. Jack and I were sitting in our living room early one autumn evening with the children, then aged three and nine, when four right-wing Curran supporters attempted to force their way into our street-level apartment. Fortunately, we had a heavy iron gate, reaching from ceiling to ground, in the small entranceway leading to our front door. The gate was locked. There were also iron bars on the windows, as well as heavy wire mesh (which I had had installed to prevent street cats from dashing in and out of the flat in summer when the windows were open.) The men were armed with lengths of iron pipe. They smashed the big windows and ripped through the wire mesh, shouting curses at Jack, "We'll kill you, you Commie bastard!" and similar threats. (He was not a member of the Party but he was defending the right of Communists to belong to the union and to hold office.) The shattering of the glass in the two large windows, the flower pots crashing to the floor, the angry obscenities of the men, terrified the children, and us as well. Jack called the police and I called Baruch, who immediately called District Attorney Frank Hogan. "One of Lawrenson's children is my goddaughter," he told him.

Hogan ordered a twenty-four-hour police guard, so for the next two months we had an armed policeman standing in front of our door, night and day, until Jack asked the local precinct to remove him. It was then December and we felt embarrassed when we would return from the movies or a visit to friends and see the poor cop standing there in the cold. "We ought to ask him in for a drink, don't you think?" I asked. "For Christ's sake, we can't ask him in for cocoa and oatmeal cookies!" Jack said. "Besides, what would we talk about?" It was during a period when we were both on the wagon and didn't even have any liquor in the house.

It was also to Bernie that I turned after a brawl outside the Sevilla, a Village bar. We had been drinking there with Herman Deehl, an NMU seaman, and Alzira Peirce, ex-wife of the painter Waldo Peirce. A Washington character, noted neither for sobriety nor propriety, was with another group. I had met him before and walked away from him on a dance floor because of his offensiveness. This night in the Sevilla, he kept trying to talk to us and made a grab at me. Jack and Deehl told him to shove off. When we left the bar and were walking home, he came running after us, shouting. Jack hit him. He went down, knocking his head on the sidewalk, and lay there. "Let's get out of here," Deehl said. "We can't go off and leave him," Jack protested. "Wait till he gets up." "He ain't gonna get up," Deehl said, ominously. At that point, the man's friends came from around the corner where, we later learned, they had attacked another NMU seaman who fought them off by swinging at them with a package he used like a medieval mace. The package contained the collected works of Lenin in thirteen volumes.

The fallen gladiator was now struggling to get up. "Okay. We'll take care of him," his friends said, so we left, thinking that was the end of it. It wasn't. The next day the papers carried an account, saying that the police were looking for the "unknown assailants" of the Washington man. They were said to have attacked him with brass knuckles and then driven off in "a large black car." Jack immediately went to see District Attorney Hogan and I called Baruch. "Sit tight," he said. "I'll call you back." When he did, he reported that the Washington man had gotten in touch with the Democratic politician Jim Farley, insisting that Jack be prosecuted. "Tell me, Helen," Bernie asked, "did Jack use brass knuckles?" I laughed. I told him again exactly what had happened. When he called back the next time, he had been on the phone to Washington to Byrnes, who was Secretary of State. "I told him that a friend of mine had knocked down what's-his-name, and Jimmy Byrnes said, 'Your friend should have killed him.' He's not very popular in Washington. Anyway, it's all right. Byrnes is going to call Farley and Hogan. I used to be quite a fighter myself, you know."

A lot of girls had gone under Bernie's bridge by then and I lost track of them, although I remember clearly the one who came after me. Bernie and I went to Condé's for dinner one evening in 1938, before I had met Jack. Condé had a new girl there, a tall, slim blonde with a certain vernal grace, who looked like a road-company Clare. She was wearing a low-cut black satin evening gown and she carried, all evening, one white lily. "How's everything back in Astolat?" I asked, a query that went unappreciated. Like Clare, she was one of those feminine types, a palm reader. She read Bernie's palm, caressing it, while Condé, who was batty about her, watched jealously. The result of that evening was that Bernie took her with him to Europe, shortly before I left for South America.

The night before they sailed, I had dinner with her. She was in love with a Spanish painter, who arrived as I was leaving. She knew that Condé was hers for the taking, but she said to me, "I'm going to stick with Baruch. It's more practical." It didn't turn out to be so, in the end, but I had to give her credit for trying. She had a three-year-old daughter by a former marriage, "a dear little near-sighted thing with thick glasses," Bernie told me, in what was for him an unprecedented show of affection for a small child. But then, as he told me afterward, on shipboard the child climbed on his lap as he sat in his deck chair. "Mr. Baruch, you ought to be President. You *look* like a President!" she chirped. When I told this to a friend, she said, "That poor kid's mother must have rehearsed her for hours."

Although Bernie frequently told me, "I don't care anything about publicity; it doesn't mean a thing to me," he subscribed to a clipping service, read everything written about himself he could lay his hands on, leapt at every invitation to be interviewed or photographed, sent forth a regular geyser of letters to the press (even to the *Daily Worker* and *The Villager*, a Greenwich Village neighborhood weekly), collected scrolls and plaques the way other men collect stamps, and, in his later years, turned down no public appearance. Newspapers carried photographs of him inspecting cheeses in Macy's to promote their "Italian Fair" sales; sitting on a New York subway bench, flanked by two City College girl students, in the 23rd Street station of the IRT at the unveiling of a sign for the Bernard M. Baruch School of Business & Public Administration; hunched awkwardly over a shovel, pretending to dig ground for the construction of the Baruch Houses, a New York City housing project on the Lower East Side. He appeared as judge at high school oratory contests sponsored by the Hearst newspapers; he sat on the dais, together with Milton Berle and George Jessel, at a dinner in honor of Bob Hope; he was chairman of ceremonies on the Mall in Central Park on "I Am an American Day"; he addressed a meeting of the Boy Scouts of Brownsville (a section of Brooklyn); he posed with the ten-millionth ball made of American rubber.

He took everything offered: the Boy Scouts' Silver Buffalo "for distinguished service to boyhood," a certificate making him an honorary member of the Daughters of the Confederacy (he had this framed and hung on his wall), *The Churchman* award, Freedom House award, American Hebrew medal, Kiwanis Club plaque for "outstanding citizen of the year," first annual American Veterans Committee award, Citizenship Day citation. You name it; he took it. For his eighty-second birthday he went to Dyerville, California, to accept a redwood bench set at the foot of the world's tallest tree (364 feet) with a plaque reading, in part: "Dedicated to Bernard M. Baruch, philosopher, philanthropist, stalwart American . . . his stature is that of the redwoods." That same year, the New York *Herald Tribune* named him as one of the hundred most important people in the world. The following year, when he was eighty-three, he attended a Danny Kaye matinee at the Palace vaudeville theater in New York, during which Kaye introduced him as "one of the greatest Americans of all time . . . whose name will go ringing down the corridors of history," a tribute that could not have been unanticipated by the recipient, who stood up and bowed, amid cheers, shouts, stamping and clapping by the audience during a ten-minute ovation. When he was eighty-six, he was still at it, writing a letter to Cecil B. De Mille to be used in advertisements as an endorsement for the film *The Ten Commandments.*

Well, he was an old man who had missed the boat in history. He was convinced that had he not been Jewish he could have been President and I suspect he was right. Certainly, he would have been a great deal better than some we've had. Still, on the balance sheet, I think we have to consider that he made his fortune from mines—gold, silver, diamonds, copper, tungsten, sulphur—and that he was either ignorant of, or indifferent to, the horrifying conditions, particularly in South America and in Africa, of the miners. Only the profits interested him, in contrast to his public expression of noble concern for "freedom," "the dignity of the individual man," etc. One example alone: he even praised that King Leopold whose notorious program of atrocities in the Belgian Congo shocked the world. Thomas Fortune Ryan and Leopold formed the Société Internationale Forestière et Minière du Congo to develop mineral resources. (This was to culminate years later in the nefarious Moise Tshombe and the murder of Patrice Lumumba.) Baruch and Dan Guggenheim joined the venture, the former commenting that diamonds were found, "making the stock a good investment."

Nor was his advocacy of democracy untainted by discrepancy between theory and practice. I remember an evening at his house when the discussion was about how to secure a certain congressional election. "How do you make sure someone will win an election?" I asked, in my most innocent voice. "The way Bernie does: a $100,000 here and a $100,000 there," Rex Tugwell said. (The handsomest member of FDR's Brain Trust, Tugwell was later Governor of Puerto Rico.)

The last time I saw Bernie he was eighty-eight. My husband was dead, so Bernie and I had dinner alone in the

East 66th Street apartment where he lived after he sold his house (which became the Grace Downs School for models and airline hostesses). He was all spruced up in black tie and dinner jacket and seemed pleased to see me. We may have argued with less fervor than in previous years but he still showed a spirited interest in explaining how much better, given the chance, he could run the affairs of the nation. When we were having coffee in his sitting room, after dinner, the butler poured us each a small drink from a bottle that was thick with dust and cobwebs. How was I to know that's the way they're *supposed* to be? "You might dust your bottles once in a while," I said to Bernie, who replied, "I see you're just as stupid as ever. You and Churchill are the only ones who have had this brandy."

He went to Europe every year for sheep cell injections from Dr. Paul Niehans in Switzerland. Once, when he telephoned me on his return, I asked, banteringly, "Did you have fun?" "Listen, Madame Fathead, he said, "you don't have much fun when you're ninety-two." The last I heard from him was the letter he wrote a few months before he died, in which he said he hoped I was happy, considering the state of the world. When I read of his death, I thought of the times I had begged him to say publicly some of the things he said privately to me and, I'm sure, to others. What could he have lost? He was old and very rich. His legend was still luminous, his word respected by the general public, if not by their elected officials. He could have made a genuine contribution time and time again, but he preferred the protective mask of safely pious platitudes. I think he just didn't have the guts. Perhaps the most depressing thing is that nevertheless he was mentally and even morally head and shoulders above so many other prominent figures on our political scene, not excluding those of today, although I admit he didn't always sound like it. I remember an incident when I was staying at Hobcaw, along with Jane Ross, ex-wife of *The New Yorker* editor, and Neysa McMein, a well-known illustrator, with her two teen-age daughters. We were invited for tea with Woodrow Wilson's widow, but I had promised the girls I would take them to a film showing in Kingstree on that day only, so I told Bernie to make my excuses. As we drove to the movie theater, the two girls were giggling and making fun of Bernie. "I'm the grown-up here," I thought. "I mustn't permit such disrespect." Aloud, I said, in a sternly reproving tone, "Mr. Baruch is a very intelligent man." I have never forgotten the response. I don't remember which girl made it, but what she said was "Is he really? You'd never think so to hear him talk."

Nine

UNDERNEATH
THE HARLEM MOON

I MET BUMPY IN THE HOT NEW
York summer of 1935. It was in the Alhambra Bar & Grill on
Seventh Avenue at 126th Street. "There's the Legs Diamond
of Harlem," Lucky said, pointing him out. (It was an inept
comparison. Diamond was a ratty sort of gangster. Bumpy
was no part of a gang. He was nothing if not independent, and
he was no rat. He had strong feelings on that subject. I once
said something about a certain trade union official turning rat
and Bumpy corrected me. "People don't *turn* rat," he said.
"They're born rat.") He came over to our table, Lucky introduced him, and he sat down and bought us a drink. He never
touched alcohol himself. "I got to keep a clear head in my
business," he said.

Even then, he was a Harlem legend. Everyone feared him;
many hated him. He had been shot at fifteen times and had
already, he told me, done time in Auburn, Attica, Clinton

and Sing Sing, not to mention briefer stays in the Tombs or the local precinct station. He was a pimp, a numbers man, and, especially, an enforcer, a persuader, meaning that he beat up people. The prosecuting attorney at one of his trials called him "one of the most vicious criminals in the history of Harlem," although I never found him anything but kind, considerate, polite (a stickler for always lighting a woman's cigaret, helping her on with her coat, opening doors for her, all the small courtesies), protective and, like many tough men, vulnerably sentimental in some ways. He kept a framed picture of Shirley Temple, age six, on his bureau; he was a pushover for a hard-luck touch; he wrote poetry about love and friendship.

Only twice did I glimpse his other side. Once, in a local Magistrates' Court, the presiding judge said something Bumpy interpreted as a racial slur and he sprang toward the bench with a snarl of such savagery that for a flash the jungle came alive in that courtroom. The other time we were standing at the bar in the Alhambra when some luckless enemy came in. Bumpy moved like lightning, and the two men were down on the floor while the crowd shrank away from them. I watched with fear and revulsion. It was not a pleasant sight. It was soon over and the inevitable loser, his eyes streaming from gouging, staggered out the door, barely able to make it. There was absolute silence in the room. Bumpy came and stood beside me again. "Is my tie straight?" he asked.

He was always immaculately dressed, in conservative taste. No sharpie styles for him, no zoot-suit, porkpie-hat fads. Like other Harlem hustlers, who were known as "the sporting crowd," he spent his money on his clothes and his car. I told him he ought to go to Sulka's for his ties and shirts, and he followed my suggestion. Other pimps and hustlers, always eager to copy his example, did likewise and I wondered what the salesmen in Sulka's thought about this sudden influx of black customers. Bumpy at that time was twenty-eight. His skin was black, he had close-cropped, frizzy hair (then called "bad hair") and shiny black almond eyes, Oriental eyes. His teeth were marvelous but often when he was amused he didn't show them in a laugh or smile. Instead, his nose would twitch like a rabbit's and the small, bright eyes would—yes, twinkle is the right word—twinkle as if he were suppressing a secret joke. I said he reminded me of a black cat I once had and he said, a little ruefully, "Don't you ever tell anyone I look like your cat!"

He was not tall, only about five feet seven inches. Gangsters coming in from Detroit, Chicago, St. Louis, other places where his reputation had spread, were always surprised when they saw him. "They're expecting some great big nigger," he explained, "and they see me and they say, 'That Bumpy? Man, that just can't be Bumpy, not that little guy.' " He had incredible physical courage, an absolutely fearless man. Even the cops respected this. "I'm one nigger they don't take downstairs in the precinct and beat his head in," he said. I was with him twice when he was shot at. The first time, it was a prearranged gun duel on a Harlem street corner. Prior to the appointed hour, Bumpy and I had dinner in a nearby restaurant. He ordered soup, steak, French fries, beans, peas, corn, salad, and he was eating it with gusto. I couldn't understand how he could be so calm. "The condemned man ate a hearty meal," I commented, nervously. "How can you do it?" "I'm hungry," he said. "There's nothing to worry about. Pay it no mind." Before he had finished, someone gave a signal and he was up and out the door like a streak. Then I heard the shots. I sat there, terrified. It wasn't more than about two minutes in all before he was back, sitting down, finishing his meal. "What happened?" "Nothin'. We both missed. Now, I'm gonna have a banana split. How about you?" "I couldn't eat a thing and I don't see how you can." "Man!" he said. "You don't know the number of times I've sat in my cell at Sing Sing and thought to myself, 'Goddam. I'd give my soul for a banana split!' " The waiter brought the dessert, piled high with whipped cream, chocolate sauce, cherries, the works. "You'll ruin your complexion," I said. "My complexion was ruined when I was born," he observed dryly.

When he had finished, we left and were driving along Lenox Avenue when a white Cadillac open sports car shot ahead of us, stopped, the driver called, "Come on, motherfucker!" and jumped out with a gun in his hand. One bullet whizzed right by me, but Bumpy was out of the car and running toward the man. He had no weapon, himself, as after the incident outside the restaurant he had thrown his gun to a friend to stash so that he would be clean if the cops came along. The gunman kept firing at him but Bumpy never took a backward step. "Someone throw me a ginger ale bottle!" he called, as he kept running toward the man, dodging the shots. I suppose the guy couldn't believe his eyes, because he didn't even wait to fire all his bullets but turned and made for his car which, luckily for him, he had left running, and off he tore, around the corner almost on two wheels. Bumpy came back to me and his eyes were glittering like iced steel. "He could have killed you," I said. "He didn't. But he sure as hell's gonna wish he had." "Don't you know the meaning of fear?" I asked him. "Lissen," he said, "when something like this happens, it's like a cool breeze blowin' through me. Man, it's beautiful . . ."

The other time was out in the street and I ran, with everyone else, all of us crowding into doorways as the bullets flew. Bumpy wasn't armed that time, either, but I think people were so frightened by his reputation that they couldn't shoot straight even when they had him at a disadvantage. (Once when I refused to believe some story of his, he said, "If I ain't tellin' the truth I hope I go out that door and some cop that don't like me come along and shoot me dead." I couldn't help commenting, "He'd have to be a better shot than most people up here.") I was also with him the night a man cut his throat with a straight razor. We were just going up the steps of a building when a man standing there said something. Bumpy turned around, the blade glistened in the light from a streetlamp, and the man ran off before I knew anything had happened. "Take a look at this," Bumpy said, holding his chin high so that I could see a thin red line around his throat. The line was blood but the cut wasn't deep. I went with him to a doctor, who sewed it up. As we drove home, I told him it reminded me of the old World War I joke about the Negro soldier who cut a Hun's throat with a razor and his pal said, "You didn't hurt him; it's just a red line," and the first soldier said, "Wait till the son of a bitch tries to turn his head!" Bumpy didn't smile but he glanced at me sidewise and murmured something like sounded like "Humph." Then his nose twitched and his eyes twinkled. "You got some sense of humor," he said. We went upstairs and made love. "I think it's better with your throat cut," I told him.

I don't want anyone to think that I used to sneak up to Harlem for assignations in the manner of many white women of that era, from Hollywood stars to New York socialites. There was nothing clandestine about my friendship with Bumpy. I told Condé about him, Irwin Shaw, Dick Sherman, my Aunt Grace, many of my friends. I took my mother to Harlem to have tea with him one Sunday and in letters from prison he would often ask me to give his love to my mother. When I took Vertès, the *Vanity Fair* artist, to meet him, Vertès did a column about him for a Paris weekly. He called it *La sombre histoire du gentil gangster* and illustrated it with drawings of Bumpy. I took other friends to meet him and one of them, who worked for Condé Nast, gave a birthday party for him in her home, with a cake and candles and all of us singing "Happy Birthday, dear Bumpy." His eyes glistened with something suspiciously like tears. It was the first birthday cake he ever had. "They don't give you none in Sing Sing," he said. I did not tell Baruch about him. Bumpy said to me that if I ever saw him, at Saratoga or anywhere, when I was with Baruch or Condé or people like that, I should pretend I didn't see him. "Listen," I said to him, "if a man is good enough for me to sleep with, he's good enough for me to speak to when I meet him on the street." It should be borne in mind that this was some forty years ago, when interracial friendships, above all, between white women and black men, were frighteningly taboo.

Not that our relationship was any big sex deal. By this I

mean that it was not one of those gee-those-black-men-WOW! sort of thing. Bumpy was not my first black lover, or even my second, nor was he the last. I was a premature integrationist. My first was Mac, a Syracuse University student whom I met in June, 1930, when I was a newspaper reporter and went along with Ann, my communist friend, and two young white Communist men to a discussion group at Dunbar Center, a Negro community center in Syracuse. After the meeting, they served tea and cookies. Our presence there would have been considered an unthinkable act of degeneracy to all the white Syracusans I knew (with the exception of Party members), who thought Jews were bad enough. After that, we met on several occasions, and I discovered that Mac was intelligent and witty, as well as good-looking. I remember he told me that whenever he met white people socially he had to spend the first five or ten minutes putting them at their ease so that they wouldn't feel they had to put him at *his* ease. He knew all about prejudice, though. When he was thirteen he tried to kill himself because the white boys in his school in Reading, Pennsylvania, used to call, "Oh lookit the nigger! Here comes the nigger," and they would throw stones at him and once they pushed him in a pile of scrap iron and he cut his face badly. At home, he took a box of kitchen matches and bit off the ends. They tasted bitter, so he cut the ends of the rest into a bowl, mashed them up, put sugar on them, and ate them. They didn't even make him sick. We used to meet at Ann's house. I helped him with his University term paper on Ecclesiastes and in return he taught me the Georgia grind, a fair enough exchange.

Frankly, Bumpy was no great justification for the Southern white man's manic sex fear of the black male. One time when he was in jail, I went to a Harlem party with some friends and there I met Canada Lee, at that time a boxer, not yet known as an actor. When I saw Bumpy again, I told him that Canada thought I was beautiful and said Bumpy was a lucky man. "Shit, man," said Bumpy. "He's a fighter. I'm a fucker." So of course I said, "Well, I certainly hope for his sake that he can fight better than you can fuck." Bumpy just laughed and said, "I guess it's all that saltpeter they give you in prison." He was a terrible dancer, too, and as for singing, he couldn't even carry a tune. "Where's all that native rhythm, that racial abandon?" I teased him. "I'm the exception that proves the rule," he said. I liked him because he was bright and brave and funny. We laughed together about the same things, and this has always meant a lot to me, with any man. We also, oddly enough, were much alike in our tastes and our beliefs. And we usually liked, or disliked, the same people.

We used to go to the places popular with entertainers and other members of the Harlem equivalent of café society: the Sunday morning breakfast dances at Small's Paradise, night spots like Dickie Wells's and other places that didn't come alive until after midnight, like the Heat Wave, the Rhythm Club, Jerry's Log Cabin, and a private club called the Turf Club, where I was usually the only white patron. Everyone knew Bumpy and he introduced me to the great black dancer, Bill "Bojangles" Robinson, whom Bumpy idolized and who used to be a fast man in a fight, himself, in his younger days. "Man, he could really go," Bumpy said. "He solid laid it." I also met Earl "Snakehips" Tucker, who was one of my favorite dancers, as well as Buck and Bubbles, actor Rex Ingram and actress Nina Mae MaKinney, the pretty star of King Vidor's film *Hallelujah!* That summer was the last year of *Vanity Fair* and Bumpy used to line up black actors, singers, dancers for me and bring them into the Condé Nast offices to be photographed for the magazine.

It was because of the magazine that I happened to be in Harlem when I first met him. In those days it was a chic thing to do to go to Harlem late at night, an extension, I guess, of the "slumming parties" (that repellently snobbish phrase) of the twenties. Because I could speak French I used to have the job of shepherding artists and photographers who came from Paris to work for Condé Nast. There were two places they all wanted to see, Coney Island and Harlem. I took them to the usual tourist haunts: the Plantation and the Cotton Club; Clinton Moore's, a dimly lit apartment-club that catered to an epicene coterie (titled male Britons flew there like homing pigeons almost the moment they hit New York) and which boasted a young black entertainer named Joey, who played piano and sang but whose *spécialité* was to remove his clothes and extinguish a lighted candle by sitting on it until it disappeared. I never saw this feat but everyone else seemed to have and I was told that he was often hired to perform at soirées of the elite. "He sat on lighted candles at one of the Vanderbilts'," my informant said.

We also always went to the Savoy Ballroom, patronized at that time only by the more venturesome madcaps from downtown. Noguchi and I tried unsuccessfully to persuade Henry Luce to go there with us that night back in 1932 when we went to his apartment after the Martha Graham recital. It is with some embarrassment, now, that I remember tugging at Luce's arm and pleading, "Oh come on! You'll love it." (It was the first time I'd ever met him or I would have known that the Savoy Ballroom was one of the last places on earth that Henry Luce would have loved.) On one of these den-mother excursions I met Lucky, a light-skinned Negro who could have passed for Portuguese, and we were having a drink with him in the Alhambra, a special treat because no tourists ever went there, when he introduced me to Bumpy. From then on, my Harlem visits were quite different. Bumpy loathed Clinton Moore's and the Savoy, and he had only contempt for white sightseers. I agreed with him, but I had accepted it, or at least gone along with it, whereas he never had and never would.

"We ain't in no zoo," he said, that first night. "How would you like it if we was to go downtown to your clubs and restaurants to stare at you people? Not that we'd get let in. So why should we let you up here? I can't no way go downtown and walk into the Ritz. No way, no how. Except maybe I'm walkin' behind you, carryin' your bags, and then they'd get took away from me by some white bellboy because they wouldn't let me inside the door." I knew he was right but it was nearly four in the morning and I had been drinking all night, so I invited him to go as my guest for tea at the Ritz that afternoon. I insisted, vehemently. He knew that I meant it. Fortunately for us both, he had more sense than I did and he refused. If he had accepted, I would have gone through with it, even cold sober, which would have proved nothing. Those were the days when the height of genteel daring in interracial relations was to serve on committees for the Urban League, and whenever white liberals met a Negro they made a point of grabbing his hand and shaking it, in situations where they wouldn't have done so if he had been white, and experiencing, I daresay, a glow of nobility. ("Gee, I shook hands with one!")

Bumpy was perceptive enough, intuitive enough, to know that while the silly bravado of my gesture may have been due to alcohol, the conviction behind it was sincere. Ever since childhood, really, I had been puzzled by, and resentful of, the insanity of racial prejudice. Perhaps this was partly an inheritance. My grandmother's father, a Methodist minister in LaFargeville, was an abolitionist and his house was a station on the underground railway for escaping slaves from the South. My great-grandmother used to go down in the kitchen early mornings to make coffee for them. "Are you sure your great-grandma didn't give those runaway slaves something more than coffee when she went down to the kitchen?" Bumpy once asked. I was so proud of my carefully nurtured tan, either from sun lamp or sunshine, a white fashion Bumpy found ironically amusing. I did get pretty dark. One time, when another Harlem pimp was looking for a white girl to work in a downtown brothel, Bumpy pointed to me and asked, as a joke, "How about her?" The man looked at me and then said, "Sure. All she's got to do is say she's Spanish."

Actually, my specific hatred of anti-Negro prejudice began at Bradford. Until I was fifteen, I suppose that if I thought of Negroes at all, it was probably as servants, Pullman porters, railway station redcaps, stage or screen comedians, dancers, singers. But in September, 1923, I was one of the seniors picked to welcome new students and their parents to Bradford. A Negro girl arrived from the South, with her father, obviously to the fearsome consternation of the school faculty members present. On the application form, where it said "Race," she had put "Negro," but no one at the school had noticed it, probably because no Negro girl had ever applied and the registrar staff were so used to seeing "White" that they never really looked. Anyway, the girl and her father were told that she would not be admitted. I was shattered by this. I thought of all the preparations she and her family must have made: buying her uniforms, getting her clothes ready (we wore Peter Thompson uniforms by day but at night we dressed for dinner in our own clothes—one dazzling beauty, Dot Toy, daughter of a Sioux City banker, never wore the same dress twice in two years), sewing Cash's woven name tapes on every single article, saying goodbye to friends and relatives, happily taking the train North—and then to be refused admittance almost as soon as she was inside the front door. Academic entrance requirements were then very high, so the girl must have been bright. She must have fulfilled all the academic requirements, as well as the social and financial references.

I got together four or five other girls and we went to Miss Sarah Coates, the principal (later to become the first head of Sarah Lawrence) and pleaded with her to let the girl stay, saying that any one of us would be happy to room with her. The answer was No. I still feel sick to my stomach, even today, when I think of it. I don't pretend that I spent my life from then on fighting for The Negro, but it certainly opened my eyes and made me think. Since that day, I have never been able to accept that anyone should be judged by color of skin, any more than by religion. (Bradford had a Jewish "quota," as did Vassar.) I believe I am one white person (the Indian strain has nothing to do with it, because I have figured out I am about one sixteenth part Indian) who is at ease with blacks and they know it, almost the instant they meet me. It's not easy to explain to people who don't get the vibrations. As Bumpy used to say, "If you don't know, you just don't know." I was not attracted to Bumpy just because he was black. Nevertheless, he was "a home boy"; and he, too, sensed the empathy.

A few days after our first meeting, he called me at my office. "I'll see if she's in," my secretary said. She looked dubious. "It's some man," she told me, "who says just to tell you his name is Bumpy." What he wanted was to ask a favor. One of his girls had been arrested and he thought I might help her. He asked me to meet him uptown to discuss it, so I did, later that afternoon, taking with me Irene Kittle, then on the staff of *Glamour*. Renee was about five feet tall. "She your bodyguard?" Bumpy said, when he met us.

His Number One girl, Jean, had been picked up for soliciting and he wanted to know if I would testify in court as a character witness, saying that she had formerly worked for me as a stenographer. I agreed and the next day I met him again with his white lawyer. "She'll get on the stand and say she's managing editor of *Vanity Fair* magazine," Bumpy explained to the lawyer, who looked aghast. "She'd never get away with it," he protested. "But it's the truth, man," Bumpy said. The lawyer, however, lost his nerve so they solved the problem by bribing the arresting cop and the magistrate. Harlem was then the choice beat for a cop on the take and the 123rd Street precinct was a gold mine. In fact, some cops even paid kickbacks to be seconded to that locality. They got paid off by pimps, whores, numbers runners and bankers, bars, night clubs, everyone. Not only the cops but also higher police officials and many judges. It was no secret, so why the testimony before the Knapp Commission investigating police corruption in New York a few years ago should have come as any big surprise is a mystery to me. I laughed right out loud when I read that New York City Police Commissioner Patrick Murphy said he was "astonished and appalled" by revelations of graft among members of his force.

Bumpy was involved in the numbers racket, off and on, and several times ran his own policy bank, as it was called. For anyone who doesn't know, this was (and is) an illegal lottery in which the bettor would pick three numbers from one to 999, inclusive, and would bet a penny, a dime, a dollar, whatever, that these three numbers would come up that day. At one time, the three numbers were taken from totals bet at a chosen racetrack. At another, the U.S. Treasury daily balances were used, or the last three figures in the New York Stock Exchange totals. You placed your bet with a "runner," of whom there were hundreds in Harlem, in cigar stores, saloons, crap games, lunchrooms and on street corners. If your number came up, you were paid six to one, minus 10 percent for the "runner." Each runner reported to a comptroller and each comptroller to a banker. Since the odds are terrific, the money rolls in, to the banker.

The policy game was brought to America by Marcellino, a Puerto Rican who got the idea from the big Cuban lotteries. He and Simeon Francis started the racket up on San Juan Hill in New York. Marcellino was a sport and a spender, and he ended up penniless. Francis, on the other hand, made no splurge, never even bought a car, took in around $10,000 a day from his bank, and retired to the West Indies to end his days in tropical ease. In 1931, at the time of the Seabury-Kresel investigation, there were four big numbers kings in Harlem: Simeon Francis, Casper Holstein, Wilfred Brandon and James Warner. Holstein was president of the Turf Club at 111 West 136th Street, where Bumpy used to take me and where I could always get in, even without him. (On my first date with Jack Lawrenson, I took him to the Turf Club and I also told him about Bumpy, then in Dannemora.) Holstein had an income at one time of $12,000 a day from the numbers, owned apartment houses all over Harlem, gave extravagant presents to white politicians, including a silver tea set as a wedding gift to an alderman's daughter, and was known to bet $35,000 in a day at Saratoga. It was his kidnapping by four white gangsters and one Negro one that raised a political stink which helped get the vice investigation started.

Brandon had three hundred collectors working for him from Harlem to Connecticut, made $25,000 a day, drove a Lincoln car with a uniformed chauffeur, and had his headquarters in an undertaking parlor on the southwest corner of 146th Street and Seventh Avenue. As for Warner, he made a piffling $10,000 a day, mostly out of the Spanish-speaking colored section, and retired to the British West Indies.

Harlem's famed Numbers Queen was Madame Stephanie St. Clair, a black woman from Martinique who came to this country from Marseilles, via Canada, in 1912. She started banking numbers in 1922, with a capital of $10,000. Two years later, she learned about graft when she paid her first $300 to a neighborhood cop. From then on, she paid police and judges. Despite this, in December, 1929, she was sentenced to three years on Welfare Island. Released on parole within one month, she burst upon the Seabury vice squad investigation like a big black thunderbolt and split it wide open. She accused a district attorney, two judges, scores of police, bondsmen and political fixers. She gave names, dates and the amounts paid out in graft. She told of a magistrate who died from the effects of a beating because he refused to pay $30,000 as the price of his appointment to the bench. She didn't tell All, but she told plenty. The big numbers kings skipped to Canada or the West Indies; and it was announced that the policy game was smashed.

Then came the "combination." Prohibition was on the wane and the big white gangsters downtown were beginning to see the writing on the wall. They cast their eyes northward and lo! there was the land of Canaan, with the rich, ripe, unplucked fields of the Harlem numbers racket, unorganized, a dog-eat-dog industry, with no cooperation among the Negro bankers. With an exalted New Deal spirit, a number of white hoods, among whom Dutch Schultz and George "Bo" Wineberg were not inconspicuous, decided to create a numbers empire. Their first step was to hire Bub Hewlett, colored gunman. They gave him $300 a week, plus expense money, and told him to "organize." His idea of organization was simple and, for the most part, effective. At the start, he hired, for a pittance, a group of black thugs. These menacing emissaries were then sent around to every Harlem numbers banker to "invite" each to join the combination. The way it worked out was that the black bankers did all the work and the white gangsters took the money. Some bankers left the combination or refused to join in the first place. Their runners were slugged, kicked in the teeth, shot at, cut with knives. An average of fifteen to twenty of them a week were tossed out of cars by night on the steps of Harlem Hospital.

As a result of these measures of persuasion, quite a few recalcitrant bankers crept back under the wings of the combination. Mme. St. Clair was made of sterner stuff. She was then a woman in her early forties, standing 5'8" in her stocking feet, black, husky, fearless. She had around ten comptrollers and forty runners working for her. She hated the Dutchman and he hated her. He was out to get her. She looked around for a henchman to serve her. She found him in Bumpy, just released from Auburn prison in August, 1932, after having been shipped around from prison to prison as an incorrigible. He was broke, he was desperate, and, at that time, he was just a bad nigger who knew no one. Madame hired him as her bodyguard. When he was not escorting her to concerts at Carnegie Hall, for she had a musical nature, he took her for walks in Central Park. The rest of the time he protected her interests and fought the Hewlett mob in one of the most violent gang wars in the history of Harlem. With fabulous personal courage, he shot it out in dark alleys, in the sinister dimness of streets off Lenox Avenue, against great odds, when the battle cry of the opposition was "Get Bumpy!"

Practically single-handed, he broke Hewlett, weakened the power of the combination, and gave the numbers game back to the blacks, until the syndicate moved back in when a well-played number hit and the Harlem policy banks couldn't pay off. Dutch Schultz lent some $150,000, but his fee was reentry into the racket. Bumpy had little truck with his mob, although they always treated him with respect and frequently tried to work out a deal with him. They once invited him to a meeting downtown at which he was the only black man. "I looked like a little fly in a bowl of milk," he told me. And once, when he got out of jail, Joe Adonis, at one time reputed to be the head of Murder, Inc., met him with a gift of money. I asked Bumpy what Adonis was like. "Like any other wop," he said. He didn't like any of those people and, at least in the days I knew him, he stood up to them, which was something no one else dared do.

Most of the sporting crowd were pimps, no matter what other line they might have. Bumpy had five whores working for him. I never saw any of them, but I heard they were all good-looking, which I could believe. He was scornful of the theory that every black man's dream was to rape a white woman. ("Lord, will I ever?" "No, nigger, never." "While there's life there's hope." "Yes, and where there's a tree there's a rope.") "You oughta see some of the dogs that come up here. I just look at 'em and shake my head. I wouldn't touch 'em with a borrowed prick." Three of his girls were white and the others so light they could pass. They all worked the streets downtown. He wouldn't have any of them in a house. I naïvely asked him what they said when soliciting. I looked incredulous when he told me they said, "Want to see a nice little girl?" "Oh come on, Bumpy. That's ridiculous." "I know it is. But that *is* what they say. Leastwise, they start off that way." Once, he told me, he got them all together for a pep talk, like the manager of Wanamakers department store used to give the staff every week, and told them they'd better hustle harder because "I'm not in this business for my health." Contrary to the beliefs of some social workers, they were certainly not held in thrall, against their will. They were in love with him, or thought they were, and one of them, Margie, a peroxide blonde whose real name was Yetta—she came from Delancey Street on the Lower East Side—committed suicide when he was sent to prison for ten years. His attitude toward them was more equivocal. "You just know a girl has got to be stupid or she wouldn't be a whore," he said to me. "Any girl who will walk the streets and work all night turnin' tricks and then come home and give all her money to some pimp who maybe beats her up and then he give her a quarter for carfare and he spend all her money gamblin' or buyin' clothes for hisself, well, baby, she *got* to be stupid. Look at Pigmeat's Della. Now there's one whore that ain't got no heart of gold. Pigmeat say he wish it was, he'd cut it out and pawn it. He knocked out her teeth and now he got to buy her new ones 'cause she can't work with no teeth. And she still love him. What kind of people is that?"

I think Bumpy was truly fond of Jean, though. He thought she looked like Barbara Stanwyck and so she did, as I discovered when she achieved newspaper prominence in February, 1937. It was revealed then that she was the Broadway Gun Girl who held up five restaurants with a toy cap pistol and was finally captured at 5 A.M. one morning while trying to rob another place on Columbus Avenue. At that time she was out on a thousand dollars bail for stabbing another girl four times in a fight over a client. (Heywood Broun, who was with Walter Winchell in the station when she was brought in, wrote a column about her coolness and utter self-possession, ending it with the words: "Just before the police matron took her out, she swept the station with a glance. We were all dirt under her feet.")

When arrested as the girl bandit, she gave her name as Norma Parker, said she was twenty-five, a Creole from New Orleans, and gave a fake address. Later, it came out that she was only twenty, Polish-American, born in Boston but reared in Brooklyn, and her name was Nellie Gutowski. An honor student at school, she ran away when she was fifteen and became a prostitute. She was seventeen when she met Bumpy, who thought she was twenty-one, that she was Italian, and that her real name was Jean Valente. She was as spirited as she was good-looking. She was also loyal. The New York *Sunday Mirror* ran her story, "My Life from Child Prodigy to Broadway's Toy Gun Girl," in six installments, and not once did she even hint at Bumpy's existence. Psychologists, psychiatrists and social workers wrote supplementary articles on "The Social Meaning" of her life and even the judge, sentencing her to an indeterminate stretch in Westfield State Farm, was sympathetic, picturing her as a lonely waif driven to prostitution who "never liked the work" and spent all her money on clothes, theaters, restaurants. Not one of them learned that she was proud of being Bumpy's top girl and that everything she earned went to him. Three months after she was sentenced, she escaped by scaling a seven-foot fence topped with barbed wire and went back to Bumpy.

Unlike his girls, I did not give him money. However, I did insist on paying for my own drinks, as I didn't think he ought to spend on me anything that came from them. I also gave him my grandfather's diamond ring, which I had reset at Tiffany's. ("Would the gentleman care to come in and choose the setting?" the salesclerk asked. When I told Bumpy, he said, "I can just see myself walking into Tiffany's and saying, 'Ah've come to see about mah ring.'") In contrast to admirers like Nast and Baruch, he gave me a silver fox cape and a diamond and platinum wrist-watch, both "hot." (On the card he wrote, "To the world's sweetest baby, from Sir Bump.") When I married Jack, although he knew all about Bumpy, he was understandably reluctant to see me wearing the gifts, so I passed them on to my mother and she wore them for years.

Because of his reputation I doubt if he ever had to pay when he took me to places like the fights at the St. Nicholas ring or to Dr. Bier's Training Camp in Pompton Lakes, New Jersey, where we watched Joe Louis work out for his fight with Max Baer in September, 1935. "I could take him," Bumpy said, when we left the camp. "He's bigger than you are," I pointed out. "Shit. He's a boxer. I'm a street fighter." He also took me to see Satchel Paige, the great Negro baseball player, in an exhibition match at Dyckman Oval held for the benefit of the Scottsboro boys, the nine black boys taken off a freight train in Alabama in 1931, charged with raping two white girls (one of whom, Ruby Bates, later retracted her accusation) and sentenced to death, precipitating a legal battle that lasted approximately twenty years, with Heywood Patterson, the most famous of the accused, given five trials and sentenced to death three times. The case was one of the great *causes célèbres* of the thirties, along with that of Tom Mooney, who was convicted of participation in the bombing of a Preparedness Day parade in San Francisco in 1916. His death sentence was commuted to life imprisonment by Woodrow Wilson. I put his picture in *Vanity Fair* in 1934, at which time he had served eighteen years. He was eventually released when it was proved that the two witnesses whose testimony convicted him had been in another town on the day of the bombing and therefore lied when they said they saw Mooney. "Free the Scottsboro Boys!" and "Free Tom Mooney!" were two of the banners with which we marched in many a May Day parade. Bumpy knew perfectly well about the phoney frame-ups but he liked to tease me by saying, "If Tom Mooney didn't rape them little white girls, what's he doin' in jail all this time?"

For Labor Day, 1935, we drove to Philadelphia. As we crossed the state line, we were stopped by a cop. Aware of the Mann Act Bumpy told him, "She's an entertainer." "What kind?" asked the cop, skeptically. "A singer. She's got a job over Labor Day in Philly and I'm her manager." Fortunately, I wasn't asked to prove my talent, and I was sufficiently tanned to offset any other suspicions. I remember the weekend chiefly because of a friend of Bumpy's named Satin Top, whose trade was that of laying down counterfeit money. He took us to all the black bars on South Street and recited a verse he had learned as a child in Mississippi: "Bull frog slidin' on the mantel piece, He hopped right off in a pan of grease. He say, 'Look out, motherfuckers, lemme pass! Here come a bullfrog wid a French fried ass.'"

Bumpy was born October 16, 1906, in Charleston, South Carolina. His parents named him Ellsworth Raymond Johnson. In the winter of 1937, when I was visiting Baruch at Hobcaw Barony, I went to see Bumpy's sister Elise, a gentle, quiet young woman who taught in a little one-room Negro school. I also visited his father—his mother was dead—in his house on Bogard Street in Charleston's Negro ghetto. (Bumpy's brother Willie was in prison for killing a white man.) The father was a kindly old soul who introduced me to a large group of friends, neighbors, and relatives as "This is Ellsworth's wife." I didn't bother to contradict him and they probably all thought I was colored, anyway. Mr. Johnson took the whole troupe of us to the colored section of Crystal Beach and bought us ice cream in honor of the occasion.

Bumpy left the South when he was a boy. I never asked why, but I can imagine that his fierce, visceral pride of race was a quality that early got him into trouble. "Down home, you know, we used to say, 'Nigger, nigger, never die, Black face and shiny eye, Georgia cracker, chew tobaccer, Spit right in my eye.' They ain't *nobody* ever spit in *my* eye." He told me that he was a second-story man when he was fifteen. "What's that?" "It means, baby, that I used to climb in upstairs bedroom windows." "You mean you were a *bur-glar?*" My tone was horrified. I'd never seen one, outside of the movies, much less met one. "Yeh, yeh, I was a burglar. I was a stickup gunman when I was sixteen." At seventeen he was sent to Elmira Reformatory but his stay there apparently had no rehabilitating effect. "Two hours after I was on the street I was on a heist."

From then on, he spent about as much time behind bars as he did on the outside and his literary tastes improved from Ella Wheeler Wilcox poems in his early days ("I had the book and everybody else was copying down his favorite poems and learnin' 'em by heart") to Thomas Paine's *The Rights of Man* and a life of Robespierre, both of which I sent him in prison, at his request. In jail, he was an avid reader, studied history and philosophy, and became an expert chess player. He never learned, however, to curb his temper or to bow his head to any man. "Any dumb gorilla can beat up people," I told him. "All right. Sure I'm a thief and a pimp and a hood. What would you have me do? Go down to Grand Central Station and carry bags for dimes, or go back to Africa and take my pants off and run around in the jungle? Lucky Luciano can live at the Waldorf but it don't matter how much money I got, I can't walk in there and get me a room. Every time I look in the mirror I see the same black face. I ain't no Paul Robeson and I ain't no Angelo Herndon.

I'm just an awful lot of black. All I got to do is stay black and die. White people ain't left us nothin' but the underworld. They made hoods and thieves outta every nigger that's got any guts."

In September, 1937, he was arrested on a charge of stabbing a man. He wrote me a note in which he said that his cell in the Tombs was as cold as a black whore's heart, adding, however that he supposed there's no place like home, be it ever so humble, and as far as he was concerned, being back in the Tombs was like coming home. He said that if I wanted to visit him there, I would have to say I was his wife because I certainly couldn't pass myself off as his sister. I did make a couple of visits, and so, apparently, did his girls, all of us claiming to be wives, until one guard remarked, "What's this guy in for—bigamy?"

He was tried, convicted and sentenced to Sing Sing for six to ten years. The *Daily Mirror* said: "Harlem is in a state of rejoicing that his reign of terror is over." It was his twenty-first arrest and third felony conviction. I went to see him again in the Tombs before he was taken to Ossining. "They'll be calling me Uncle Bumpy by the time I get out," he joked. He served the entire ten years, three months of it in solitary the first year. He beat up a guard and was then sent to Dannemora, known as the Siberia of New York State prisons. He was knifed four times in the mess hall the first day he was there. He was only permitted to write to relatives, so he claimed I was his sister. "My Dear Little Sister: I am developing into quite a basketball player. At first I thought that I would die of fatigue but I stuck it out. I received a letter from my lawyer in which he quoted 'Stone walls do not a prison make nor iron bars a cage.' If that is correct, then I have been badly kidded by someone. Your brother, Ellsworth Johnson. Number 94048."

When he got out, I saw him again, briefly, in the winter of 1948. I went up to Harlem looking for him because Condé warned me that I ought to get my letters and photographs back. I told him Bumpy would never do anything to harm me but he said, "You don't know, Helen, and neither do I, how ten years in prison might change a man. You're happily married and you have two small children." As soon as I saw Bumpy, I knew I had nothing to fear. I never saw him again.

Once, sometime later, I took the late magazine editor George Wiswell to meet him, but Bumpy had been picked up a few hours earlier on a dope-selling charge, although narcotics had been one thing he stayed away from. "It's a Federal rap and you just don't fool with them Feds." Many of his friends thought he had been framed because he tried to drive the pushers out of Harlem and he fought the Mafia. I don't know. Anyway, he served fifteen years, first in Alcatraz; later, when they closed The Rock, in Lewisburg. He came home to Harlem in 1963, when he was fifty-six years old, and was "welcomed like a conqueror," according to the *Amsterdam News*.

In 1967 he was arrested on a federal indictment charging conspiracy to transport and distribute narcotics. The arrest came after a movie-style car chase that began in front of his Lenox Avenue apartment house and ended on the Van Wyck Expressway. The agents believed he was on his way to Kennedy Airport to board a plane for the Caribbean. Their search of his car and person revealed no trace of narcotics. He was freed on $50,000 bail and the case was still pending when, in July, 1968, he died of a heart attack while eating in a Harlem restaurant with a friend.

Three clergymen and one bishop officiated at his funeral in St. Martin's Episcopal Church on Lenox Avenue at 123rd Street. He was buried with a rosary and a St. Christopher's medal on his folded hands; there were more than seventy elaborate floral pieces; singer Billy Daniels sang "My Buddy"; the church was jammed and crowds lined the streets outside, while police officers stood on surrounding rooftops. The church's pastor emeritus, the Reverend John Johnson (no relation to the deceased), said in a eulogy that the warden of Alcatraz had told him that Bumpy was "an amazing man." Reverend Johnson went on to say: "He chose his course and he followed it with his eyes open. He had a code of ethics. He was not a coward and he never betrayed a friend. He had good manners and was generous to a fault. He decided early in life not to be a clown, a flunky or a beggar. He despised phonies and hypocrites . . . Maybe there was no other way for him to be a man. . . ."

Jimmy Breslin wrote a column about him, portraying him as a sort of Robin Hood. I wouldn't have said so, although, of course, he did spend fifteen years inside after I last saw him, which gave him plenty of time to do a lot of reading and thinking. Before I ever met him, Lewis Lawes, Sing Sing's famous warden, told him, "Ellsworth Johnson, you could have been a great leader of your people." He was, I believe, born too early. With his brain and his fearless spirit, he could have been a tremendous asset to the Black Power movement, if he had been a young man in recent years. I have no doubt where he would have stood in the struggle.

Ten

THE CASE OF THE NEAR-SIGHTED SPY

THERE WAS A PERIOD IN MY life when several people thought I would make a great spy. The first time this was broached, I was flabbergasted. A man I knew called me and said it was important that I meet him at the Washington Square Arch in Greenwich Village because there was something he could not discuss over the telephone. His tone was so urgent that I was curious, and I went. When I arrived, my friend was with another man who looked like an old grey mouse. The mouse said he was going to give me an opportunity to serve my country. It seemed there was a man living in the Ansonia Hotel, at West 73rd Street and Broadway, who was believed to be the link between Trotsky, then alive in Mexico, and his followers here. The idea was that I should take a room on the same floor, strike up an acquaint-ance, get into the link man's room and, presumably when he was not looking, steal his secret papers. I burst out laughing.

"You must be daft," I said. "For one thing, I'm not going to lurk around a hotel trying to pick up some character. I'm no good as a lurker. For another, I'm blind as a bat. I'd probably steal his laundry list. Who ever heard of a near-sighted spy?"

I convinced them it was a terrible idea and that was that. However, in the spring of 1938 I received an approach from another quarter, a request from intermediaries to visit the ninth floor of Communist Party headquarters on East 13th Street. I was not a Party member but I certainly was close, and when anyone said "ninth floor" I knew it meant top officials. The Spanish Civil War was still going on, and I felt more strongly about it than about any other international event before or since, so I would have done almost anything to help those who in my opinion were on the side of the angels. It turned out that what they had in mind was South America. I talked chiefly with a Venezuelan I was to know only as Ricky. Ricky had figured out that we were relatives because he was married to my second husband's first wife's sister. I pointed out that this was scarcely an intimate bond and anyway I had been divorced for two years, with my second husband married to his third wife, but Ricky laughed and made the stunningly inapposite comment that it didn't matter because all American women were frigid, pronouncing the last word with a hard "g."

He wanted to know if I could go to South America and get some information for them. I said I had never been there but would love to do so and was sure I could arrange a trip to write travel articles for various glossy magazines. What information was it he would like me to get? His reply floored me. "We want you to survey the canals in the south of Chile from a strategic military point of view." I gulped. When I started to murmur that I wasn't exactly qualified for this kind of task, he interrupted. "These canals could be very important in another world war. In the 1914–1918 war an entire German squadron hid there." "What were they doing hiding in the south of Chile? The war was more than five thousand miles away." Patiently, he explained: Vice-Admiral Graf von Spee's East Asiatic Cruiser Squadron of the Imperial German Navy used the canals as a base, slipping out to attack British ships en route to Argentina for wheat and meat, and at one time catching a British fleet and shattering it. In the next war, Ricky said, the nation that controlled those canals would have a military advantage. I told him I believed him but I didn't think I was the right person to investigate. "You will be fine," he said. "Besides, we don't have anyone else."

I arranged to write articles for *Vogue, Harper's Bazaar* and *Town & Country,* and these assignments secured me free passage on Grace Line ships. Baruch gave me letters of introduction to several American ambassadors and also got his friend Gordon Rentschler, president and director of the National City Bank of New York, to notify the bank's managers in various South American cities to give me every assistance. Armando Zegri, a Chilean journalist, gave me letters to friends in Santiago, and John Wheeler, head of the North American Newspaper Alliance syndicate, wrote me a To Whom It May Concern letter of accreditation. No one had an inkling of the true purpose of my trip, except Ricky and his comrades, who were unable to give me a single name or lead—with the exception of Chile, where the Communist Party was legal—because they had lost all their contacts through the brutal police-state repression of military dictatorships. They wanted me to track down, if possible, any underground resistance groups and report their analysis of the Axis (Germany-Italy-Japan) penetration of the continent. Ricky told me to write in code to a woman named Olga in Coney Island. I had to memorize her address and then destroy it. I was going cold into the unknown and I suppose I should have been apprehensive, but I'm afraid I took a rather larky attitude, and I sailed blithely off on the *Santa Lucia* on July 2, 1938, thinking that if my fellow passengers only knew what I was up to, they would be nudging each other and whispering, "Who is that beautiful international spy?"

I soon was on friendly terms with the most spectacular of the first-class passengers, Colonel Ricardo Astudillo of Ecuador, president of his country's railroad, who had been to

North America to buy second-hand locomotives. He was over six feet, looked like a cross between Victor McLaglen and Wallace Beery, and was a full-blooded Quechua Indian, known to his countrymen as El Macho (because, so they said, he had three balls), a hero of border wars, former Secretary of War, of the Navy and Aviation, of Public Works, of Education, *and* the Premier of Ecuador, all more or less at the same time. Intelligent and courageous, he had been adopted as a small boy by a white Ecuadorian landowner who gave him his own name and sent him to school, unheard of for the general run of wretched, poverty-stricken Quechuas, descendants of the Incas.

If I had any notion of traveling inconspicuously, it was dispelled at the first port, Colón, where I was met by reporters probably alerted by the Grace Line publicity department. This was to be the pattern along the west coast: front-page articles, photographs, even, in one paper, a banner headline. As the reason I was considered newsworthy was because I had written *Latins Are Lousy Lovers*, one might have expected hostility from the press, but instead the coverage was intoxicatingly flattering. ("Not only is she young and good-looking, but she has a magnetic personality and is extraordinarily quick on the trigger" . . . "Her lethal quality is that indefinable something which causes a man, even when out with his wife or the Number One Girl Friend, to stop dead in his tracks and drool . . .") Naturally, I lapped it up, but I also considered that it established my cover.

Colonel Astudillo was met at Colón by Colonel Olmedo Alfaro, Ecuadorian consul general, and, instead of going through the canal on the ship, the three of us crossed the isthmus by train to Panama City, where Alfaro had arranged for us an audience with President Arosemena, following which he took us to meet the governor and then led us on a dizzy tour of the military barracks, the jail, two hospitals and the air base, ending with a drive into the countryside, past guayacan trees in bloom and acres of yellow frangipani, to see the ocean and a pile of old stones where, so he informed us, came Balboa once upon a time, exclaiming,

"How *pacific* are your waters!" When we returned to Panama City, the newspapers were out, proclaiming my arrival, as a result of which an ex-president, Harmodio Arias (in Panama every third president is named Arias, or so it seems), gave a champagne supper in my honor in a local grog shop somewhat inelegantly called the Balboa Beer Garden. He had practically convened a special session of congress, and I was the only woman among thirty-six men. The various senators and congressmen kept leaping to their feet to propose gallant toasts, the gist of which was how much my visit was going to further the cause of international good will. The supper ended on this high diplomatic note, and Astudillo and I went off to inspect the night clubs, rejoining our ship the next day. (Eighteen years later, when I returned to Panama to do a piece for *Esquire*, the telephone rang in my suite at the El Panamá Hotel and a male voice said, "The last time you were in Panama I was a little boy. Now I am grown up and I would like to meet you." It was Harmodio Arias' son. I didn't see him but I like to think that I had become a family legend.)

Astudillo left the ship at the lovely, glistening port of Guayaquil. I went ashore with him and he introduced me to a group of railroad executives, one of whom ceremoniously presented me with a complete set of Ecuadorian railway timetables, something I had always wanted. We also visited the navy, which at that time consisted of two ships. I inspected only the flagship, the *Eloy Alfaro*, formerly an American millionaire's yacht. The crew was lined up at attention when we came on board, and the officers, who were very handsome, took me to the lounge, where they plied me with champagne and cookies, played their jazz records, and kept trying to shoo away the sailors, who were peeking in the portholes and winking at me. Although I hadn't gleaned much heavy information from these parergal flings, I dutifully mailed a "Dear Olga" letter, the first and the last, before Astudillo took me back to the ship. He wanted me to give him my contraceptive diaphragm so he could have it copied and introduce its use among the Indi-

ans. I refused this historic opportunity to control the Ecuadorian birth rate, selfishly insisting that I might need it on
the rest of my trip, an idea that sent the colonel into such a
snit that I promised I would stop off on my return voyage.

Things were duller on shipboard without him. The next
port was in Peru, where we didn't stay long enough for me
to do my Mata Hari impersonation, which was just as well
because Peru was then one of the worst of the military dictatorships, with the infamous distinction of having pioneered
in the Americas the use of electric-shock torture on the geni-
tals of political prisoners. Haya de la Torre, head of the
anti-government Aprista movement, was in hiding, and all
overt opposition to the regime had been crushed. A United
States ambassador who happened to mention the word
democracy in a radio speech was promptly cut off the air,
without his knowledge, so that he went on and finished his
speech but nobody in Peru heard him. I learned this much
over pisco sours at the San Isidro Country Club in Lima,
where my informant, a journalist, was careful to keep his
voice low, as in those days a man was considered a dangerous radical in Peru if he thought people ought to have the
vote, and by people he need not mean peasants or workers
but just the middle class.

In Arica, our first Chilean port, we took on a few special
passengers: Norman Armour, the American ambassador, and
some rich Chileans with whom he had been deep-sea fishing.
They were all very drunk and remained in that state the
rest of the voyage, so I didn't present my letter from Baruch.
I did so later, in Santiago, and attended a party at the
embassy, where the ambassador's condition was the same as
on shipboard. I gathered it was chronic. His attitude toward
Chileans, with the exception of a few multimillionaires, was
one of contemptuous and patronizing condescension, as was
that of the National City Bank manager and also the latter's
wife. I went with the wife to a bridge party, all North American women, where the idea of scintillant conversation was
to discuss how ignorant and stupid the "natives" were. I
found this to be a prevalent attitude among our diplomatic

representatives throughout Latin America. The last thing they were interested in, or knew anything about, was the welfare of the common people in the countries to which they were posted. Their chief aim was to bolster the fascist few. Nor can I see today that our policy has improved much in the last quarter century, especially in view of the obscene alacrity with which we recognized the present Chilean junta, another shining example of what we call "the free world," meaning "safe for business." Our plunder of South America in modern times (and the methods we have condoned, or connived at, in order to achieve this) makes the conquistadores look like the Salvation Army.

I spent a total of five weeks in Chile. The *Santa Lucia* docked at Valparaiso eighteen days after we left New York, and if it had been one more day I would have jumped overboard, I was so bored with the cruise passengers. I took a train to Santiago and checked in at the Ritz. Itching for some action, I didn't even wait to unpack but went out on the street, found a newsstand, bought a newspaper I could see was Communist, looked up the address on the masthead, hailed a taxi and told the driver to take me there. "*¿Como no?*" he said, which is a Spanish phrase meaning, "Why not?" used in response to practically everything. (Ask a waiter to bring you coffee and he says, "Why not?" Tell him you want your bill and he says, "Why not?" Remark that it's a beautiful day and he says, "Why not?")

In contrast to the soporific shipboard life, the effect of dry land was so energizing that I galloped around Santiago that first day as if I were bringing the news from Ghent to Aix. At Communist headquarters I asked for the two men whose names Ricky had given me. It turned out one was a senator, the other a *diputado*, and congress was in session, but that didn't stop me. I went there, managed to talk to them during an interval, made an appointment for another meeting, and left them bemused, I'm sure, although I obviously endeared myself to Carlos Contreras, who was also head of the Communist Party, when he asked if I was a Party member and I replied, "*No, pero soy muy simpática,*" thinking

I was saying that I was sympathetic, but actually saying, "No, but I am very charming."

It was still afternoon when I left the parliament building, so I had a quick lunch in a café and took another taxi to *La Hora*, a newspaper in opposition to the government, published and edited by Anibal Jara (who later became Chilean ambassador in Washington) to whom I had a letter of introduction. He was a swarthy, burly man with jowls that suggested a perpetual melancholy, misleadingly so, because he was a humorous, friendly man with a hedonist's enjoyment of life. We chatted a while and he asked me to have dinner with him that evening. I left his office, couldn't find a taxi, had no map and no idea where I was, except that it was a long way from the Ritz, and, after walking around for an hour, realized that I was completely lost. Some spy. It was after six and already dark because July is winter in Chile. In desperation I walked up to a house and rang the bell. The family was at tea but when I explained my predicament they insisted that their little boy would take me back to my hotel, which he did, a long trolley ride for which he wouldn't let me pay, and delivered me at the Ritz at seven-thirty. I dashed to my room and changed for dinner. Then I sat and waited. When it got to be after ten o'clock, with no sign of Anibal, I decided that he must have come before I returned to the hotel. I was starting to undress when the phone rang. He was in the lobby. He hadn't mentioned any hour and I didn't know that dinner in Chile, for those who could afford to eat, began around ten at night, probably because "tea" consisted of hors d'oeuvres, chicken, three or four vegetables, sandwiches, salad, pie, cakes, ice cream, candy, nuts and fruit.

The weeks that followed were hectic. Juggling engagements with bankers, ambassadors and their group, with Anibal and his friends, and with the Party, I was busily buzzing around Santiago like some demented bee. A presidential election campaign was in progress, in which the Popular Front candidate, Pedro Aguirre Cerda, congressman and lawyer, former Minister of Education and ex-professor of economics at the University of Chile, was running against the enormously rich Gustavo Ross, who was backed by President Alessandri and the notorious Chilean oligarchy of "fifty families." The campaign against Aguirre Cerda was bitter and vicious. Everyone expected trouble and Anibal bought a machine gun to put on the roof of his building. I went to interview General Carlos Ibañez, a semi-fascist ex-president (contrary to some reports, the present Chilean junta is not the first military government: General Ibañez was head of state in 1933 and again in 1935) who we expected might lead some sort of coup. He received me haughtily, demanding to know why North American newspapers would send someone so young and, worse yet, a woman. (And when at the home of a friend I met Pablo Neruda, a Communist and even in those days a famous poet, he asked me peevishly, "Why didn't they send Hemingway or Steinbeck?")

Anibal arranged for me to interview President Alessandri, but in a fit of insane capriciousness I refused to keep the appointment and, instead, made Anibal take me around to record shops where I listened to *cuecas* and popular Chilean songs. When I got back to the Ritz that night, my room had been ransacked by the *carabineros*, with suitcases broken open, everything turned over. I called Anibal, packed up, checked out of the hotel and moved to his house. He said I would be safer there and, besides, he had central heating. The next night we were at a dinner party when he received a telephone message that the President had expelled me from Chile for insulting him by failing to keep my appointment. Anibal called Alessandri's secretary and made it clear that he would consider it a personal affront if I were expelled. His newspaper had considerable prestige, so the expulsion order was canceled.

Meanwhile, I knew that sooner or later I had to do something about those damn canals. I told Anibal that I wanted to see the southern part of the country for my travel articles. The lakes were supposed to be fantastically beautiful and there was great skiing in the south. He saw me off at the railway station when I left by sleeper with a ticket to Puerto Montt, intending to play it by ear from there. Almost everything near Puerto Montt was German-dominated. German was the language; schools were taught in German, not Spanish; young men born in Chile went to Germany to do military service and then returned; the Nazi salute and "*Heil Hitler!*" were customary; the area was openly pro-Nazi. Krupp had made a trip there to sign an agreement giving him the valuable forest concession. In the adjoining location in Argentina, cheek by jowl with Chile, Fritz Thyssen, steel baron of the Ruhr and, like Krupp, a top Hitler backer, had made a visit to the coal mines the previous year and air bases were under construction there. I learned all this in Santiago and as I thought about it on the train I couldn't imagine how I could find out much more, especially as my knowledge of German was limited to a few blunt expletives mischievously taught me by George Grosz on a blind date when he first arrived in New York from Germany in 1932 and J. P. McEvoy had called me and asked me to take Grosz beer drinking. Certainly, I couldn't see myself asking questions about the strategic military significance of the canals! The more I pondered my mission, the more it appeared absolutely ludicrous. The next day I got off at Talca, a third of the way to my destination, spent the night in a small hotel, and took a train back to Santiago. I told Anibal I had changed my mind because I was freezing, which was no lie, as in the Talca hotel I went to bed with all my clothes on, including sweater and winter coat, and even then had to have the manager send up a coal-burning brazier, causing him to collapse with giggles because what I said in Spanish was "I am very cold. Please send me up a Brazilian."

I was queasy about staying longer in Chile, thinking that the way I had mucked up my trip south might look suspicious, so I left by plane for Rio. Our ambassador to Brazil was then Jefferson Caffery, known throughout Latin America as Señorita Caffery because of his predilection for stalwart young men. When I was living in Cuba, he was our ambassador there, and his favorite boyfriend, a mulatto pimp named Maceo, used to buy shirts and ties at El Encanto store and say, "Charge them to the American ambassador." This of course has nothing to do with diplomatic ability, provided they tend to their knitting and put business before pleasure. After all, we had an Under-Secretary of State who was caught *in flagrante delicto* on a train with a Pullman porter, and there are many other examples, not excluding Dag Hammarskjöld. The only disadvantage was that Latin Americans, with their mystique of *machismo*, had a tendency to feel insulted when we sent them ambassadors less than 100 percent heterosexual. Caffery was away while I was in Rio, but I saw other people from the embassy, as well as some rich Brazilians whose sister was married to a friend of Baruch's. The younger brother, I was disturbed to learn, had volunteered to fight with Franco and had been invalided home. He told me this while I was a dinner guest in his house, so I couldn't adequately express my shock at meeting for the first time someone who had actually fought for Franco. The older brother was nicer and even, to a minuscule degree, faintly liberal, a perilous attitude under the dictator Getulio Vargas, as Brazilian jails were over-crowded with people who had neglected to realize this. (*Plus ça change, plus c'est la même chose!*)

Prior to my visit, Bertram de Jouvenal, a French writer, came to Rio, was overheard in a café expressing opinions critical of the regime, and was hauled off to jail, an experience also undergone by a titled Englishwoman staying in my hotel. I was therefore wary of attempting to locate any political underground. I decided the best way was through a careful perusal of newspapers. Eventually, I came across a book review, the phrasing of which seemed to me an indication. (To the politically developed, a turn of phrase that would be unremarkable to an average reader will register a signal, somewhat in the way a dog can hear certain sounds inaudible to humans.) I looked up the writer in the telephone directory, decided against calling, in case his phone was tapped, and took a taxi to his house, giving the driver an address five blocks away. (I had the sense, this time, to buy a map.) I walked around for a while, fearful I might be watched, and finally went to the house. The maid wouldn't let me in, but she brought a lady out to talk to me. The lady said there was no one there of that name, I must have the wrong address. I explained who I was and what I wanted. She asked me to wait and closed the door, returning shortly with two men who spoke Spanish. (My Portuguese was atrocious.) We talked and then they, too, went back in the house. They reappeared to ask me to return the following day for lunch, but they had not admitted that they knew the man I was seeking. He was there all the time. When I went for lunch, he had asked some friends to meet me, lawyers, doctors, professors, writers, all of whom had been in prison and some of whom had been tortured, although they were about as radical as, say, someone like Arthur Schlesinger, Jr., today. Their crime was the advocacy of democracy. We talked all afternoon. I learned that the Communist leader, Luiz Carlos Prestes, known as The White Knight, had been imprisoned for years, tortured, and kept in solitary confinement. They had not been able to break him, although one of his associates, a German, had gone insane from the treatment, and a young Communist from the United States had been thrown from a window into the prison yard, breaking his back. The United States ambassador at the time, prior to Caffery, refused to make inquiries, giving as his excuse the archetypal American phrase "We have to play ball with the government." (Prestes never did crack and was eventually released during a more relaxed later period. The last I heard of him, some years ago, he was living on a ranch near São Paulo.)

From Rio I flew to Buenos Aires, where the National City Bank manager met me at the airport with his chauffeured limousine. I certainly hadn't told him I was coming, so he must have put Panagra Airways on notice to advise him if and when my name appeared on a passenger list. A solicitous host, he gave a luncheon for me at the ultra-fashionable Jockey Club and had set up such a full social schedule—the races, polo, dinners, a house party at the haci-

enda of Argentina's richest rancher, cocktail parties—that I
had difficulty extricating myself long enough to tend to my
spying. I telephoned a schoolmistress I had met on the boat
and through her met Eduardo Araujo, a popular congressman known as *El Joven Diputado* (The Young Congressman), a member of the Radical Party. In Latin America any
party called the Radical Party was, and still is, considerably
less radical than the British Labor Party today. Neither
socialist nor in any way Marxist, it was more like the liberal
wing of our own Republican Party. Araujo took me around
to cafés frequented by novelists and poets who were political
dissidents. Quite simply, we eavesdropped until we found
the right people and then I took it from there. I was told
to see a man in Montevideo, a Dr. X (doctor of philosophy,
not medicine), who knew the entire underground apparatus
on the continent. Uruguay at that time was completely
democratic. Twenty-five years ago, South America was filled
with repressive dictatorships. Chile and Uruguay were the
exceptions. Look at South America today. This is progress?

I went to Montevideo, a half-hour flight, and thought how
pleasant it was to be again in a free country instead of one
where people with frightened eyes walk the streets. Dr. X
was a charming, cultivated man, bedridden with some illness the nature of which I did not inquire. He received me
graciously, while deploring my government's policy of trying
to put down any democratic movement but supporting ruthless, terroristic dictatorships. I spent the afternoon there and
he gave me a comprehensive outline of the political situation
on the continent.

I was back in Santiago in time for an abortive putsch organized by General Ibañez. Even though we had been expecting it, the violence, when it came, was a shock. There is an
old Chilean proverb, "*Gata con guantes no caza ratones*"
("Cat with gloves on catches no mice"), and the troops
didn't handle anyone with gloves. At one point they fired
into a crowd of which I was a member and we all ran in
terror, trying to scramble and squeeze into buildings. I just
missed being crushed by the slamming shut of a huge iron

door as I slid past it, the last person to get inside. I was lucky. It only took the skin off my arm. A group of Ibañez' misguided young followers trapped in a government building were bayoneted in the back and caught in cross-fire even though they had their hands up in surrender. Thirty of their mutilated bodies lay in the morgue, where a friend of mine photographed them. I sent the pictures, with a report of the putsch, to Harry Luce, thinking *Life* might use them, in view of the impending Chilean election. He sent me a friendly cable, thanking me but saying that *Life* was not interested in Chile. In Buenos Aires I had told the National City Bank man that I thought there would be a Chilean coup, so he must have thought I had a crystal ball. He flew to Santiago to ask me about the coming election. When I said that Aguirre Cerda would win, he couldn't believe it because he knew, as I did, that the government candidate was offering 300 to 400 pesos a vote in the interior and 1000 pesos in Santiago, no small bribes when the wage of the average Chilean worker was one peso a day. I left Chile before the election, but my prediction came true. The masses of the Chilean people are stubbornly democratic, which is why I doubt that they'll placidly resign themselves to the reign of the present junta, although it was reported in the British magazine *Time Out* that the ineffable Henry Kissinger did assure his friend Julio Nuñez, close associate of the Edwards family, the richest family in Chile, that the United States would back efforts to overthrow Allende, "short of a Dominican-style intervention." I therefore assume that our government will endeavor to hearten the junta. Long live Kennicut Copper!

When I left New York I didn't intend to stay in Ecuador, so I had no visa for that country. The Ecuadorian consul in Santiago was a little old man who looked like Donald Meek in the movies. He was so near-sighted that he had to peer at all my papers through a large magnifying glass, which gave the procedure a Sherlock Holmes air. After I managed to satisfy him that I was not insane, not even feebleminded, not a professional beggar, not a menace to public health, had never served more than four years in jail (that's what the rules specified), did not traffic in prostitution, had never been expelled from Ecuador and was not Chinese, he said I could leave my passport and come back in forty-eight hours.

My friend the colonel met my ship in Guayaquil. He took me to Quito and into the interior, places like Riobamba, Ambato and Banõs, an amazing little town with hot mineral springs, located on the edge of the jungle at the headwaters of the Amazon. The drive from there through the Andes has the most magnificent scenery, rivaling anything in the world: a rich profusion of incredible colors and the sudden miraculous beauty of pure white waterfalls leaping brilliantly forth from the green and violet-blue rocks. The train trip from Guayaquil to Quito was probably the most startling railway journey on earth. I suppose today everybody goes by plane, but at that time the little train seemed to cling to the sides of colossal mountains, teetering along, crawling up a narrow track carved out of solid rock. At some points, twisting and turning dangerously, the train barely inched along, and the engineer got out and walked in front of it to see that the tracks hadn't been broken by ice thaws. Every once in a while he had to shoo the Indians off the tracks as they trudged along in their bright-colored ponchos, doing God knows what way up there above the clouds, the desperately poor Indians who stared at us with implacable, hungry eyes.

I met some of the politicians and representatives of other groups in whom I was interested. I don't know who is president there today but in the past they have had some interesting specimens, including an alcoholic one turned out of office by the army because, stepping forward at the airport to greet the president of Chile, he was so pickled he fell flat on his face.

It was twenty years before I saw the colonel again. In 1958, by then a General, he looked me up in New York. He had come for treatment of an old war wound, and in the hospital he turned on his radio. The program happened to be an interview with me. As he flatteringly told me, "I heard your voice and recognized it before they said your name."

After he left the hospital, he had dinner with my children and me and some friends in my Greenwich Village apartment. The mountains of Ecuador seemed far away and long ago.

On the ship home from Guayaquil there was a Czechoslovakian named Willy Eisner, who had been traveling around South America selling enamel for chamber pots. He and I and a young German stuck together, playfully calling ourselves "the German spy, the Czech spy and the American spy." Of course we meant it as a joke. The German, also a salesman, showed us a business letter from his firm, delivered to him at the first port. It ended with *"Heil Hitler!"* Willy and I teased him, asking scornfully, "They don't *really* put that on ordinary business letters, do they?" The German looked so miserable with embarrassment that we dropped the subject.

Our happy trio was disrupted when the news of Munich came over the ship's radio. Britain had persuaded Czechoslovakia to accept the Nazis, although the Czechs were ready to fight and Russia would have supported them if France honored her military pact with the Czechs. Hitler would have been stopped and there would have been no World War II, in the opinion of the military experts, including General Halder, Chief of the General Staff of the German Army in 1938. Nicholas Kaldor, Professor of Economics at Cambridge and British government advisor, has quoted General Halder as saying that the German army was totally unprepared for war in September, 1938. Her available forces were inferior to those of Czechoslovakia, without even taking into account those of Russia, France and Britain. The German General Staff (von Brauschitz, as well as Beck, Witzleben and others) felt Hitler was leading them into a military disaster, but their plan to remove him from power was ruined by the announcement of Chamberlain's arrival in Munich. Czechoslovakia had 500 tanks on the border and a striking force of 340,000 men ready for action and, according to General Halder, would have been capable of stopping Hitler single-handed. To Britain must go the underestimated infamy of betraying Czechoslovakia, persuading Beneš, her president, not to fight, and influencing France, as well, to refuse to join with Russia in resisting Hitler's advance.

I was so obviously distressed when I heard the news that my tablemates were puzzled. "We didn't know you were Czechoslovakian," one of them said. "I'm not." "Well—uh—why are you upset? I mean, why should you care?" This was the general attitude among the cruise passengers, but the rest of the voyage was for Willy and the German, far more than for me, a sad and worried one. I left the ship at Havana, where I was to be godmother at a Cuban christening, and arrived in New York two weeks later. Almost everyone thought Chamberlain at Munich had secured peace, at least for us and our European friends. With this "I'm all right, Jack" attitude, nobody gave a damn about the Axis penetration of South America. John Wheeler of the North American Newspaper Alliance said, "There's no interest in Latin American politics." He had expected me to write sprightly little pieces about Latin lovers or the picturesque peons—*the sun was setting as I rode my burro to the shores of Lake Titicaca where I ferried across the blue lagoon, carrying the burro on my back, pursued by quaint Jivaro Indians laughingly aiming their poison blow darts at me and chanting, "Pale-face make yum yum long pig stew . . ."*

In Rio, the *New York Times* correspondent, Brazilian but a naturalized United States citizen, had said to me, "When you go back to New York, please tell my editor Edwin James that all my dispatches are censored and that the censor puts his gun on the desk in front of him while he reads them." When I repeated this to James, he said, "Frankly, I don't believe you." "I promised to deliver this message and I have delivered it," I said, and walked out of his office. I did write five travel articles (*Vogue, Town & Country, Harper's Bazaar*). The editors were pleased and the Grace Line was pleased. Two years later I wrote for *Town & Country* a criticism of our Good Neighbor policy that was reprinted in the Spanish edition of *Readers' Digest* and evoked some complimentary letters from Latin Americans ("shows a marvelous grasp about conditions in Spanish America," "the most intelligent article I have seen on the subject," etc.). I never did do my report for Ricky, but Earl Browder, then head of the C.P.U.S.A., came to see me in my one-room flat in the Village and I gave him a detailed rundown on the South American political underground. I also wrote, at Baruch's request, an analysis of Axis activities there, which Bernie gave to Cordell Hull, then Secretary of State, and, some time later, a long memorandum which he gave to Nelson Rockefeller, then coordinator of Inter-American Affairs. It obviously made no impression on him, but you could scarcely expect the owner of vast latifundia in Venezuela to see eye to eye with the average peon on the need for reforms.

The month after my return, I spent Thanksgiving with the Luces at Mepkin. Another guest was Sir William Wiseman, head of British Military Intelligence in Washington during World War I. He made several cryptic remarks about my South American trip and I was puzzled. However, I didn't pursue the matter. Sometime later, in New York, I received a call from him. I was living with Jack Lawrenson at the time and wondering how I could get him to marry me. One Sunday while we were still asleep the telephone rang. It was Wiseman, inviting me to come to dinner. When I went back to bed, Jack asked sleepily, "Who was it?" "That was Sir William Wiseman," I said grandly. "He wants me to come to dinner at his house to meet the Duke and Duchess of Roxburghe." "Oh, stop kidding. Was it your mother?" Jack said and went back to sleep, while I lay awake thinking, "What will I wear?" It turned out the Duke couldn't come and I remember the Duchess chiefly for her impressive bosom. The other guests were Tex McCrary (not yet married to Jinx), the British head of the privately owned Argentine electricity corporation, and another woman. During dinner, Wiseman asked what we thought of Chamberlain's Munich agreement. The Duchess said, "Oh, it definitely means peace!" and the others agreed. McCrary said he had talked to "the man in the street," a phrase that always amuses me because it usually means taxi driver, doorman, waiter, or someone equally ready to say what he thinks the questioner wants to hear, if the latter is obviously well-heeled.

I said nothing, so Wiseman asked me directly. "I think it means war," I said. "Chamberlain saved Hitler from what would have been defeat. I think it is inevitable now that we will all have to fight him eventually." The others thought I was batty, except, perhaps, Wiseman, who looked at me sharply and said, "That is an interesting opinion." The next day he telephoned and asked me to lunch, where he said to me, "Have you ever considered intelligence work?" "Not seriously." "You could be useful." I told him there was not a chance. "I'm too lazy, too cowardly, too selfish. Besides, I'm in love."

My last offer in the espionage field took place at Café Society Downtown, the left-wing night club in the Village, where a meeting was arranged with a mysterious Russian. I was told that he was the top Soviet agent in the United States, responsible only to the Kremlin, and that none of the local Party people, not even Browder, knew of his existence. I was warned that I mustn't breathe it to a soul. He wanted me to be a spy for the Soviet Union at the New York World's Fair of 1939, which he evidently expected to be a hotbed of espionage and maybe it was. He looked like photographs I saw years later of Rudolf Abel, the Soviet agent who was exchanged for Gary Powers on that bridge. He wore very thick spectacles that magnified his eyes and gave him a sinister look, reminding me of a character in the 1934 version of Hitchcock's *The Man Who Knew Too Much*. (This was the first version, made in England, with Edna Best and Leslie Banks, not the later feeble remake with Doris Day.) He put his face close to mine and talked in a low, cold tone. There would be, he said, any amount of money, but I must realize that once I entered their employ I could never leave it. I would be at the World's Fair in Flushing that year; the next year I might be in China. He talked about "iron discipline," a bum way to recruit someone like me, and made it sound as enticing as joining the Wehrmacht. I was terrified. I went home and telephoned Jack, who had been in Boston for two months and of whose return I was beginning to despair. "I can't tell you what's happened," I said, "because my phone could be tapped this minute. But if you don't come home right away I'm going to be a spy in Flushing and then in China and you'll never see me again." I hung up. He came home and we got married and no one ever again asked me to be a spy.

Eleven

THE WATERFRONT YEARS

I MET MY LOVE IN STEWART'S Cafeteria on 8th Avenue above 14th Street. He was on his way to the men's room.

I was sitting at a table with my friend Irene, no longer a Condé Nast receptionist but on the editorial staff of *Glamour* magazine, and her husband Harold, a longshoreman. They had long wanted to meet Baruch, so I took them to his house for dinner. We left there at ten and, back in the Village, stopped at Stewart's for coffee. It was June, 1938. "Lawrenson's holding court there in the back, I see," Harold said. "Who's he?" I asked. "He's one of the founders of the National Maritime Union, a hell of a guy. No rough, tough, jolly Jack Tar type. Very smooth, with brains, guts. Terrific orator, a spellbinder."

A few minutes later he walked by our table, a tall, broad-shouldered, lean-faced man with a neat mustache and an unmistakable air of distinction that sometimes led people to call him "the poor man's Anthony Eden." He stopped to speak to Harold, who introduced him. When he came back from the Gents, instead of returning to his own table, he sat down with us. When we left, he walked us home to West 12th Street and promised to come to a party we were giving to raise money for The Shape Up, the rank-and-file publication of the reform group within the ILA (International Longshoremen's Association). Harold was astounded. "I never saw him pay that much attention to a girl," he said, after we were inside the building where I had a one-room flat on the same floor as their apartment. "Lawrenson doesn't run after girls. He doesn't have to. All he has to do is stand still and wait for them to throw themselves at him."

I said he wasn't my type.

He showed up at our fund-raising party but I was too occupied playing co-hostess to pay attention to him and not long afterward I sailed for South America, without giving him a thought. In fact, I forgot about him. Things were different on his part. All that summer he hung around New York. Years later, his closest friend told me that when he asked Jack why he didn't ship out, the answer was that he was waiting for me to come back from South America.

I had been home a week in October when I went with Harold and Irene and another couple to the Welcome Inn, a lively bar on Sixth Avenue, frequented mostly by merchant seamen. Jack's friend was there and he went to the telephone booth and called Jack at home. "She's back. She's here." In a short time, Jack showed up, casual, controlled, aloof, as always. He spoke to me briefly, then went to the bar to join friends. An hour or so later, he came back and had a beer with us. That was all. But the next afternoon he telephoned me and asked if I'd care to meet him for a drink. I did. We began at 5:00 P.M., went to the Turf Club in Harlem at 4:00 A.M., and ended up in my flat at dawn. I missed a dinner engagement and the theater and I didn't care. I didn't even bother to telephone to cancel them. I think I knew from that night on that I'd rather be miserable with him than happy with anyone else. There was no other way. He was I, and I was he, to an extent we both realized and often commented on in the next nineteen years. Our reactions, whether intellectual or emotional, were identical. Our standards, our values, were the same. We thought alike about everything: politics, people, books, films, theater, paintings, bars, fashion, cats, even climate. Most couples disagree in some areas. We didn't. Nor were we ever bored with each other. I don't mean that it was roses all the way, because it certainly wasn't. There was tension, anxiety, heartache, with nagging and tears from me. Ireland sober is Ireland free. "Did you swear on your mother's grave," I once demanded in exasperation, "that you'd never leave a bar before closing time?" But always, underneath, as we both knew, was an indestructible bond.

My life for the next dozen years was to be bound up with the waterfront. Actually, the connection had begun five years earlier, when I was on *Vanity Fair* and became interested in the longshoremen. Irene and I were sharing a flat when she met Harold at a party. They fell in love and were married. He had had a variety of odd jobs: merchant seaman, carpenter, walk-on actor, model for life classes at the Art Students League. Through a friend of mine, a port captain in the mercantile marine, I got him a job on the docks. It wasn't long before he met Sam, a quiet, dedicated man who was trying to organize rank-and-file protest against the corrupt, gangster-controlled longshoremen's union headed by Joe Ryan, ex-streetcar conductor, ex-docker, a bloated, pig-like creature who ruled the waterfront by terror. The dockers had the highest accident rate in all of industry, and not just in their work. The union officials were gunmen and racketeers appointed by Ryan, often paroled to him direct from prison. They sold union books for whatever they could extort and permitted men to work only in return for kickbacks, a practice made possible by the shape-up, a method of hiring that consisted of two hundred to three hundred men lining up in a semicircle twice a day, waiting for the foremen to pick the ones to get work. Besides the kickbacks, members in many of the union locals were forced to pay back 40 to 50 percent of their wages in other rackets: they had to pay each month in advance to barbershops, but if they ever showed up to get haircuts, they'd never work again; they bought their groceries at exorbitant prices from certain dealers; if they needed money, they got loans at 20-percent interest rates; they even had to patronize particular liquor stores, bars, whorehouses. The gangsters' annual take from all these services was estimated at one time as $350 million a year, which included what they stole from ships' cargoes. There were never any union meetings or elections. From time to time small groups of brave men raised their voices in protest and died on a silent street or a vacant lot, by the bullet, the knife, the garrote, the club, or else lived on in that sick, shamed silence of men who have had fear beaten into their bowels. Sporadic official investigations caused a temporary tsk-tsk from the citizenry and accomplished nothing.

The shape-up system of hiring, which bred the corruption, was abolished in England in 1912 and on the West Coast of America by Harry Bridges in 1934. On the East Coast, as far back as 1916, Mayor Mitchell's commission to investigate the waterfront condemned the practice, as did one in 1937 by District Attorney Tom Dewey. Two investigations by William O'Dwyer, one when he was district attorney in Brooklyn, one when he was mayor of New York, failed to change the situation, despite reams of testimony about murders, mayhem, extortion, racketeering. The terror went on. "I have never heard of any violence on the waterfront," commented Joe Ryan, who went to eight o'clock Mass every morning, liked to eat at Canavaugh's, wore hand-painted ties, custom-made suits and silk underwear, and whose annual dinner of the Joseph P. Ryan Association was attended by New York City mayors, police commissioners, chief magistrates, district attorneys, Mafia bigwigs, high-ranking members of the Catholic hierarchy, shipowner executives and, usually, Ryan's close pal, William McCormack, a multimillionaire waterfront tycoon through his stevedoring operations, right-hand man to O'Dwyer, Knight of Malta, friend of

Owney Madden. True, in 1953 Ryan was indicted for stealing $45,000 in union funds, at which the union accepted his resignation and gave him an "irrevocable" pension of $10,000 a year for life, pin money in comparison with what he had salted away. He was succeeded by Capt. William Bradley, a bumbling tugboat captain, and the gangster element remained in control.

I came into the picture in 1933. We used to raise money for the rebel groups. We met them and their womenfolk in their homes or at small gatherings like the one I went to in Harlem with Harold, Irene, Sam and his wife, given by the Deep Sea Social Club, a group of black longshoremen who served for refreshment, I recall, a sort of liquid T.N.T. called King Kong. Some of the rebel longshoremen were members of the waterfront section of the Communist Party. Most were not, but they recognized that the Party members were leaders in the fight to reform the union. I used to go out occasionally with Dutch, a German who had been a member of the Spartacus Club back home in Hamburg. He had gone to sea in a windjammer at the age of twelve, later shipped on Norwegian whalers and then on steamships, but had worked on the docks since coming to America. "Dutch is our prop longshoreman," Sam said, at one of our fund-raising parties attended by several magazine editors and their uptown friends. "Go ahead, Dutch. Act tough. Spit on the floor." Dutch took a shine to me and told me, "Every day I see you is a holiday. My heart goes like popcorn."

My involvement in waterfront activity at this stage was largely confined to sympathy and extremely minor gestures. When Japan attacked China, we stopped wearing silk stockings and boycotted Japanese silkworms by switching to rayon hose. (Nylons hadn't been invented.) I still was not a Party member, but I could see that the Communists were the only ones who seemed to be doing anything to alert people to the dangerous events abroad. In 1933 a small group of my Communist friends (including Anne, an artist's wife, who was six months pregnant) went on board the *Bremen*, ostensibly as visitors seeing off departing passengers, and handcuffed themselves to the rails, displaying placards protesting the persecution of Jews in Germany. They were sent to jail for thirty days. In California, Bridges' longshoremen held thirty-five work stoppages in a vain attempt to stop shipments of scrap iron to Japan, for which they were frequently beaten up by police, arrested and jailed. In Frisco they refused to load supplies for the German ship, the *Karlsruhe*, and after Mussolini invaded Ethiopia in 1935, they tied up the *Cellini*. Any similar action was impossible on the East Coast, but my friends doggedly continued to mimeograph leaflets and pass them out on the docks.

After I met Jack the focus, as far as I was concerned, shifted to the merchant seamen, although many of the longshoremen and their wives remained my friends. In July, 1939, Sam came to our apartment. A friend of his, Pete Panto, had been mysteriously missing for two weeks. Panto had been organizing a revolt against gangster rule of the six Italian longshore union locals in the Red Hook section of Brooklyn. The last meeting he called was attended by 1,200 men. One evening he received a telephone call. With him in his rooming house at the time was the brother of his fiancée Alice, to whom he was to be married the following week. Panto told him that he had to meet two men and that if he didn't show up by ten o'clock the next morning, the brother should notify the police and also the rank-and-file committee he had organized. There had been no trace of him. A Citizens Committee, headed by Marcy Protter, a Brooklyn lawyer who represented the Panto group, went to see O'Dwyer to ask him to investigate the disappearance. The then Brooklyn District Attorney accused Protter of merely seeking publicity for the committee and called his information "fiddle faddle." Sam wanted to know if I could think of any way to bring the case to the public. I called and wrote to several radio program producers and one of them was interested. I wrote a basic script and arranged for the radio men to meet Panto's mother and his fiancée, who both agreed to appear on the program. They came to the studio for preliminary talks but on the day of the program rehearsal they didn't show. A hasty trip to Brooklyn revealed that they had been threatened and were obviously terrified. They refused to appear on the program and it was dropped.

In January, 1941, nearly a year and a half later, Panto's body was found in a quick-lime pit in Lyndhurst, New Jersey. He had been trussed up and garrotted, strangled with wire. The location of the grave was disclosed by Abe Reles, a member of Murder, Inc., who also described eighty-four other murders. According to Reles, Panto was murdered by Albert Anastasia, Mendy Weiss and James Ferraco. Albert Anastasia was the head of the waterfront section of Murder, Inc., which in itself was a subsidiary of that great under-world organization in which Frank Costello, erstwhile kew-pie doll manufacturer and habitué of The Colony, and Joe Adonis were the upper crust. Reles said the gorilla who did the strangling told him, "Gee, I hated to kill that kid but I had to do it for Albert because Albert had done a lot for me."

Despite this testimony and the finding of the body, District Attorney O'Dwyer kept Reles in custody for eighteen months and never pressed for an indictment of Anastasia. Three other Panto case witnesses who had agreed to testify were murdered and Reles, while guarded by police in the Half Moon Hotel in Coney Island, was killed by a fall from a window. O'Dwyer sadly remarked that his "perfect case" had gone out the window with him, although the Reles testimony was corroborated by a fellow member of Murder, Inc., Allie Tannenbaum. His statement naming Albert Anastasia was simply filed away and no action taken. At a later Crime Commission hearing, Joseph Hanley, who had been Assistant District Attorney at the time, swore under oath that O'Dwyer ordered him off the case. The Anastasia brothers continued to boss the longshore union locals, and Joe Ryan referred to the Albert Anastasia Social Club as "a crusade against Communism on the waterfront" and called Anthony "Bang Bang" Anastasia "a fine anti-Communist."

So that's the way it was. Men wrote books and plays and films about the waterfront murders and made money from them, but Panto's killers were never indicted, and the docks remained corrupt and terrorized. When Jack and I went to see Brando in *On The Waterfront* I had to restrain him from walking out, he was so disgusted. To those of us with an inside view, there were too many inaccuracies, omissions, distortions. A truthful film about labor unions has yet to be made. I believe it's a long time before it will be, if it ever will.

Jack was a year older than I was, born in Dublin in October, 1906. Despite the name, he was totally Irish. His mother was a Fogarty and her mother was a Murphy. His Lawrenson ancestor had come from Denmark in the eleventh century when the Danes invaded Ireland and were defeated by Brian Boru. I don't know much about his family background because his sister and brothers all told different stories. Nor had he himself escaped that mythomania seemingly endemic to the Celtic peoples. I once did a little mental arithmetic and then asked him, "How come you led the Irish Revolution at the age of ten? Didn't your mother object?"

As far as I can figure out, he left Ireland when he was ten, after his mother's death, and lived in London with his father, but under what circumstances or what the father did for a living I never learned. I do know, from Jack's seaman's papers, that he went to sea when he was thirteen, in 1920, on a ship called the *Prinz Ludwig*, and apparently on that first voyage he felt the call that has enticed men since prehistory. For some men, going to sea is a job. For others, like Jack, it is the necromantic mystery, the true vocation. I often felt that he never should have left. Living shoreside, I think he always knew what Jerry Allen in her biography of Conrad has called "the profound maladjustment of the sailor away from the sea." He didn't quit until our marriage. He sailed below, in the black gang, as wiper, fireman, watertender, oiler, preferably on tankers. With inverted snobbery, tanker stiffs tended to consider themselves a cut above passenger ship crews in the marine pecking order, and the engine room black gang above others. None of them wanted to be officers and they all loathed Navy sailors. They were the gypsies of the sea, the last of the romantics, fiercely independent. Jack London termed them "the alley cats of the world," and *Fortune* magazine said of them, "You are dealing, in fact, with the true proletariat of the western world, the homeless, rootless, and eternally unmoneyed. They are tough, knowing, free." This was only partially true. Their home was a ship. They spent their money in waterfront bars and shipped out with the slogan "One turn of the propeller and all debts are paid." They were true internationalists. They sailed the world; they drank and talked and argued with men of all nations and races; they knew the score.

They also were, many of them, surprisingly well read. While I was diligently reading *The American Mercury* at Vassar, Jack was reading it at sea and discussing the contents with shipmates. He also used to buy *Vanity Fair*, and there were few writers whose names were unfamiliar to him, even if he hadn't read them. Where he differed from his mates was in the poised, cool, superior, aristocratic appearance and manner that made him seem arrogant to some people but masked a sensitive and uncompromising idealist. Baruch called him "a zealot," but to me that conjures an image of some wild-eyed ranter, which he surely was not. Baruch also said that he looked "like an English lord," an affront to Jack's Irish pride, but it was true that his looks, speech and general bearing were so authoritatively patrician that even the snootiest headwaiters, although of course they didn't know him, thought they ought to. On the rare occasions when he left the waterfront environs, perhaps celebrating a birthday or an anniversary, we could go anywhere without a reservation, the Pump Room in Chicago, The Colony, "21" or El Morocco in New York, and Jack was immediately and deferentially conducted to a good table.

He was equally at ease in those places and in the rowdiest waterfront bars. He could also hold spellbound a packed Madison Square Garden meeting. *The Reporter* magazine called him "a brilliant orator and tactician," while John Cort, writing in *Commonweal*, referred to him as "that fascinating character, the intellectual, charming, and slightly sinister-looking seafarer whom they call 'Old Silver Tongue.'" He had a marvelous voice, deep, with no trace of brogue, but a well-bred accent that often disconcerted people or misled them. We spent one New Year's Eve with friends at the Café Latino and among the guests was Marcus Goodrich, whose book *Delilah* had been a recent best seller. Someone who didn't know us mentioned the waterfront and Goodrich launched into a vehement denunciation of CIO waterfront organizers, whom he called murderers, rapists, thieves, arsonists, thugs, "the scum of the earth." Changing the subject, he turned to Jack and asked, "Are you a writer, too? Or what do you do?" "I'm a CIO waterfront organizer," Jack said calmly. There was a brief, deep silence. Then Goodrich, rallying gamely, said, "Well! I think that calls for champagne," and signaled the waiter.

Jack was nineteen when he first joined a marine union during a brief shore leave in Baltimore. Four years later he became a member of the International Seamen's Club, a forerunner of the militant rank-and-file movement in the American merchant marine. From then on, he was an active trade unionist as well as seaman. He was elected Secretary of the National Strike Committee during the 1936–1937 seamen's strike out of which the NMU was formed, although not without opposition from shipowners, Joe Ryan and his goons, representatives of the American Legion, the ISU (International Seamen's Union), the reactionary union from which the rebels broke away, and the police. In New York, mounted police, whom we called "Mulrooney's Cossacks," trained their horses to rear up, pinning pickets and demonstrators with their forelegs. Twenty-eight men were killed and over three hundred wounded before the new union was formed. Jack's name as one of the nine founding members was on the CIO charter granted to the NMU by John L. Lewis, and his union book was Number 5.

In those first years, an attempt was made to destroy the new union by infiltrating shipowners' stooges, labor spies and agents of the Railway Audit and Inspection Company, a deceptive name for an organization that was one of two thousand similar groups in America which provided "industrial service" to employers, namely, strike-breakers, spies, agents provocateurs, strong-arm men, and union-busting equipment that varied from tear gas bombs to Thompson machine guns, all under the time-honored camouflage of "fighting the Reds." It was an old tactic then and it still works today. (Ask the Greek colonels, the Chilean admirals, the Brazilian generals.) Back in the nineteenth century, Jay Gould of Wall Street said, "I can hire one half of the working class to kill the other half." Depressing as it is to have to admit it, he was right.

According to testimony before the LaFollette Civil Liberties Committee, the thug agencies, of which the best known were Pinkertons, William J. Burns, and Railway Audit, at one time or another numbered among their clients some of the most respectable names in industry, such as Bethlehem Steel, Borden Milk, Curtis Publications, Frigidaire Corp. of New York, Pennsylvania Greyhound Bus Company, Western Union, even Quaker Oats and Campbell Soup. Railway Audit, whose NMU plant was a man named Ray Carlucci, was working for, among others, the Isthmian Line, a subsidiary of U.S. Steel, Standard Oil, the Grace Line and the Luckenbach Steamship Company.

One of the shipowners' paid agents, Walter Carney, wrote a confession while in the Tombs in which he said, "One thousand dollars were passed to Jerry King and S. Lemmon in the Standard Oil office on the 22nd floor of Radio City, on their promise to sabotage the oil agreement and change the leadership, as they wanted Jack Lawrenson out of the way." Jack had negotiated for the union the first industry-wide tanker agreement. At a subsequent meeting in a hotel room, King, Lemmon, and Frederick Phillips (a contact for the American Legion) were told "to get rid of Jack Lawrenson at any cost." Squads armed with baseball bats invaded the union hall on 11th Avenue, and there were beatings with tire chains in the Gulf ports. At least two men were killed, but at last the spies were exposed and driven from the union. It was ironic that many years later, ESSO of New Jersey offered Jack a well-paying job as Labor Relations advisor. He wouldn't have considered it for a split second. Popular with the union membership and respected even by his enemies, he had a profound, even stern, integrity. He was a man who could not be corrupted, or even momentarily tempted, by money, power, love, his personal safety, the security of his family. An FBI dossier on NMU officials, compiled during the late forties, and copied in part for me by a secretarial contact in their office, said of him, "Lawrenson is an incorruptible man." That he was. Arguing with other union members in our apartment once, he said flatly, "I'd rather see my wife and children starve to death." I knew he meant it, and I respected and admired him for it. I wouldn't have had him otherwise. Some men are men of inviolable honor and principle. Most men aren't. They're more flexible, as the House Committee on un-American Activities and similar groups were to make only too manifest in years to come, when not just the lowly seamen but also top Hollywood and Broadway celebrities ratted on their friends and associates. Contrary to Elia Kazan's sniveling paid advertisement in newspapers, proclaiming his patriotism, they didn't do it for the good of their country. They did it for the good of their purses.

There was nothing in the world that could have turned Jack Lawrenson into an informer or a fink. When he thought the Communists were right, he worked with them. When he thought they were wrong, he said so. He wore no man's collar. He had to do what he thought was right, even when, in the end, it destroyed him. His integrity was unquestionable but, lest I make him sound too heroic, let me hasten to add that he was otherwise somewhat less than a paragon. He never was on time for anything. Indeed, he seemed to have no consciousness of time nor any regard for the hours he kept people waiting. The thing was that they did wait. Oh, not trains or planes: he missed a lot of those. People waited. Those with business appointments, those with social engagements, even doctors and dentists. No matter how angry or frustrated they became, he always managed to carry it off. He seldom apologized and when he did, his excuses, even if not plausible, were accepted. He maintained in public a reserve that went beyond normal reticence. He was neurotic and Irish, a tautology, I suppose, if ever there was one, with all that implies, the best and the worst. (His favorite writer was Sean O'Casey, his favorite poet Yeats. He knew great portions of their work by heart.) And, of course, he loved, as I did, too, the fluid, vivid life and bonhomie of crowded bars, the tougher, the better. When he left the house to buy a paper or cigarets, I never knew whether he'd be back in five minutes or five hours or, in one case, five days. It was never a matter of other women. It was the lure of the pub, deep in his Irish blood, not for the drink itself but for the ambience, the easy, masculine camaraderie, especially strong among the seamen. They could stand at a bar for hours on end, buying rounds of beer, matching picket cards, swapping reminiscences of ports from Capetown to Odessa, talking union endlessly, talking ships. "The *Omacheechee?* She was an up-and-down job." "That faker's as phoney as a nine-dollar-bill. He couldn't organize a piss-up in a brewery." "I'm sittin' in the Cyclone Cafe in Madagascar when in comes this broad and she walks right over to my table and says, 'Hello, Fine and Dandy.' Christ, it was Hot Ass Annie from Liverpool." "The coal was slack and full of slate and that's what fucked the four to eight!"

He couldn't tear himself away, and I didn't blame him. Sometimes, too, he showed an almost suicidal flair for danger. On one of our first dates he took me into a waterfront saloon that was the hangout of the shipowners' agents who had been offered money to kill or maim him. Several of the goons were there and the atmosphere was electric with tension and menace. Blissfully unaware of the cause, I had a wonderful time. I suppose the only reason we emerged unscathed was because Joe Kay, a seaman friend who accompanied us, although admittedly frightened, had the wit to tell the bartender that I was a member of District Attorney Dewey's staff, and the word was passed around.

At other times, he could be infuriatingly remote. Clare Luce wanted to meet him, so she came down to Café Society on Sheridan Square, where Irene and I were giving another fund-raising party for the longshoremen. I had told Jack she was coming. She was sitting with a group of us when he strode right past our table and didn't even say Hello. He went straight to the bar, where he stayed with some other seamen and longshoremen. He never came near us. After Clare left, I stayed a while longer but then I, too, went out. He evidently saw me leave, because he sent a friend, Kitson, to stop me. "You tell him to go fuck his mother!" I shouted, livid with fury, and took a taxi home. He came right over. I was hooked and I knew it. He was, too, and he knew it. The difference was that he fought it. When he was in Boston during the tanker strike in the winter of 1939, he stayed on, even when the strike was over. During this period, Irwin Shaw called me and took me to the movies. I even remember which one: Sam Jaffe in *Gunga Din*. Irwin had met Jack, perhaps at that Café Society party. He was quite funny about it. He said, "I dreamed the other night that he was a midget." (Jack, a little over six feet, was several inches taller than Irwin.) I said to him, "Look. I truly love this man and I never want to do anything to offend or dishonor him." Irwin stared at me in disbelief. Then he said, "You dumb bastard, what are you going to do if he doesn't marry you? Go into a convent?" To everyone's surprise, we did get married. When he heard of the wedding, Harold's comment was, "Why doesn't someone give them each a gun and let them shoot each other?"

We were married in City Hall, with only three seamen present. Afterward, Jack and I spent the evening alone together in Reddington's, an Irish bar on Greenwich Avenue. We certainly didn't notify the press, but the *World-Telegram*, obviously short of news that day, ran a report and my picture on the front page, right under their banner headline, with a line over the photograph: Helen Norden Again to Wed—But No Latin. *Time* magazine announced the wedding in their Milestones column, spelling Jack's name wrong and calling me "sexational penwoman," while a Hearst Sunday supplement devoted a page to an emetic story entitled "Rescued!" (*It took Irish John to snatch lovely Helen from the blistering back-talk of the sentimental señors.*) I was thankful Jack left town the day after the wedding and was gone for two weeks, as he would have found the publicity too embarrassing to tolerate. When Condé or other friends asked, "Where's Jack?" I replied, "Oh, he's gone to New Orleans on his honeymoon."

Actually, he went to the second national NMU convention, where he helped draft the union constitution, generally acknowledged at the time as the most democratic trade union constitution in the country. All the convention delegates were poor and had to double up in cheap hotel rooms. Jack made local history by forcing his hotel to let him share his room with Ferdinand Smith, a black Jamaican seaman. The NMU was the first union to break the color bar in meetings in Louisiana, Texas and other Southern states. They also pressured shipowners into accepting integrated crews, called in those early days "checkerboard crews." Ferdinand, one of the NMU founders, with Union Book No. 2, was the union secretary for many years, despite occasional mutterings of discontent or envy from some of the union brothers of his own race, who at one time confronted him, chanting, "You like white ass!" Nevertheless, he was given a testimonial banquet at the Hotel Commodore in 1944 "in recognition of his outstanding service to labor, the Negro people, and the nation." Joe Curran, who five years later in his successful drive for dictatorial power was to connive at Smith's expulsion from the union, along with other "Reds" who had first put Curran in office and kept him there, was chairman of the banquet. Among the sponsors were Congressman Emanuel Celler, theatrical producer Kermit Bloomgarten, sculptor Jo Davidson, blues singer Libby Holman, Frederick Vanderbilt Field, Marshall Field, Mrs. Elinor Gimbel, Albert D. Lasker, José Ferrer, Langston Hughes, Adam Clayton Powell, Jr., and many others, all of whom seemed as horrified as Jack and I were when the orchestra burst into a medley of what they may have considered appropriate tunes, including "Old Black Joe" and "Swanee." We all tried to talk as loudly as possible, in an attempt to drown the sound.

No other trade union had such a mixture of social background. In most other unions, such as the miners or the subway workers, for example, there was, and is, a homogeneity of family background totally lacking among merchant seamen, who are of all races, all nations, with varying degrees of culture and education. This was especially true of the NMU in the early years, which had a membership of contrasting social strata, from poets to bank robbers, sharecroppers to professors, and at least one ex-Trappist monk. Our group hung out every night in the Welcome Inn, a home away from home, with "Mexicali Rose" the jukebox favorite, occasional knife fights or scuffles and shouts of "You politically undeveloped sonofabitch! You Menshevik bastard!" but for the most part an atmosphere of ebullient roistering. Everyone knew everyone else and whoever was in port at the time would come there and join us. The occasional outside stranger who wandered in off the street might not know what to make of us, but he was usually well treated, as long as he didn't unwittingly offend, like the insurance salesman who joined our table once, during a political argument, and made the innocent mistake of saying to Dominick James Gavin, startlingly handsome in a black turtleneck sweater, "I can see you are a gentleman," at which Gavin sprang at him, exclaiming, "No sonofabitch can call me that!"

Among the best nights were ones that Showboat Quinn was there. Showboat, a loyal friend to Jack and me both, was born in Towamba, a cattle station in Queensland, Australia, where his Irish great-grandfather had been sent as a convict for throwing a rent collector down a well. The family prospered, and Showboat was sent to Britain at the age of fourteen to attend boarding school. He never showed up at the school. Instead, he bummed around England, ending up with a traveling circus as cage boy, which meant he cleaned the animals' cages. Fired for hitting a lion on the head with a broom, he was shanghaied in Liverpool, working as a coal-passer on the ship. He jumped ship in Las Palmas, in the Canaries, worked for a whorehouse there, and then went back to sea. Apart from a spell as bellhop at the Lambs Club in New York and busboy at Reubens, he spent his life at sea, and a charmed life it seemed to be.

He was what you might call accident-prone. He joined the rank-and-file rebels against the old International Seamens Union and was almost beaten to death in Houston in 1935. "Four goons came in my hotel room. They kicked my teeth in and they kicked three of my ribs to smithereens. I crawled to a window and busted the glass. I grabbed a piece and yelled, 'The first sonofabitch that comes near me I'll cut his head off.' They left the hotel and I went to the hospital." He was shot at by goons in Port Arthur and again in Galveston. In Newport News, during the 1936 strike, he was stabbed in the abdomen by finks, for which he was sentenced to a year in jail for trespassing. He sued the Baltimore & Ohio Railroad for false arrest. The case was thrown out and so was he. In the 1937 strike he had an ear cut half off in a knife fight, and his chin and nose bore other knife scars. He had his throat cut in Boston and, en route to the hospital, said, "Tell the boys I died for the union." In New York, drunk, he fell out of a third-story window and broke his back. He was in a plaster cast for six months. Found to have TB, he was ordered to the marine hospital in Fort Stanton. Instead, he shipped out for Africa. He was arrested for picketing in Durban and fell overboard from his ship in Lourenço Marques. Back in New York, he walked in front of a truck and went to St. Vincent's Hospital, but only an arm was broken. He got in a fight, fell over a fire hydrant and fractured a shoulder. Somewhere, somehow, he met a rich girl who took a fancy to him and kept him as a pet in her uptown apartment until he got bored and split. The last time I saw him, he was rushing along 8th Avenue, wearing a motheaten fur cape. "I'm on my way to the North Pole," he said. He was understandably a legend among the seamen, perhaps because he typified the swashbuckling sort of life they liked to imagine they once had. Dauntless, funny, seemingly indestructible, he finally died of cancer.

Although there was no one quite like Showboat, there were others who came and went in the nights at the Wel-

come Inn: Low Life McCormick, who was arrested with
three other seamen in another foray onto the *Bremen*, where
they tore down the swastika flag from the mast; Ding Dong
Bell, who, before going to sea, taught a men's Bible class in
Pittsburgh and who met his doom when he walked out of an
open sixth-floor window, under the alcoholic impression that
it was a door; Red Graham, who put the "Internationale"
on a whorehouse jukebox in Norfolk and persuaded the girls
to display a sign reading "Only CIO men welcome here,"
and who once poured whisky on the wooden leg of the poet
Orrick Johns and set fire to it; Fitzsimmons, who, when I
first met him, discussed interior decoration and said to me
solemnly, "If there's one thing I know, it's chintz!" He was
torpedoed in World War II, but survived to serve as technical advisor to Alfred Hitchcock on *Lifeboat*, starring Tallulah
Bankhead, an act we never allowed him to live down. And
there was Big Dan McDuffy, of whom it was said that when
visiting red-light districts he used to pay little boys a dime
apiece to run beside him shouting "Big prick! Big prick!"
There were also the men whose names I never knew but
slivers of whose conversations have remained imbedded in
my memory: "I was in the U.S. Marines in '27 and '28. Leo
Berman and me. We was the only Jews chasing Sandino."
"My mother was a ballerina. She danced on eggs before all
the crowned heads of Europe." (Yes, that's exactly what the
man said.) "He's the guy who turned the bees loose in Gimbels." And so he was. During a strike of store employees, he
took a large brown paper bag filled with bees into the store
and emptied them out, causing shrieking women shoppers
to flee onto 34th Street and Broadway from every exit.

Our closest friends were No Pants Jones, good-looking,
easygoing, bright and witty; Moe Byne, a quiet Lithuanian
who caught the old Joe three times from black whores in
Zanzibar and who usually sat in a back booth at the Inn,
playing pinochle; Fine and Dandy, who sometimes brought
a strange blond girl named Lily Prime, a name that seemed
to fit her pale, disdainful, offbeat beauty; and Kitson, who
would, I believe, have given his life for Jack. His language

was pungent with phrases like "He don't know his ass from the Fourth of July," "There I sat, like a prick at a Polack wedding," "So I says to him, 'I don't mind your shoving an umbrella up my ass, but you don't have to try to open it.' " He referred to girls as "split-tails" or, even more picturesquely anatomical, "the bearded clam"; and men he disliked were prickeroos, as in "That prickeroo says to me, 'I'll make a hospital case out of you' so I tell him back, 'I'll make a morgue case out of *you!*' " When drunk, he went in for long recitations of old Wobbly songs that went on and on and on, verse after verse, a litany of radical folk heroes, although his favorite passage, recited with stentorian relish, was: "When children die by thousands in the mills, When jeweled hands reach down and take the gold their blood distills!"

Our drink was mostly beer, but gallons of it, per person. We would start around six and when the Inn closed, Jack and I, sometimes with friends, would repair to an after-hours place in a rickety tenement on Cornelia Street and drink until the delicatessens opened at eight in the morning and we could buy more beer to take home. When I was pregnant with our first child, I asked my fashionable, upper-East Side obstetrician, "What about drinking?" He wanted to know what I drank, and when I said, "Only beer," he said, "Oh, that's all right, then. How many beers do you normally have in an evening?" "About fifty," I said. He almost fell off his chair. It was true. In fact, it was probably an underestimate. Looking back, I am amazed at my stamina. If I had five beers today, I'd throw up or pass out or both. But back in those years I could keep pace with any man and out-drink many of them.

When the last call for drinks came at 4 A.M. in the Welcome Inn, it was nothing for us to order "Forty beers." The waiters would bring them and line them up on the long table in our booth. Of course, we didn't drink them all by ourselves. There would be a group of us, perhaps seven or eight. The manager let us stay until we finished every drop, a procedure sometimes accompanied by singing IRA songs like "Kevin Barry" ("Shoot me like an Irish soldier, Do not hang me like a dog"); radical songs ("The workers' flag is deepest red") and old-time I.W.W. songs, of which my favorite was:

> In the gloom of mighty cities,
> Mid the roar of whirring wheels,
> We are toiling on like chattel slaves of old,
> And our masters hope to keep us
> Ever thus, beneath their heels,
> And to coin our very life blood into gold.
> But we have a glowing dream
> Of how fair this world will seem
> When a man can live his life secure and free;
> When the earth is owned by Labor
> And there's joy and peace for all
> In the Commonwealth of Toil that is to be.

Jack joined in with his resonant baritone when he had drunk enough to overcome his customary restraint, and so did Lard Ass Jenkins. They were the two best singers. A lighter note was often injected into the repertoire by Deehl, a tubby little man who preferred less militant songs with lyrics like "I've got a girl named Annabella, She's got a cunt like an open umbrella." ("I once knew a girl who had one like a pocketbook," Harold said.) Deehl used to sail as busboy on passenger ships and was a radical by association rather than conviction. He liked to tell of a strike during which he was in charge of the food supplies and received a package that contained one can of sardines and a note, "With best wishes from the Staten Island YCL." (Young Communist League.) My favorite among his stories was when a passenger ship captain known as Bullshit Bower was advised by his purser that he really must make an effort to converse with the passengers at his table in the First Class dining room. Deehl, as busboy, overheard his initial effort at small talk: "The barracuda masturbates its food just like a human being." During World War II, Deehl went to classes and became a radio operator. As often happens, his militancy decreased as his wages rose. But I shall always remember him kindly because in Bremerhaven he met a one-legged whore for whom he felt so sorry that when he returned to New York he sent her a wooden leg.

The Pilot was a weekly newspaper written, edited and read by NMU members. A major section was devoted to letters from ships' crews, containing reports of meetings and resolutions passed. Along with demands for ice cream twice a week and requests for Palmolive soap, were diatribes against "scab-herding finks," "company stooges," "shipowners' rats," and denunciations of gas hounds (not to be confused with gash hounds) or "characters," as they were frequently termed. Despite their prodigious drinking bouts ashore, NMU members frowned on drinking aboard ship or even in ports during a voyage if it led to fighting or disruption. Thus, the crew of the tanker *Gertrude B. Kellogg* sent in a resolution that read: "WHEREAS, ex-Bo's'n McD. took advantage of his 230 pounds to bulldoze people and declare himself while drunk and beat up members of the crew, namely, three men, and WHEREAS, while this ship was in drydock in the port of Philadelphia, Tuesday, April 11th, he assaulted Roy Groft at 2:30 A.M. and ended by pulling a knife, waking all hands amidship and aft and throwing the ship into a state of confusion, and WHEREAS, his suitcases were immediately set ashore and he was put off the ship at 3 A.M., therefore be it RESOLVED, that we, the crew, thank Joe Stealan and Roy Groft for the efficient and effective way they exited the slave-driving bulldozing buckeroo bo's'n."

I have a special affection for the *Gertrude B. Kellogg* because we had a cat named Irwin who went to sea on her when he was scarcely more than a kitten. We gave him to a friend who was sailing on her and he became the ship's cat. Dogs are never on ships because they don't adjust to the seafaring life, but cats do, and seamen are fond of them. When the *Gertrude B. Kellogg* went into drydock for repairs, the crew took up a collection to send Irwin to a cats' boarding home until they were ready to sail again.

The Pilot carried advertisements of waterfront bars such as Moulin Rouge, "the Well Known Diversion Establishment on the Panama Canal," Mickey Mouse Bar in Santos, Brazil, and my favorite, the Itty Bitty Bar, run by "Marie and Margie" in Corpus Christi, Texas. Proprietors of these *boîtes* had to mind their p's and q's or they might find themselves boycotted as the result of a letter like this one: "The crew of the Nira Luckenbach would like to have published that the Friendship Bar on Twig Street in Tampa is unfair to honest seamen. During the month of May the proprietor of this notorious bar pulled a gun on three of the crew members when he was caught short-changing a member. This notorious parasite has shot at other seamen in the past but fortunately his aim was as rotten as his honesty."

The newspaper also carried world news of interest to members, union news, political resolutions from crews—the tug *Buttercup* was the first ship on the Great Lakes to go on record for the freedom of India—and reports of disasters, such as the fate of the sand dredge *Nevasink*, which sank with all hands. At one period I wrote a weekly column about the NMU Ladies Auxiliary, which I helped to organize and for which I drafted the original constitution. Seamen's wives, like their husbands, were a mixed bag. They included writers, social service workers, prostitutes, teachers, factory workers, librarians, domestic workers, as well as housewives. The organizing group met several times at my place, where I served coffee and Fig Newtons and from one of whom, I'm afraid, Jack and I caught crabs. That was the only source we could figure, as the embarrassing little *Phthirius pubis* appeared following a meeting where several of the members used our bathroom.

The main objective of the Ladies Auxiliary was not social, but to acquaint women relatives of seamen with the aims of the union and get them involved. In the beginning, the NMU was the most democratic and progressive of all trade unions. Every member was free to speak his mind, and the slogan "An injury to one is an injury to all" was taken literally. During those halcyon early years, before it became regimented like other unions and arbitrarily dominated by venal old men, the NMU was always in the vanguard of the labor movement, in the fight against any form of racial prejudice, in the antifascist struggle. When the North American Committee for Spanish Democracy wanted to send a relief ship in 1937 with supplies for the Spanish government, they came to the NMU for a crew. The ship, the *Erica Reed*, sailed with a crew of all NMU volunteers. They were bombed by fascist planes in the Barcelona harbor but got away. More than a thousand seamen went to Spain to fight against Franco. The Abraham Lincoln Brigade members I knew personally were all NMU men who believed that the defense of democracy lay on the Ebro.

During World War II, members of Colonel Wild Bill Donovan's OSS, the forerunner of the CIA, interviewed the NMU Spanish vets, questioning them in a pathetically naïve attempt to learn their "motivation." *What* made them fight with such dedicated determination? *Why?* The earnest Secret Service men were truly puzzled. They could have understood soldiers fighting in a foreign civil war as mercenaries, but this was something alien to their comprehension. Still, they recruited some of the NMU vets as volunteers to be parachuted into Yugoslavia on behalf of the Allies.

Over six thousand merchant sailors were killed at sea in World War II. They were blown to bits in explosions, drowned, burned to death in seas of flaming oil from torpedoed tankers. Many died from starvation and exposure on rafts and in lifeboats. They were being torpedoed before America entered the war, at a time when our ships carried no guns, when lifeboats were not equipped with food and supplies, and there were no destroyer convoy escorts. The seamen could have made three times the money by working in shipyards or war industries, but they stuck to the sea, carrying the vital supplies. The shipping companies made millions. When a ship was sunk, the shipowner collected insurance, paid for by the government. In June, 1946, Senator George Aiken of Vermont and Representative Richard Wigglesworth of Massachusetts asked for an investigation of the Maritime Commission and the War Shipping Administration, after the U. S. Comptroller General reported that over $8 billion of their funds were not properly accounted for. Nothing came of it. On the other hand, when a ship was sunk, the crew's pay stopped. Even if the men spent months in hospital, burned, blinded, or otherwise injured, they received no money unless and until they shipped out again. If the men were killed, their wives received $5000, but there was so much red tape that this took months to collect.

Many of our friends were torpedoed, one of them three times in twenty-four hours. Asleep in his bunk when the first torpedo hit, he was blown into the sea, swam a half-mile back to the ship, which was still afloat, and was torpedoed again forty minutes later. He found two shipmates swimming in the water and the three men held hands all night to keep from getting separated in the darkness. At dawn they saw an empty life raft and swam to it. A rescue ship picked them up and that afternoon the rescue ship was hit. Another three men Jack knew spent thirty-nine days on a raft in the South Caribbean, living on raw fish and seagulls, drinking their own urine. "Constitution" Gurnee, whom both Jack and I knew, was twenty-four days on a raft, the only final survivor of seven men. "Sharks was following us a lot. The second assistant engineer was the first to go. He stood up, said, 'Fuck this. I'm going down to the corner and get a beer,' and went over the side." When Gurnee sighted land on the last day, he had been alone for two weeks.

The war role of these men went unpublicized, except in *The Pilot.* I did what I could to remedy this. I wrote a radio play and articles for *Collier's, Harper's,* and an obscure magazine called *The American Seaman.* The *Harper's* article was reprinted in a college textbook of war writing, probably because it was the only one the publishers could find that dealt with the merchant marine. Also, with this same piece I became the unwitting contributor of a considerable amount of dialogue and some of the action in the film *Action in The North Atlantic,* starring Humphrey Bogart. The author of the film script had lifted large portions from my article, an act reluctantly confirmed by Warner Brothers' lawyer. My goal was not to make money out of the seamen, so I signed a release in exchange for a thousand dollars. "And what are you going to do with the money?" the lawyer asked. When I told him that I was going to buy war bonds for my children, he said, unctuously, "Mr. Warner will be so pleased." Mr. Warner ought to have been pleased, and the lawyer, too. I ran into a girl friend of the latter who told me that he confided in her that he had been promised a sizable bonus by Warner Brothers if he could get me to settle for $10,000. Oh well, they don't call me The She Wolf of Wall Street for nothing.

Probably my most useful contribution was getting Harry Luce to run an eight-page feature in *Life*, presenting the NMU members as the heroes which indeed they were. We were in the Luce car, on our way back to their Connecticut house after the Grace Moore party. Jack wasn't with us because he was in Detroit. Clare was dozing with her head on Harry's shoulder and he and I were talking about the dinner, during which Stanton Griffis had assured us that nobody was making a nickel out of the war, not even Eugene Grace, while Mrs. Lawrence Tibbett had said that we must all make sacrifices and she was cutting down on her servants. "I was in the kitchen the other day, mixing the salad dressing, and my butler said to me, 'I hate to see you doing that, madam,' but I reminded him that it was wartime."

Along this vein, I told Harry that Hermès was making chic leather gas masks for rich Parisiennes and Molyneux had designed clothes for the fashionable to wear in air-raid shelters. "It takes all kinds," he said in disgust. "Speaking of sacrifices," I said, "we had a friend named Blackie Castle who was eaten." Admittedly, this was a gambit difficult to ignore. He wanted to know what I meant, so I told him. Blackie had been at our apartment the previous Christmas Eve, when he helped Jack to put together an indoor swing for our little girl. He told us that when he was a kid in Ireland, his family was so poor that their Christmas dinner often consisted of bread and tea. "Once, I had an orange." He had served five years in the New Jersey State Penitentiary for shooting and wounding a cop during a night-club holdup. In prison he read Marx and Engels, and when he came out he joined the NMU. Once, between ships, he went for a ride in a friend's car and told him, "Drive by the State pen. I just want to see the old homestead once more." He stayed chatting with us that Christmas Eve, but we never saw him again. His ship was torpedoed and he was in a lifeboat with several shipmates. The others spent twenty-one days in the lifeboat, but Blackie, injured in the explosion, died after twelve days. We heard the story from one of the survivors. When Blackie was getting weaker, he called the bo's'n over and said, "There's no sense in all of us dying. I never was much good alive. I can be some good dead." He explained exactly how to split the back of his thighs and other details. As soon as he died, the bo's'n followed his instructions, and they ate him. As I explained to Luce, this was not the sort of thing we wanted publicized, although it was not a unique case, but we did want recognition of the war job the seamen were doing. He questioned me closely and said he would see that something was done. He kept his word. When the pictures and story appeared in *Life* in August, 1942, I sent him an appreciative note and received in return a telegram: "Am delighted you like it. Deepest thanks for inspiration. See you soon. Harry Luce."

During those war years Jack was the NMU vice-president in charge of organizing on the Great Lakes, where for twenty-five years the Lake Carriers Association had prevented any attempt to unionize the fresh-water seamen. The employers had a lot at stake. There were fifteen hundred vessels carrying iron ore, coal, grain, limestone and oil, among other cargoes, and the tonnage sometimes exceeded that of the Atlantic, Pacific and Gulf ports combined. Jack began his organizing drive in 1941 and won National Labor Board elections among Lakes seamen employed by Bethlehem Steel, Inland Steel, Jones & Laughlin, Midland Steel, International Harvester. His headquarters were in Detroit but he traveled constantly to all the Great Lakes ports. I visited him in Detroit, Cleveland and Chicago, attended meetings, met the seamen and their wives, and at the opening of the

NMU hall in Milwaukee, was one of the hostesses serving beer.

The toughest organizing nut to crack was Ford, whose company owned a fleet of Great Lakes ships. The Ford security chief, the notorious Harry Bennett, had successfully crushed any attempt to organize Ford employees on land or water. Bennett was an ex-sailor and ex-boxer who was brought to old Henry Ford in 1916 by Arthur Brisbane, the famous Hearst columnist and master of the banal phrase. According to Booton Herndon in his book *Ford*, Brisbane saw Bennett in a street fight and took him to Henry, who hired him to keep the unions away, a task he performed with the aid of a small army of thugs. He built up a spy network in every part of the factory and, as Herndon wrote, kept the workers in line through fear in "one of the most sickeningly brutal episodes in industrial history." Any worker suspected of harboring union sympathy was visited in his home by one of Bennett's goon squads and beaten mercilessly in front of his wife and children. Herndon tells of one case where a man who had no connection with the Ford company expressed interest in the trade union movement during a chat with a neighbor. The Ford thugs, out to nip in the bud such subversive talk, got his twin brother by mistake and beat him to death.

When Jack first met Bennett, he wrote me, in October, 1941: "He's a little guy. Thinks like a mobster, talks like one, but he's the last guy in the world you'd think was one. I spent two whole days beating his ears and finally he agreed to negotiate for everything he's got that floats. I've drafted the contract." As a result, all unlicensed personnel on Ford ships became NMU members. It wasn't an easy job for Jack, and potentially a dangerous one, but he did it well, with the immensely valuable aid of Bill Taylor, a handsome, quick-witted, cynical man from the United Automobile Workers. Taylor took me on a tour of the Ford Tool & Die plant where, as we walked along the narrow catwalk in this inferno of shattering din, I found it so unbearable that I could not understand how men who worked there could survive with their minds intact. People who have never been inside a place like that could not possibly realize the environment's destructive inhumanity. The wonder is not that men strike for higher wages, but that they can be persuaded for any amount to work in such a place.

I attended CIO conventions in Detroit and Chicago with Jack, who was a delegate. In Detroit, the delegates were singing "Hello, Joe, whaddya know? Old man Ford's got the CIO!" In Chicago I first met Harry Bridges. Jack, of course, knew him already, and later in New York he was to be a guest in our home on several occasions. The Bridges story is one of the epics in American history. No other man has had such an impact on the labor movement as this brilliant, shrewd, cocky, hawk-faced Australian ex-seaman, son of a prosperous Tory realtor in Melbourne and an Irish mother. Admitted to the United States in 1930, four years later he brought longshoremen out on strike in all West Coast Pacific ports. On what came to be known as Bloody Thursday, July 5th, the Governor called the National Guard, equipped with riot guns, sawed-off shotguns, revolvers, clubs, vomit gas. Hospitals were put on wartime basis. At the end of the day, two thousand troops marched onto the Embarcadero (the San Francisco waterfront) with machine guns and bayonets. Two pickets were killed, one hundred injured. Four days later, San Francisco labor hit the bricks in a general strike. Forty thousand men, women and children paraded through the city, eight to ten abreast, to the music of Beethoven's funeral march. Rich residents fled town and throughout the country newspapers warned that Moscow was trying to seize San Francisco. The strike lasted ten days. It ended when FDR appointed Archbishop Edward J. Hanna, of the Catholic archdiocese of San Francisco, as head of an arbitration board. The result was the first coast-wide contract in the industry, the hiring hall to replace the iniquitous shape-up, a six-hour day and a thirty-hour week. Three years later, Bridges formed the ILWU (International Longshoremen's and Warehousemen's Union), was elected president, seceded from Joe Ryan's union, and joined the CIO.

That was only the beginning of the Bridges story. For seventeen years the U.S. government tried to deport him, a process that involved five separate trials, two hearings before the Supreme Court, a resolution introduced in Congress to impeach Secretary of Labor Frances Perkins for her failure to deport him, and a bill passed by a vote of 330 to 42 in the House of Representatives, the Allen Bill, introduced by Rep. Allen of Louisiana, the first time in history that Congress tried to pass a law for the sole purpose of deporting one specific man. The bill died in the Senate. In a Supreme Court decision in 1944, Justice Frank Murphy said, "Seldom if ever in the history of this nation has there been such a concentrated and relentless crusade to deport an individual because he dared to exercise that freedom which belongs to him as a human being and is guaranteed him by the Constitution."

It wasn't over yet. In September, 1945, Bridges became a citizen and in May, 1949, he and his two naturalization witnesses, both officials of his union, were indicted for criminal fraud, based on the fact that when asked during the naturalization proceedings if he belonged to the Communist Party or ever had belonged, Bridges replied, "I have not. I do not." He was tried in San Francisco, where paid government witnesses testified against him. His citizenship was revoked and he was sentenced to five years in prison. His two naturalization witnesses received sentences of two years each, and even his lawyers received jail sentences. Again, his case went to the Supreme Court, which set aside the sentences in June, 1953, and restored his citizenship. Two years later, he was again arrested and stood trial on the same charge, this time a civil action. (The time before had been a criminal fraud action.) To his credit, Judge Louis Goodman threw out the charges, and the U. S. Department of Justice finally gave up.

For nearly twenty years Bridges had been under constant surveillance by police, the FBI and private operatives. Every telephone he used was tapped; his hotel rooms were bugged. At one period, an attempt was even made to frame him on

a murder charge, with perjured testimony and evidence con-
sisting of a set of dentures found in a lake and said to
belong to the murder victim. The frame-up collapsed when a
dance-hall girl admitted that she had driven the supposed
victim to the airport and watched him board his plane out
of town. Because of her refusal to go through with her part
of the frame, she was brutally beaten up, nose smashed,
teeth knocked out, ribs broken. "I couldn't bring myself to
lie about Harry Bridges," she said. "My brothers and my
father belong to his union."

Naturally, the two decades of persecution made him a
trade union hero. A favorite record on the jukebox of The
Anchorage, a bar opposite the NMU headquarters in New
York, began, "Oh the FBI is phoney, the bosses they are
scared. They can't deport six million men, they know, And
we're not going to let them send Harry over the seas. We'll
fight for Harry Bridges and build the CIO." It became a
collectors' item because it was withdrawn and in the subsequent recording the reference to the FBI was deleted.

Harry Bridges was not a card-carrying member of the
Communist Party for the same reason Jack wasn't when he
helped found the NMU. The Communist Party did not permit anyone to join who was not a U. S. citizen. I doubt if
Bridges ever was technically a member, even after he
became a citizen, although there was no question where his
sympathies lay. Nowadays, he is a respectable old labor
chieftain, lauded by shipowners and civic worthies, practically an Establishment figure himself, a far cry from the
Bridges of yesteryear. If he made any protest during the
Vietnam war, I certainly never read or heard of it. Ah well
—no matter what he may have become in his old age, no
one can take away from him what he once meant to American labor and his contribution to it.

A man of totally different caliber from the beginning was
Joe Curran, for thirty-six years president of the NMU until
he retired in 1973 with more than a million dollars in
severance pay and pension benefits. It could not be said of
him that he traduced his principles because he never had

any. Always an oaf, with a mean conscience and bumptious manners, he was never one of our group, never even one of the Welcome Inn set. He was not a likable man.

According to profiles in *Time* and *The New Yorker*, he was born in 1906 on New York's Lower East Side. He never knew his father or his father's name or occupation. His mother was a servant and he doesn't know much about her, either. He claims to be Irish and has always played on it, but none of the true Irishmen in the union, the ones born in Ireland, believe that he has a drop of Irish blood. The Dies Committee stated that their investigations showed him to be of Ukrainian parentage, but their assertions were often less than gospel. The waterfront rumor was that he is Lithuanian or Polish. I would opt for the latter. From infancy he lived with a German baker in Westfield, New Jersey. Always slow-witted, when he left school at fourteen he had only made it as far as the fifth grade. In the early union years, he was inarticulate and thought he could solve all problems by bellowing. He was the puppet of the Communists. They picked him to head the NMU because he seemed good type-casting: a rough, ignorant, truculent sailor, native-born, invincibly working-class. When he left school he worked as an office boy for Gold Medal Flour Company but started going to sea at sixteen. He was a bo's'n when, with prompting and priming, he led the 1936–37 strikes. A noisy man with a plug-ugly face, he stood 6' 2", weighed 217 pounds, had a lumbering walk, small, beady ophidian eyes, a broken nose, thick and straggly, a bald head and an ash-grey complexion. He was variously known as Ham Head, The Pope, and No Coffee Time Joe, the last because as a bo's'n he refused to allow men time off for coffee break.

The Party coddled him, flattered him, coached him. They picked a bright, literate girl, Dorothy Snyder, to be his secretary. She wrote his letters for him because he couldn't spell and he couldn't dictate. In the first years, she also wrote his weekly column in *The Pilot*. Other Party members wrote his speeches. When he first was interviewed for newsreels, the few simple words he spoke had to be printed on large cardboard signs placed above the camera. He does have an animal cunning and, over the years, he learned how to handle himself, although even then he would say things like "It ain't germane." Once he sent an official a telegram that read, "Must see you immediately at once."

He may never have been literally a Party member, although Foghorn Russell who was, told me that the merchant marine Party section used to be called The Travelers Club, and that he once stood right behind Curran in line to pay his dues. Certainly, everyone from the Dies Committee to the newspapers labeled him a Red and during one period Joe Ryan announced to the press, "Harry Bridges is here running the strike and Joe Curran is in Moscow sending him the money." Curran was indeed in Moscow at the time, being feted by functionaries, but he wasn't relaying any Moscow gold. In 1937, *Fortune* magazine quoted him as saying, "Communists make good unionists." Most of the other NMU officers, secretary, treasurer, vice-presidents, port agents, patrolmen (the officials elected to settle beefs for ships' crews), were Communist Party members, as was the union lawyer, Curran's own secretary and most of the other staff employees. His second wife, Rhetta, and her sister had both gone to Commonwealth College, in Arkansas, with my old Syracuse Communist friend Ann. If not Party members, they were certainly very close. Rhetta, a husky, red-headed girl from one of the Dakotas, formerly worked in a rubber factory in Akron, Ohio, and met Joe when she was going to sea as a stewardess. They named their only child Joe Paul, after Paul Robeson, who was the boy's godfather. (After he turned against his mentors, super-patriot Curran revoked Robeson's honorary membership in the NMU, an exaggerated gesture of disclaimer.) Furthermore, on one occasion in our Charles Street apartment, Curran telephoned William Z. Foster (head of the C.P.U.S.A. before and after Earl Browder), to consult him about union policy. I heard the conversation.

In view of all the above, therefore, I could scarcely believe my ears when, following his apostasy, I heard Joe tell Tex McCrary in a radio interview, "I didn't even know what a Communist was until after World War II."

The reasons for a man's ideological change of heart can be intellectual or emotional, but they can also be economic. Curran started at a salary of $100 a week, fixed by the union constitution in 1939. At the same time, Jack was elected chairman of a committee to organize all shipping companies not then under contract. His salary was $35 a week. He always denounced the inflated salaries of other trade union officials, the "piecards," and successfully fought any move to raise NMU salaries above the maximum of $150 a week for Curran and $125 for the vice-presidents. (He also argued that all officials should go back to sea for a year after a certain length of time in office, but this was never accepted.)

In the first convention after Curran succeeded in taking over the union and ousting anyone who disagreed with his dictatorship, including Jack, all salaries were raised, with Curran's getting the biggest boost. "These gains would never have been possible if Lawrenson was still in the union," he commented truthfully. During his last years as president, his salary was over $85,000 a year, plus an expense account, plus a Cadillac, plus other emoluments. When he retired with his additional million, of the 50,000 union members only some 28,000 were working, and *their* annual wages averaged $3,000.

His opponents claimed that officials had been raiding the union treasury and that large sums had been made in various real-estate deals. Curran and M. Hedley Stone, the Treasurer, an ex-Communist, were the only two who controlled the funds. They refused at all times to have the books audited by an outside public accountant. The takeover of the union was accomplished in an atmosphere created by the Korean War and the later era of McCarthyism. It was not without opposition, however and it is time to set the record straight.

Jack was not expelled from the union. Nor did Curran

oppose him because he was a Communist. Jack had been a member of the Party but had dropped out some years before, as Curran knew. Curran fought him and forced him out of office because Jack defended the right of Communists to be members of the union in accordance with the NMU constitution. He also attacked Curran's attempt to silence all criticism and freedom of speech in the latter's extraordinarily worded proposal to amend the constitution to deny membership not only to Communists but to any member who wrote or spoke, or who "inspired" anyone else to write or speak, anything which "discredited" any official of the union. In a speech to the membership Jack said, in part: "I am against the persecution of any member or official because of his religious or political views. I am for the right of every member to express his views freely on all questions confronting the membership, believing that such free expression strengthens our union and safeguards the union's inner democracy. I am against machine domination of our union, regardless of whether it is imposed by cliques, groups, political parties, or officials."

Curran refused to let *The Pilot* publish the speech or refer to it, and he illegally removed Jack from the duties to which he had been elected by the membership as vice-president in charge of *The Pilot*, Education and Publicity.

Booed at meetings which rejected his proposals, denounced by ships' crews, even faced with charges brought against him for violation of the union constitution and for misappropriation of funds, and presented with a federal court order restraining him from interfering with the elected officials, Curran turned to strong-arm methods and rigged meetings. He called on the police with the claim that the "Reds" were about to seize the union headquarters. Hundreds of police and goons covered every entrance to the union hall and anyone known to oppose Curran was beaten up and his union book yanked, thereby denying him his livelihood. In New York, Curran hired thirty hoods at ten dollars per diem, and thousands of dollars were spent hiring dumping squads in ports throughout the country. Even so, the ports of

San Francisco, Baltimore and Boston voted overwhelmingly against Curran, and the crews of many ships, including the *America*, largest ship in the merchant marine, went on record against him. He permitted no word of any of this in *The Pilot*. He called a meeting in the St. Nicholas Arena to oust Jack as vice-president, but, despite a phalanx of police and the goon squads, the membership voted to support Jack. As he walked to the microphone, he was given an ovation. He spoke for forty-eight minutes and finished to cheers and applause, with members rushing to shake his hand. Not one member spoke against him, with the exception of ex-Communist Neal Hanley, the secretary and a Curran supporter, a pitiful figure, trying to rig his conscience. It was Curran's first setback since he took over the New York port with the help of goons and cops.

A meeting called by Jack in Tom Mooney Hall in Astor Place on a Sunday morning was raided by forty Curran thugs, who hurled a traffic stanchion through the plate-glass doors and attacked with tire irons, knives, clubs, bricks, iron bars. Our friend Bob McElroy was standing guard on the ground floor. He gave a signal with the elevator bell and then, as the *New York Times* reported, "He put on a creditable performance of Horatius at the bridge against the invaders" until others rushed downstairs from the meeting to help him.

National elections were held in 1950. Jack won hands down in New York, where the voting was supervised by the Honest Ballot Association. In the other ports, however, members had to mark their ballots in view of strong-arm men. Jack was defeated, 13,301 to 8,353 by John McDougall, a Curran man from New Orleans. More than half the membership either didn't vote or else had their ballots thrown out by Curran men on various excuses, such as failure to seal the envelope with the right kind of tape.

Jack retired his union book. Obviously, it would have been suicidal for him to continue as a member. For two years we had lived in a vicious climate of menace: he was mugged on the street at night; Curran's goons tried to smash their way into our home to kill him; he received so many threatening telephone calls in the night that we had to get an unlisted number. What affected him most was not what had happened to himself but the sight of democracy destroyed in the union he did so much to help build and which meant so much to him. "You had a moral victory," I told him. "That's been the story of my life," he said, grimly. "Moral victories, and a failure at everything else." It wasn't true. A valiant, brilliant man, he made a real and selfless contribution to his fellowmen. When I first went to Mexico in 1955 I made a point of seeing Lombardo Toledano, head of the Confederation of Latin American Workers. I told him I did not want to leave Mexico without paying my respects to him. He knew about Jack and what had happened in the NMU. "Tell him," he said, "that for his integrity I salute him."

In the remaining years of Jack's life, an inner desolation possessed him. As for Curran, he eventually turned against his co-conspirators and squeezed them out until only he, of the original men who founded the NMU, remained at the helm of his one-man union. (Contemplating this, the Communist hierarchy must have experienced a certain empathy with Dr. Frankenstein.) Today, he lives in retirement in Boca Raton with his million-plus, an old man beneath my contempt.

Twelve

"HENCE, LOATHED MELANCHOLY"

Milton

WHEN JACK DIED I THOUGHT, "I have two choices: either I kill myself or I go on living."

I was being theatrical. There wasn't a chance of my choosing the first way. There were our two children, so obviously I would go on living for them. Even without them, however, I am far too interested a spectator to want to leave the arena. "*You*'ll never commit suicide," Clare Luce once said to me, almost resentfully, and the tone with which she emphasized the "you" implied that there was something wrong with me and I didn't have sense enough to know it.

I have scant capacity for brooding. It may be true that most men lead lives of quiet desperation, but I lead one of quiet content, snug in my invisible cocoon of self-spun magic. I wake up cheerful and brisk every morning, doubtless an obnoxious trait to those who can't even say Hello until they've had their coffee or their pill. It puzzles people who think I ought to be miserable or dissatisfied or depressed or worried, because it is a common assumption that no one is really happy, at least not for long at a time. Some twenty years ago, my friend George Wiswell got a job with one of the top book publishers. He called me and said he had a great idea for a book I could write. Despite my paralyzingly lethargic attitude toward work, I met him for lunch, because I liked him and enjoyed talking with him. I expected that he would suggest I write something flippant about sex, as ever since the Latins piece, editors seemed to think I was a sort of comical Baedeker of the bedroom. It turned out this was not at all what George had in mind. He wanted me to write a book about how to be happy, because he said I was the only truly happy person he'd ever known. Everyone else was going to psychiatrists, or drinking to escape, or getting ulcers, or having nervous breakdowns, or taking pills to sleep and pills to stay awake; and they all felt sorry for themselves. His idea was for me to reveal my secret formula for happiness and then we'd all make a lot of money and that would make *him* happy. I informed him that it was embarrassing enough to be considered a sex expert without becoming Pollyanna the Glad Girl sex expert.

When I went home, I told Jack I didn't know the secret, anyway. He said, "I do. You're happy because you have no ambition." I asked him to explain, so he did. "You're not disappointed because you haven't attained a set goal, because you've never had a goal. You've no guilt feelings about cutting people's throats to get ahead; you don't have to suck up to anyone in order to use them or make 'contacts.' There's no sweat. Failure is unimportant if you don't crave success. But you can't write a book and say that the secret of happiness is to have no ambition. That's un-American!"

I thought about it and decided he was right. Well, partially right. Other people are always saying how much they love a challenge. Actors being interviewed say they accepted a role "because it was a challenge." Newspaper Jobs Wanted advertisements tell of "dynamic, aggressive man looking for job that offers challenge." Not me. There's no use throwing down the gauntlet in front of me and daring me to pick it up. "Pick it up yourself," I'd say. I couldn't keep writing on my sickbed, like Katherine Mansfield or Robert Louis Stevenson; I couldn't knock out a best seller longhand on brown paper grocery bags while sitting at the kitchen table surrounded by my six children, or have fourteen novels rejected by thirty-odd publishers and, undaunted, keep plugging away. I have no desire to fight my way to the top, overcoming all obstacles, so I can be a bank president or chairman of the board of U.S. Steel. I don't want to be an ambassador and settle Trieste. If I hadn't had to earn my own living, I would have been content not to amount to a row of pins. I lack the competitive instinct to win, to be first, to be best. I don't want to row alone across the Atlantic or be the first woman pogo-stick jumper to hop nonstop from Nome to Nyack. When opportunity knocks, my reaction is to hide under the bed and stuff cotton in my ears. Go away. Tell 'em I'm not here.

Recently, I saw a prune-faced boffin pontificating on TV about pot smoking among the young. I burst out laughing when he said earnestly, "And the most damning thing about it is that it destroys the competitive instinct!" This is what they can't stand, the inadmissible character defect. I was born with it, and I consider myself lucky.

Many people probably think I've been a fool. I suppose it is true that I haven't "made the most" of what talent and opportunities I've had. I certainly haven't contributed anything to the world, or made my mark, or lusted after fame and fortune. I could look back on mistakes, humiliations, failures, and writhe with embarrassment, but I don't. I consider that I have been a fortunate woman and have had a happy life, by and large. I can survive tragedy, not through self-delusion but through acceptance. I accept. I don't mean that I accept cruelty or hypocrisy or injustice. I accept whatever happens to *me*. What you lose on the swings you win on the roundabouts.

I have lived in different worlds and learned to speak with many tongues, although never as a native of the inner circles.

I have been forever an observer, no matter how involved I might appear, how adaptable. Even today, I can grit my teeth and be gracious. I can suffer fools and bores. I have accepted everything as part of the pilgrimage through the brief, tenuous miracle of existence, always aware of the unimaginable infinity of the universe, secure in my conviction that regrets are fruitless and that depression is a selfish luxury of the ego. I am enough of a Pelagian to believe that man, "although aided in various ways by divine grace, is virtually the author of his own salvation." In the final analysis, each of us is responsible for what we are. We cannot blame it on our mothers, who, thanks to Freud, have replaced money as the root of all evil. Just because his own mother pushed him down a flight of stairs, a couple of generations have been brought up to trace their weaknesses and insecurities to the womb from whence they came, a device that has proved for many a fatuously easy escape from self-knowledge and self-discipline. I am immensely grateful for the gift of life. I refuse to waste it in worry or in the minor martyrdoms we all could seize, to dwell on, to bemoan. In fact, the secret of happiness may be learning not to cry over spilt milk.

About the Author

HELEN LAWRENSON was born in a village in upstate New York and attended Vassar College. She was managing editor of *Vanity Fair* magazine and is the author of *Latins Are Lousy Lovers*. Mrs. Lawrenson has contributed to magazines such as *Harper's*, *Harper's Bazaar*, *Vogue*, *Town & Country*, *Look*, *Holiday*, *Glamour*, *Mademoiselle*, *Cosmopolitan*, *McCall's* and others. Sixty-six of her articles have appeared in *Esquire*, and she has contributed to British magazines as well as other foreign publications.

Mrs. Lawrenson now lives in London. She is the widow of Jack Lawrenson, a co-founder of the National Maritime Union.